RabbitMQ in Action

RabbitMQ in Action

DISTRIBUTED MESSAGING FOR EVERYONE

ALVARO VIDELA
JASON J.W. WILLIAMS

MANNING
SHELTER ISLAND

For online information and ordering of this and other Manning books, please visit
www.manning.com. The publisher offers discounts on this book when ordered in quantity.
For more information, please contact

Special Sales Department
Manning Publications Co.
20 Baldwin Road
PO Box 261
Shelter Island, NY 11964
Email: orders@manning.com

Manning Publications Co.   Development editors: Maria Townsley, Cynthia Kane
20 Baldwin Road   Technical proofreader: Jerry Kuch
PO Box 261   Copyeditor: Benjamin Berg
Shelter Island, NY 11964   Proofreader: Katie Tennant
                                  Typesetter: Dottie Marsico
                              Cover designer: Marija Tudor

ISBN 9781935182979
Printed in the United States of America
1 2 3 4 5 6 7 8 9 10 – MAL – 17 16 15 14 13 12

To my grandfather, Maximiliano Godoy,
who showed me the ways of life. Gracias.

—A.V.

To Mama, Papa, and my sister J'aime.
Your love, support, and faith in me
has made it possible to climb mountains...
and to God who always carries me to the other side.

—J.W.

brief contents

contents

12 **Smart Rabbits: extending RabbitMQ   216**

foreword

Welcome to *RabbitMQ in Action*. If you're like me, possibly you're thinking, "Should I read past page one?" Alas, too many technology books are written and published, and not all merit more than superficial attention. So let me invite you to read on, if you think this description fits you:

- You want a practical way to learn about push technology, streaming data, and other messaging patterns.
- You want to achieve professional-level expertise with RabbitMQ, including best practices for design and running in production.

In other words, this book is not just a guide to RabbitMQ. It teaches fundamental design patterns across many use cases. It shows why more applications are using them—and what the "dos" and "don'ts" are.

What are these patterns? If you've ever wanted to draw a picture of your system as an information flow or network, rather than as a stack, then you're probably using messaging, or are ready to do so. You may be thinking of data delivery, nonblocking operations, or push notifications. Or you want to use publish/subscribe, asynchronous processing, or work queues. All of these are patterns, and they form part of the design canvas known as *messaging*.

Messaging is a critical capability: it enables software applications to connect and scale. Applications can connect to each other as components of a larger application, or to user devices and data. Messaging is essentially asynchronous in that it decouples applications by separating the sending and receiving of data. The wonderful thing is that this connection pattern works in the same way at any scale.

Scale is the point. The dominance of the internet as a basis for application delivery has made scale the critical factor in application design. Thinking small is no longer acceptable. Recently the term *big data* has become fashionable. But everything is *big* now, compared to only a few years ago.

For example, the number of mobile-connected devices will exceed the number of people on earth soon, probably in 2012. As I write this, Facebook is about to IPO. CTO Bret Taylor said that "Facebook would have been a mobile application if the technology had been available when Mark Zuckerberg was building it in his dorm room."

Take a moment to think about that. Most applications used to look like this: you load a document or get data from a database, do some processing, and write the results to disk. Future applications will look more like Facebook: always on, cloud hosted, and accessible anywhere. Input and processing are continuous and automatic, and deliver a filtered stream of information that the user wants, as it happens.

These levels of automation, reach, and scale are impossible without adopting a very specific set of design patterns. It is these patterns that you can learn in this book. Derek Collison, one of the originators of modern messaging technology, memorably described messaging as enabling "data in motion." It's hard to imagine an application that doesn't need to move data. So messaging is everywhere.

This book gets you started immediately. The patterns are presented as code examples that you can run, and the authors take special care to help you operate your system as well. With Jason J. W. Williams and Alvaro Videla, you have access to experts who've been running large-scale RabbitMQ systems for years. This book is a natural culmination of their outstanding work sharing these experiences with the community.

After you get a feel for RabbitMQ, it's very easy to get help and find more examples via the extensive RabbitMQ user community, regardless of which languages you're writing code in. This makes RabbitMQ an excellent choice for your messaging needs.

I hope this has whetted your appetite to turn the page and read on. There will be messages, and there will be rabbits, and all will be revealed.

ALEXIS RICHARDSON
COFOUNDER AND FORMER CEO
RABBIT TECHNOLOGIES, LTD.

SENIOR DIRECTOR
VMWARE CLOUD APPLICATION PLATFORM

preface

Writing this book has been like discovering RabbitMQ itself—encountering a problem that needed solving, but not knowing what the solution looked like. Until May 2010, we didn't even know each other. We both had been active in the RabbitMQ community for the past two years, but we'd never actually bumped into each other. Then one day a conversation with Alexis Richardson (Rabbit's CEO at the time) introduced Alvaro and me to each other, and made what you hold in your hands possible. What we had in common was a desire to write down in a single place all the knowledge we had acquired about RabbitMQ the hard way. Back in 2010, that knowledge was (and today still largely is) scattered across the internet in a smattering of blog articles and terse technical tutorials. In other words, we both wanted to write the book we wished had existed when we started with RabbitMQ two years earlier.

Neither of us came from a traditional messaging background, which made us fast friends and has largely informed the tone of *RabbitMQ in Action*; we wanted this book to be accessible for folks who've never heard of a queue or a binding before. In fact, when each of us discovered RabbitMQ, we didn't even know what "messaging" was or that it was the solution to the problems we were having. My (Jason's) situation was that my company needed a way to take the spam reportings we received from our customers and process them out-of-band from our main stream of incoming messages. In Alvaro's case, his company had a social network whose member communication system was creaking under the load of a 200 GB database. Like so many others who've come to messaging, both us had first tried to solve our queue-centric issues using database tables. Problems, like ensuring that only one application instance consumed any particular queue item, plagued our attempts at a database-driven solution and sent us looking for a better way. After all, we knew we couldn't be the first people in the history of software to have these issues.

The solution for both of us came in a surprisingly similar way: a friend at Plaxo told me to check out this "RabbitMQ thing" as a way to solve my queue-centric problems, and an Erlang colleague of Alvaro's in China gave him the same advice. Halfway around the world, both of us discovered RabbitMQ in the same way, and in response to trying to solve almost exactly the same problem! In fact, since you're reading this book about RabbitMQ, it's likely that similar challenges have led you to discover RabbitMQ in the same way. That speaks to the fact of why RabbitMQ is so popular: it easily solves the basic problems of distributing data that each of us runs into again and again when trying to scale the software that we build.

Our hope is that *RabbitMQ in Action* will help you design solutions to those challenges more quickly and easily with RabbitMQ, so you can spend more time writing the software that will change the world and less time getting up to speed on the messaging broker that will help you do it. Perhaps, along the way, RabbitMQ will introduce you to an awesome coauthor who will become the lifelong friend you never expected.[1] This book is a product of how much we love writing software, and our hope is that it will help you do the same in ways you never thought possible.

ALVARO VIDELA
DÜBENDORF, SWITZERLAND

JASON J. W. WILLIAMS
BOISE, IDAHO, UNITED STATES

---

[1] They say that coauthor relationships have a worse "divorce" rate than marriage. It's not a bad comparison, since writing a book together requires the constant give-and-take and mutual respect that it takes to make living in close quarters work. So it's been an unexpected blessing to not only be able to write a book, but to discover a friend whose ideas can live in close quarters with yours and make a whole far greater than you could achieve alone.

acknowledgments

Only two names appear on the cover of this book, but there are many more without whom it would not exist. First and foremost, we'd like to thank Alexis Richardson, RabbitMQ's CEO when we started writing. Without his recommendation, Manning would not have come knocking on our inboxes, and we would never have written a book together. We also thank him for providing the foreword to our book. In that vein, we need to express our utmost gratitude to the RabbitMQ team for continual help and answers to our incessant questions about the minutiae of Rabbit. In particular, we owe a thank you to Matthew Sackman and Matthias Radestock, without whom the chapters on clustering and RabbitMQ internals would not have been possible.

Above all, we owe an incalculable debt of gratitude to Jerry Kuch from the RabbitMQ team. Jerry volunteered countless hours repeatedly reviewing drafts of each chapter for accuracy, including doing the "official" technical review of the completed book by himself. Every time we needed clarification or advice outside our experience, Jerry was always a quick IM away. He was never cranky and never complained about being our point person on the RabbitMQ team. If you find yourself discovering little picadillos you never knew about Rabbit's operation, you likely have Jerry Kuch to thank. He truly made this a better book, and is a fantastic engineer.

At Manning, we cannot thank our primary development editor Maria Townsley enough. Maria kept us writing and on track. She put up with our work schedules, and our feast-or-famine style of delivering material. Above all she was our advocate and fought for what was important to us. If you enjoy the style of *RabbitMQ in Action*, thank Maria as she carried the flag for it. We also need to thank Cynthia Kane tremendously for getting us through the final chapters and into print. Cynthia stepped in as our final development editor when we were set in our ways. She adapted to our work style, and treated the book as if she'd been invested in it with us from day one. Cynthia was truly our third-base coach and got us home.

Finally, we'd like to thank our dedicated readers, who bought the book during Manning's Early Access Program (MEAP), as well as our reviewers: Barry Alexander, P. David Pull, Bruce Snyder, Tony Garnock-Jones, James Williams, Patrick Lemiuex, Bruce Lowekamp, Carlton Gibson, Paul Grebenc, Richard Siddaway, Gordon Dickens, Gene Campbell, Karsten Strøbæk, Jeff Addison, David Dossot, Daniel Bretoi, and Ben Rockwood. You were not paid, and yet you gave us detailed feedback and thoughtful advice as if the book were your baby too. This book is immeasurably better in ways unforeseen by us because of you. Thank you.

Alvaro

I would like to thank my wife Silvana for being always there supporting me during the writing of this book. How many movies we did not watch and how many times we did not go for walks together because I was writing this book? I don't know…but all I can say now is, thanks for understanding. Another big thanks goes to my mom for always believing in me. After all, writing a book is a family effort. I'd also like to thank my ol' pals at The Netcircle in China where I caught the rabbit fever and made them hear the word *RabbitMQ* too many times a day. Finally, I would like to thank Jason; Manning presented me with a coauthor and I ended up with a great friend.

Jason

I can never thank my parents and my sister enough for their support and love during this process. They believed in me and urged me forward—including making sure my derrière was pushed out the door to the coffee shop to write when I didn't feel like it. They always believed I would complete this book, even when the end looked so far away.

I'm lucky enough to call my parents my partners in the startup we founded together, and as partners, I owe them and DigiTar a huge debt for never complaining when writing cut into work hours, and for giving me the flexibility to balance both. Without our company, I would never have been driven to discover Rabbit or write the blog tutorials that led to being invited to write this book. Among the many blessings and opportunities DigiTar has given me, this book is one of them.

Finally, thank you to Alvaro. You are the friend I never knew existed, my ever steadfast compatriot in arms, and truly my brother from another mother. Thank you for being an unexpected blessing.

about this book

RabbitMQ is an open source message broker and queueing server that can be used to let disparate applications share data via a common protocol, or to simply queue jobs for processing by distributed workers. It doesn't matter whether your project is big or small: RabbitMQ can adapt to your needs. Do you want to quickly prototype one of your application components in language *X* and be sure you can easily switch it tomorrow to a more performant language? RabbitMQ can help you by decoupling the communication protocol. Do you need to be able to process image uploads for your social website as they arrive, while adding or removing workers with ease? You can use Rabbit queues to store jobs and let the broker perform the load balancing and job distribution for you. Problems like these can be easily and quickly solved by using RabbitMQ; this book is here to show you how to best implement your architectures around messaging.

Programming your application is one thing—keeping your application up and running is where the challenge starts. Don't worry; this book also covers best practices for RabbitMQ administration, clustering, securing, and monitoring, so you can also learn the operational side of things.

Finally, we'll get into RabbitMQ's brain and those inner details that will let you understand the system resources used by the broker so you can perform capacity planning while you design your architectures. Also, you'll learn how to extend the broker by installing plugins and by creating your own, because, why not? Get your editor ready because you'll be coding in Python, PHP, Erlang, Java, and C#.

Roadmap

Chapter 1 explains the origin of the AMQP protocol, how RabbitMQ was born, and what industry problems it came to solve. Next, you'll install the server and create your first Hello World program that will send data via RabbitMQ.

Chapter 2 immerses you in the world of messaging. We go from basic concepts up to seeing how to map those concepts in AMQP (the protocol used by RabbitMQ). Once you're past that, you'll learn about message durability and what happens in the life of a message from being published to getting consumed on the other end of the network.

Chapter 3 shows the basics of server management. You'll see how to start and stop nodes, how to configure permissions, and how to get statistics about what's happening on the server. And we give you some useful tips for troubleshooting the server.

Chapter 4 teaches you about messaging patterns and best practices. You'll learn about fire-and-forget models, RPC architectures, and much more.

Chapter 5 starts a series of three chapters on RabbitMQ clustering and setup for high availability. Here you'll set up a RabbitMQ cluster both on your local machine and on physical servers. You'll learn how to upgrade a cluster of RabbitMQ nodes and how to use mirrored queues.

Chapter 6 discusses how to load balance a set of RabbitMQ brokers using HAProxy while teaching how to create smart messaging clients that know how to reconnect to the broker in case of failures.

Chapter 7 ends the series on high availability by explaining how active/standby broker pairs work. You'll also learn about the Shovel plugin that allows RabbitMQ to replicate data across data centers.

Chapter 8 is where RabbitMQ administration goes visual. You'll learn about the RabbitMQ Management plugin and its web interface, but we don't stop there: we also perform an overview of the REST API offered by the plugin.

Chapter 9 builds from the previous chapter by explaining the REST API in detail. Here you'll learn how most of the administration tasks can be performed from your code by using this API. Provisioning new users and virtual hosts for your applications was never so easy.

Chapter 10 teaches you how to monitor RabbitMQ, from Nagios checks to using AMQP and the REST API to monitor the server internal state. You'll learn what you can do to detect problems before they happen.

Chapter 11 explains in detail the inner workings of exchanges (the routing algorithms used by RabbitMQ). We go into the details of the resources used by your messaging fabric to see what to expect from your architectural decisions. We also cover the security side of things by teaching you to enable SSL connections for your applications.

Chapter 12 ends the book by showing how to extend RabbitMQ's behavior both by adding new plugins created by others and by creating your own plugin.

Code conventions and downloads

All source code in listings or in text is in a `fixed-width font like this` to separate it from ordinary text. Code annotations accompany many of the listings, highlighting important concepts. In some cases, numbered bullets link to explanations that follow the listing.

Since one of RabbitMQ's greatest strengths is gluing together applications written in different languages, we use both Python and PHP as the primary example languages (with a little .NET and Java thrown in for good measure in the appendixes). But we want our examples to be as widely usable as possible to readers from all languages. Since we can't convert every example into every language, we've posted a Github repository so you can contribute too: https://github.com/rabbitinaction/sourcecode.

In the official Github repository you'll find the latest versions of the example code from the book, along with a number of those examples already converted by other readers into languages like Ruby. Don't see your favorite language? Fork the repository and add it! Then just send us a pull request and we'll do our best to incorporate your versions of the examples. (Note: you must use the same BSD license as our code for us to pull your changes in.)

If you'd like the canonical and truly "official" copies of the examples from *RabbitMQ in Action*, you can download them from the publisher's website: http://manning.com/RabbitMQinAction. The exact code as it appears in the latest published edition of the book will always be posted there.

Author Online

The purchase of *RabbitMQ in Action* includes free access to a private forum run by Manning Publications where you can make comments about the book, ask technical questions, and receive help from the authors and other users. You can access and subscribe to the forum at www.manning.com/RabbitMQinAction. This page provides information on how to get on the forum once you're registered, what kind of help is available, and the rules of conduct in the forum.

Manning's commitment to our readers is to provide a venue where a meaningful dialogue between individual readers and between readers and the authors can take place. It isn't a commitment to any specific amount of participation on the part of the authors, whose contribution to the book's forum remains voluntary (and unpaid). We suggest you try asking the authors some challenging questions, lest their interest stray!

The Author Online forum and the archives of previous discussions will be accessible from the publisher's website as long as the book is in print.

About the authors

ALVARO VIDELA is a developer and architect specializing in MQ-based applications. He speaks about RabbitMQ at conferences throughout Asia, Europe, and the U.S.

JASON J. W. WILLIAMS is CTO of DigiTar, a messaging service provider, where he directs design and development, including using RabbitMQ for real-time analysis operations since 2008.

about the cover illustration

The figure on the cover of *RabbitMQ in Action* is captioned "A farmer from Lumbarda, island of Korcula, Croatia." The illustration is taken from a reproduction of an album of Croatian traditional costumes from the mid-nineteenth century by Nikola Arsenovic, published by the Ethnographic Museum in Split, Croatia, in 2003. The illustrations were obtained from a helpful librarian at the Ethnographic Museum in Split, itself situated in the Roman core of the medieval center of the town: the ruins of Emperor Diocletian's retirement palace from around AD 304. The book includes finely colored illustrations of figures from different regions of Croatia, accompanied by descriptions of the costumes and of everyday life.

Lumbarda is small fishing village of approximately 1,200 inhabitants. It is situated on the northeastern coast of the island of Korcula, one of a number of small islands in the Adriatic off the western coast of Croatia. The farmer on the cover is wearing his work clothes, not one of the colorful and richly embroidered costumes that are typical for this region, worn only on Sundays and other special occasions. His everyday outfit consists of well-patched brown trousers and a brown vest worn over a white linen shirt, and a straw hat on his head. He is smoking a pipe, leaning on a spade, and, appropriately enough, looking down at a white rabbit, in a moment of rest from his toils.

Dress codes and lifestyles have changed over the last 200 years, and the diversity by region, so rich at the time, has faded away. It's now hard to tell apart the inhabitants of different continents, let alone of different hamlets or towns separated by only a few miles. Perhaps we have traded cultural diversity for a more varied personal life—certainly for a more varied and fast-paced technological life.

Manning celebrates the inventiveness and initiative of the computer business with book covers based on the rich diversity of regional life of two centuries ago, brought back to life by illustrations from old books and collections like this one.

Pulling RabbitMQ
out of the hat

1

This chapter covers

- The need for an open protocol—AMQP
- Brief history of RabbitMQ
- Installing RabbitMQ
- First program—Hello World

We live in a world where real-time information is constantly available, and the applications we write need easy ways to be routed to multiple receivers reliably and quickly. More important, we need ways to change who gets the information our apps create without constantly rewriting them. Too often, our application's information becomes siloed, inaccessible by new programs that need it without rewriting (and probably breaking) the original producers. You might be saying to yourself, "Sure, but how can message queuing or RabbitMQ help me fix that?" Let's start by asking whether the following scenario sounds familiar.

You've just finished implementing a great authentication module for your company's killer web app. It's beautiful. On every page hit, your code efficiently coordinates with the authentication server to make sure your users can only access what they should. You're feeling smug, because every page hit on your company's world-class avocado distribution website activates your code. That's about when your boss walks in and tells you the company needs a way to log every successful and failed permission attempt so that it can be data mined. After you lightly protest that that's the job of the authentication server, your boss not so gently informs you that there's no way to access that data. The authentication server logs it in a proprietary format; hence this is now your problem. Mulling over the situation causes a four-aspirin headache, as you realize you're going to have to modify your authentication module and probably break every page in the process. After all, that wonderful code of yours touches *every* access to the site. Let's stop for a moment though. Let's punch the Easy button and time warp back to the beginning of the development of that great auth module. Let's assume you leveraged message queuing heavily in its design from day one.

With RabbitMQ in place, you brilliantly leveraged message queuing to decouple your module from the authentication server. With every page request, your authentication module is designed to place an authorization request message into RabbitMQ. The authentication server then listens on a RabbitMQ queue that receives that request message. Once the request is approved, the auth server puts a reply message back into RabbitMQ where it's routed to the queue that your module is listening on. In this world, your boss's request doesn't faze you. You realize you don't need to touch your module or even write a new one. All you need to do is write a small app that connects to RabbitMQ and subscribes to the authorization requests your auth module is already publishing. No code changes. Nothing you already wrote knows anything has changed. It's so simple a smile almost breaks out on your face. That's the power of messaging to make your day job easier.

Message queuing is simply connecting your applications together with messages that are routed between them by a message broker like RabbitMQ. It's like putting in a post office just for your applications. The reality is that this approach isn't just a solution to the real-time problems of the financial industry; it's a solution to the problems we all face as developers every day. We, the authors, don't come from a financial services background. We had no idea what "enterprise messaging" was when we needed to scale. We were simply devs like you with an itch that needed scratching: an itch to deal with real-time volumes of information and route it to multiple consumers quickly. We needed to do it all without blocking the producers of that information … and without them needing to know who the final consumers might be. RabbitMQ helped us to solve those common problems easily, and in a standards-based way that ensured any app of ours could talk to any other app, be it Python, PHP, or even Scala.

Over the next few chapters, we'll take you on a ride. It starts by explaining how message queuing works, its history, and how RabbitMQ fits in. Then we'll take you all the way through to real-world examples you can apply to your own scalability and interoperability challenges … ending with how to make Rabbit purr like a well-oiled machine in a "downtime is not acceptable!" environment.

This is the book we wished was on the shelves when we entered the messaging wilderness. We hope it will help you benefit from our experience and battle scars and free you to make amazing applications with less pain. Before we're done in this chapter, you'll have a short history of messaging under your belt, and RabbitMQ up and running. Without further ado, let's take a look at where all this messaging fun started.

1.1 Living in other people's dungeons

The world of message queuing didn't start out the dank and cramped one it is today, with most folks subservient to lock-in overlords. It started with a ray of light in an otherwise byzantine software landscape. It was 1983 when a 26-year-old engineer from Mumbai had a radical question: why wasn't there a common software "bus"—a communication system that would do the heavy lifting of communicating information from one interested application to another? Coming from an education in hardware design at MIT, Vivek Ranadivé envisioned a common bus like the one on a motherboard, only this would be a software bus that applications could plug into. (See http:// hbswk.hbs.edu/archive/1884.html.) Thus, in 1983 Teknekron was born. A freshly minted Harvard MBA in his hand and this powerful idea in his head, Vivek started plowing a path that would help developers everywhere.

Having the idea was one thing, but finding a killer application for it was something completely different. It was at Goldman Sachs in 1985 that Ranadivé found his first customer and the problem his software bus was born to solve: financial trading. A trader's stall at that time was packed to the brim with different terminals for each type of information the trader needed to do his job. Teknekron saw an opportunity to replace all those terminals and their siloed applications. In their place would be Ranadivé's software bus. What would remain would be a single workstation whose display programs could now plug into the Teknekron software bus as consumers and allow the trader to "subscribe" to the information the trader wanted to see. Publish-subscribe (PubSub) was born, as was the world's first modern message queuing software: Teknekron's *The Information Bus (TIB)*.

It didn't take long for this model of data transfer to find many more killer uses. After all, an application publishing data and an application consuming it no longer had to directly connect to each other. Heck, they didn't even have to know each other existed. What Teknekron's TIB allowed application developers to do was establish a set of rules for describing message content. As long as the messages were published according to those rules, any consuming application could subscribe to a copy of the messages tagged with topics it was interested in. Producers and consumers of information could now be completely decoupled and flexibly mixed on-the-fly. Either side of the PubSub model (producer/consumer) was completely interchangeable without breaking the opposite side. The only thing that needed to remain stable was the TIB software and the rules for tagging and routing the information. Since the financial trading industry is full of information with a constantly changing set of interested folks, TIB spread like wildfire in that sector. It was also noticed by telecommunications and especially news organizations, who also had information that needed timely delivery to a dynamically changing set of interested consumers. That's why mega news outfit Reuters purchased Teknekron in 1994.

Meanwhile, this burgeoning new segment of enterprise software didn't go unnoticed by Big Blue. After all, many of IBM's biggest customers were in the financial services industry. Also, Teknekron's TIB software was frequently run on IBM hardware and operating systems … all without the boys in White Plains getting a cut. Thus, in the late '80s IBM began research into developing their own message-queuing software, leveraging their extensive experience in information delivery from developing DB2 (see http://www-01.ibm.com/software/integration/wmq/MQ15Anniversary.html). Development began in 1990 at IBM's Hursely Park Laboratories near Winchester, United Kingdom. What emerged three years later was the IBM MQSeries family of message-queuing server software. In the 17 years since, MQSeries has evolved into WebSphere MQ and is today the dominant commercial message-queuing platform. During that time, Ranadivé's TIB hardly disappeared into the bowels of Reuters. Instead it has remained the other major player in enterprise messaging, thriving through a renaming to *Rendezvous* and Teknekron's re-emergence as an independent company in the form of TIBCO in 1997. The same year, Microsoft's first crack at the messaging market emerged: Microsoft Message Queue (MSMQ).

Through all of this evolution, *message queuing (MQ)* software primarily remained the domain of large-budgeted organizations with a need for reliable, decoupled, real-time message delivery. Why didn't MQ find a larger audience? How did it survive the information boom that was the late '90s internet bubble without experiencing explosive adoption? After all, everyone today from Twitter to Salesforce.com is scrambling to create internal solutions to the PubSub problems that The Information Bus solved 25 years ago. Two words: vendor lock-in. The commercial MQ vendors wanted to help applications interoperate, not create standard interfaces that would allow different MQ products to interoperate or, Heaven forbid, allow applications to change MQ platforms. Vendor lock-in has kept prices and margins high, and commercial MQ software out of reach of the startups and Web 2.0 companies that are abounding today.

As it turned out, smaller tech companies weren't the only ones unhappy about the high-priced walled gardens of MQ vendors. The financial services companies that formed the bread and butter of the MQ industry weren't thrilled either. Inevitably, the size of financial companies meant that MQ products were in place from multiple vendors servicing different internal applications. If an application subscribing to information on a TIBCO MQ suddenly needed to consume messages from an IBM MQ, it couldn't easily be done. They used different APIs, different wire protocols, and definitely couldn't be federated together into a single bus. From this problem was born the *Java Message Service (JMS)* in 2001 (see http://en.wikipedia.org/wiki/Java_Message _Service). JMS attempted to solve the lock-in and interoperability problem by providing a common Java API that hides the actual interface to the individual vendor MQ products. Technically, a Java application only needs to be written to the JMS API, with the appropriate MQ drivers selected. JMS takes care of the rest … supposedly. The problem is you're trying to glue a single standard interface over multiple diverse interfaces. It's like gluing together different types of cloth: eventually the seams come apart and the reality breaks through. Applications could become more brittle with JMS, not less. A new standards-based approach to messaging was needed.

1.2   AMQP to the rescue

In 2004, JPMorgan Chase required a better solution to the problem and started development of the *Advanced Message Queuing Protocol (AMQP)* with iMatix Corporation (see http://en.wikipedia.org/wiki/Advanced_Message_Queuing_Protocol#Development). AMQP from the get-go was designed to be an open standard that would solve the vast majority of message queuing needs and topologies. By virtue of being an open standard, anyone can implement it, and anyone who codes to the standard can interoperate with MQ servers from any AMQP vendor.

In many ways, AMQP promises to liberate us from the dungeons of vendors and fulfill Ranadivé's original vision: dynamically connecting information in real time from any publisher to any interested consumer over a software bus.

1.3   A brief history of RabbitMQ

In the early 2000s, a young entrepreneur out of the London financial sector cofounded a company for caching Java objects: Metalogic. For Alexis Richardson, the theory was simple enough: use Java objects for distributed computing and cache them in transit for performance. The reality was far different. Varying versions of the Java Virtual Machine, as well as differing libraries on the client and server, could make the

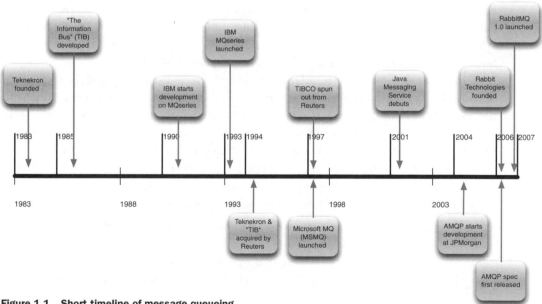

Figure 1.1   Short timeline of message queueing

objects unusable when they arrived. There were too many environment variables in the real world for Metalogic's approach to be widely successful. What did come out of Metalogic was Alexis meeting Matthias Radestock.

Matthias was working for LShift, where Alexis was subleasing office space while at Metalogic. LShift at the time was heavily involved in language modeling and distributed computing contracts for a major software vendor. The background in these areas triggered Matthias's interest in Erlang, the programming language that Ericsson had originally developed for their telephone switching gear. What grabbed Matthias's attention was that Erlang excelled at distributed programming and robust failure recovery, but unfortunately at the time it wasn't open source. In the meantime, Metalogic had closed operations and LShift was in the process of winding down their primary distributed computing contract. But Alexis had learned two valuable lessons from his experience at Metalogic: what works in a distributed computing environment, and what companies want for those environments.

Alexis knew he wanted to start a new company to solve the problems of communicating in a distributed environment. He also knew the next company he started would be open source and build on the model just proved successful by JBoss and MySQL. Looking back at where the Metalogic solution had run into problems, Alexis started to see that messaging was the right answer to distributed computing. More important, in the tech world circa 2004 a huge gap existed for open source messaging. No one was providing a messaging solution except for the big commercial vendors, and while "enterprise" open source was flourishing with databases (MySQL) and application servers (JBoss), no one was touching the missing component: messaging. Interestingly, it was in 2004 that AMQP was just starting to be developed at JPMorgan Chase. Through his background in the financial industry, Alexis had been introduced to the principal driver of AMQP at JPMorgan, John O'Hara (future founder of the AMQP Working Group). Through O'Hara, Alexis became acquainted with AMQP, and started lining up the building blocks for what would become RabbitMQ.

Around 2005, Alexis cofounded CohesiveFT. He and his cofounders in the U.S. started the company to provide an application stack and tools for what has today become cloud computing. That a key part of that stack would be distributed messaging seemed obvious to Alexis, who (still in the same office as LShift) started talking to Matthias about AMQP. What was clear to Matthias was that he'd just found the application he'd been looking for to write in Erlang. But before any of this could get started, Alexis and Matthias focused on three questions that they knew would be critical to an open source version of AMQP being successful if it was written in Erlang:

1   Would large financial institutions care whether their messaging broker was written in Erlang?
2   Was Erlang really a good choice for writing an AMQP server?
3   If it was written in Erlang, would that slow down adoption in the open source community?

The first issue was quickly dispatched by a financial company who confirmed they didn't care what it was written in if it helped reduce their integration costs. The second question was answered by Francesco Cesarini at Erlang Solutions: from his analysis of AMQP, the specification implied an architecture present in every telephone switch. In other words, you couldn't pick a better implementation language than Erlang for building an AMQP broker. The final question was put to rest by an entirely different messaging server: ejabberd. By 2005, *Extensible Messaging and Presence Protocol (XMPP)* had become a respected standard for open instant messaging, and one of the foremost implementations was the Erlang-based ejabberd server package by Alexey Shchepin. ejabberd was widely in use by many different organizations, and its implementation in Erlang didn't seem to be slowing anyone down.

With the three major questions answered, Alexis and Matthias convinced CohesiveFT and LShift to jointly back the project. The first thing they did was contract Matthew Sackman (now a core Rabbit developer) to write a prototype in Erlang to test latency. They quickly discovered that using the distributed computing libraries built into Erlang produced incredible latency that was comparable to using raw sockets. There was also the question of what to call this thing: everyone agreed on Rabbit. After all, rabbits are fast and they multiply like crazy, making it a great name for distributed software. Not the least of the reasons for this choice is that Rabbit is easy to remember. Thus, in 2006 Rabbit Technologies was born: a joint venture between CohesiveFT and LShift that would hold the intellectual property for what we know today as RabbitMQ.

The timing couldn't have been more perfect because, around the same time, the first public draft of the AMQP specification had become available. As a new specification, AMQP was rapidly changing. This was an area where Erlang proved critical. By using Erlang, RabbitMQ could be developed quickly and keep pace with a moving target: the AMQP standard. Amazingly, version 1.0 of RabbitMQ was written in only two and a half months by core developer Tony Garnock-Jones. From the beginning, RabbitMQ has implemented a key feature of AMQP that differentiates it from TIBCO and IBM: provisioning resources like queues and exchanges can be done from within the protocol itself. With the commercial vendors, provisioning is done by specialized staff at specialized administrative consoles. RabbitMQ's provisioning capabilities make it the perfect communication bus for anyone building a distributed application, particularly one that leverages cloud-based resources and rapid deployment.

That brings us to today, where RabbitMQ is used by everyone from small Silicon Valley startups to some of the largest names on the internet. That's perhaps the best thing about RabbitMQ, and the thing that surprised its founders: its largest block of users are tech firms, not financial companies. RabbitMQ fulfills Ranadivé's vision for the rest of us with smaller budgets and the same real problems. That's what drew us to RabbitMQ. We didn't know that we were looking for message-queueing software. All we knew was that we had real problems to solve integrating applications and serving high transaction loads. RabbitMQ provides a powerful toolkit for solving those problems, and brings to the masses the rich history of messaging … and finally a pluggable information bus for everyone that needs one.

1.4   Picking RabbitMQ out of the hat (and other open options)

Today, RabbitMQ isn't the only game in town for open messaging. Options like ActiveMQ, ZeroMQ, and Apache Qpid all providing different open source approaches to message queuing. The question is, why do we think you should pick RabbitMQ?

- Except for Qpid, RabbitMQ is the only broker implementing the AMQP open standard.
- Clustering is ridiculously simple on RabbitMQ because of Erlang.
- Your mileage may vary, but we've found RabbitMQ to be far more reliable and crash resistant than its competitors.

Perhaps the most important reason is that RabbitMQ is incredibly easy to install and use. Whether you need a simple one-node setup for your workstation, or a seven-server cluster to power your web infrastructure, RabbitMQ can be up and running in about 30 minutes. With that in mind, it's about time we fired up the little critter.

1.5   Installing RabbitMQ on Unix systems

So far we've discussed the motivation behind the AMQP protocol and the history of the RabbitMQ server. Now it's time to get the broker up and running and start doing cool stuff with it. The operating system requirements for running RabbitMQ are flexible because we can run it on several platforms including Linux, Windows, Mac OS X, and other Unix-like systems. In this chapter we'll go through the process of setting up the server for a generic Unix system (all examples and instructions in the book assume a UNIX environment unless otherwise noted). Since RabbitMQ is written in Erlang, we need to have installed the language libraries to run the broker.

1.5.1   Why environment matters—living la vida Erlang

We recommend that you use the latest version of Erlang, which at the time of this writing is R14A. You can obtain a copy of Erlang from its website (http://www.erlang.org/). Please follow the installation instructions provided there. By running the latest version of Erlang on your system, you'll be sure to have all the updates and improvements for the foundations RabbitMQ will run on. Every new release of Erlang includes performance improvements that are worth having.

Once you have RabbitMQ dependencies solved, create a folder where you can perform our tests. Assuming that you're running a Unix-flavored system, fire up a terminal to start typing commands:

```
$ mkdir rabbitmqinaction
$ cd rabbitmqinaction
```

1.5.2 Getting the package

Then download the RabbitMQ Server from the server download page: http://www.rabbitmq.com/server.html. Select the package for a generic Unix system and download it:[1]

```
$ wget http://www.rabbitmq.com/releases/rabbitmq-server/v2.7.0/\
rabbitmq-server-generic-unix-2.7.0.tar.gz
```

Your next step is to unpack the tarball and change to the `rabbitmq_server-2.7.0` directory inside the package:

```
$ tar -xzvf rabbitmq-server-generic-unix-2.7.0.tar.gz
$ cd rabbitmq_server-2.7.0/
```

1.5.3 Setting up the folder structure

You're nearly ready to start the broker, but there are a couple of folders to create before you do that. The first one is where RabbitMQ will write the logs. You can look into this folder in case you need to troubleshoot your installation. The second folder is for the Mnesia database that RabbitMQ uses to store information about the broker, like queue metadata, virtual hosts, and so on. Type the following commands at the terminal:

```
$ mkdir -p /var/log/rabbitmq
$ mkdir -p /var/lib/rabbitmq/mnesia/rabbit
```

You may need to run those commands as a super user. If you have to do so, then don't forget to *chown* the folders to your system user.

> **TIP** When we run RabbitMQ in production, we usually create a `rabbitmq` user and then we grant the folder privileges to that user instead of running all the commands with a normal user account.

1.5.4 Firing Rabbit up for the first time

Now you're all set to fire up the server. Type the final command to do so:

```
$ sbin/rabbitmq-server
```

RabbitMQ will output some information about the startup progress. If all went as expected, you'll see ASCII art of the RabbitMQ logo and the message `broker running`, as seen in figure 1.2.

Now open a new terminal window and check the status of the server. Type the following:[2]

```
$ cd path/to/rabbitmqinaction/rabbitmq_server-2.7.0/
$ sbin/rabbitmqctl status
```

---

[1] Pre-build installation packages for RabbitMQ are available for Windows, Debian/Ubuntu and RedHat (RPM) from http://www.rabbitmq.com/download.html.

[2] If you installed from an RPM or Ubuntu/Debian package, you may need to run `rabbitmqctl` as root.

```
Terminal — beam.smp — 80×39
mrhyde:rabbitmq_server-2.7.0 mrhyde$ sbin/rabbitmq-server
Activating RabbitMQ plugins ...
0 plugins activated:

+---+  +---+
|   |  |   |
|   |  |   |
|   |  |   |
|   +---+   +-------+
|                   |
| RabbitMQ  +---+   |
|           |   |   |
|   v2.7.0  +---+   |
|                   |
+-------------------+
AMQP 0-9-1 / 0-9 / 0-8
Copyright (C) 2007-2011 VMware, Inc.
Licensed under the MPL.  See http://www.rabbitmq.com/

node            : rabbit@mrhyde
app descriptor  : /git/rabbitmqinaction/av_scratchwork/examples/broker/rabbitmq_s
erver-2.7.0/sbin/../ebin/rabbit.app
home dir        : /Users/mrhyde
config file(s)  : /etc/rabbitmq/rabbitmq.config
cookie hash     : oNANSQ6MP0092ATN9U7Hgg==
log             : /var/log/rabbitmq/rabbit@mrhyde.log
sasl log        : /var/log/rabbitmq/rabbit@mrhyde-sasl.log
database dir    : /var/lib/rabbitmq/mnesia/rabbit@mrhyde
erlang version  : 5.8.5

-- rabbit boot start
starting file handle cache server                            ...done
starting worker pool                                         ...done
starting database                                            ...done
starting codec correctness check                             ...done
-- external infrastructure ready
starting plugin registry                                     ...done
starting auth mechanism cr-demo                              ...done
```

Figure 1.2   RabbitMQ welcome message

As you can see in figure 1.3, this command will output the status of the broker, the running applications, and nodes. At this point you have a RabbitMQ broker running in your computer with the default configuration.

Let's review what we did:

- Downloaded the server package
- Unpacked it in a tests folder
- Set up the required folder structure
- Started the RabbitMQ server
- Checked the server status

With those easy steps you got started with RabbitMQ. Now more theory about *messaging*, and then we'll start running some examples against the broker.

1.6   *Summary*

Now you can see why we love RabbitMQ so much. Despite being the progeny of technology from the financial industry, it's dead simple to set up. You get complex routing and reliability features pioneered by folks like TIBCO and IBM but in a package that's easier to manage and use. And the best part, it's open source! We've shown how far messaging has come in the past 30 years, from a simple software bus linking together

```
⬤⬤⬤                    Terminal — bash — 87×28
mrhyde:rabbitmq_server-2.7.0 mrhyde$ sbin/rabbitmqctl status
Status of node rabbit@mrhyde ...
[{pid,7595},
 {running_applications,[{rabbit,"RabbitMQ","2.7.0"},
                        {ssl,"Erlang/OTP SSL application","4.1.6"},
                        {public_key,"Public key infrastructure","0.13"},
                        {crypto,"CRYPTO version 2","2.0.4"},
                        {os_mon,"CPO  CXC 138 46","2.2.7"},
                        {sasl,"SASL  CXC 138 11","2.1.10"},
                        {mnesia,"MNESIA  CXC 138 12","4.5"},
                        {stdlib,"ERTS  CXC 138 10","1.17.5"},
                        {kernel,"ERTS  CXC 138 10","2.14.5"}]},
 {os,{unix,darwin}},
 {erlang_version,"Erlang R14B04 (erts-5.8.5) [source] [64-bit] [smp:2:2] [rq:2] [async-
threads:30] [hipe] [kernel-poll:true]\n"},
 {memory,[{total,25627552},
         {processes,10422296},
         {processes_used,10407064},
         {system,15205256},
         {atom,1139097},
         {atom_used,1137479},
         {binary,76104},
         {code,11346167},
         {ets,901984}]},
 {vm_memory_high_watermark,0.3999999999441615},
 {vm_memory_limit,2865407590}]
...done.
mrhyde:rabbitmq_server-2.7.0 mrhyde$ ▊
```

Figure 1.3   Checking RabbitMQ status

financial traders, to message routing monsters that are the beating heart of everything related to financial exchanges, to the manufacturing lines at semiconductor fabs. Now you have that kind of power running on your dev laptop, and we've only finished chapter 1! With RabbitMQ running, it's time to dive into the building blocks of messaging: queues, bindings, exchanges, and virtual hosts. Let's see how they all fit together and get Rabbit saying "Hello World"!

Understanding messaging

2

This chapter covers

- Messaging concepts—consumers, producers, and brokers
- AMQP elements—exchanges, queues, and bindings
- Virtual hosts
- Message durability
- The life of a message from producer to consumer

When you say *messaging*, programmers think of a lot of different things. Email and IM come most readily to mind, but these models aren't what we mean when we talk about messaging in terms of RabbitMQ. Messaging in RabbitMQ has some elements in common with email and IM, but is a completely different paradigm. For example, while AMQP, like email, stores messages for consumers who aren't online, those messages are routed based on tags that are much more flexible. Also different from email, the messages have no set structure and can even store binary data directly. Unlike IM protocols, AMQP hides the sender and receiver from each other. There's no concept of presence. As a result, you have a flexible infrastructure that encourages pervasive decoupling of your applications. AMQP messages can be routed one-to-many both in a broadcast pattern or selectively, as well as one-to-one. With IM you typically only get one-to-one.

Since AMQP messaging is different from other messaging protocols, we'll spend the next few sections explaining the lingo and building blocks of AMQP. If you have a good basis in enterprise messaging systems like TIBCO or IBM's MQSeries, a lot of this will be familiar. Because RabbitMQ's focus is on application-to-application messaging, it's important to understand the concepts of that messaging pattern clearly. Let's start by forgetting the client/server distinction we've had ingrained in us and begin figuring out consumers and producers.

2.1 Consumers and producers (not an economics lesson)

If you've ever worked with software that uses a network, you're probably used to thinking about clients and servers. Whether it's a browser and a web server, or your app and a MySQL server, you have someone making requests and someone servicing them. You could call it the food truck model. Your app places the order and the food truck fulfills it. The source of the data you want *is* the food truck server. This model is usually how we try to understand anything that involves our app and a service. So with this new messaging approach, you might ask, who's the customer, who's the food truck, and how do I order?

That's the problem though. RabbitMQ isn't a food truck; it's a delivery service. The data your app gets from RabbitMQ is no more served from Rabbit than the package you pick up was produced by FedEx. So let's think about Rabbit as a delivery service. Your app can send and receive packages. The server with the data you need can send and receive too. The role RabbitMQ plays is as the router between your app and the "server" it's talking to. So when your app connects to RabbitMQ, it has a decision to make: am I sending or receiving? Or in AMQP talk, am I a producer or a consumer?

Producers create messages and publish (send) them to a broker server (RabbitMQ). What's a message? A message has two parts: a payload and a label. The payload is the data you want to transmit. It can be anything from a JSON array to an MPEG-4 of your favorite iguana Ziggy. RabbitMQ doesn't care. The label is more interesting. It describes the payload, and is how RabbitMQ will determine who should get a copy of your message. Unlike, for example, TCP, where you specify a specific sender and a specific receiver, AMQP only describes the message with a label (an exchange name and optionally a topic tag) and leaves it to Rabbit to send it to interested receivers based on that label. The communication is fire-and-forget and one-directional. We'll get more details about how RabbitMQ interprets the label later when we talk about exchanges and bindings. For now, all you need to know is that producers create messages and label them for routing (see figure 2.1).

Consumers are just as simple. They attach to a broker server and subscribe to a *queue*. Think of a queue as a named mailbox. Whenever a message arrives in a particular mailbox, RabbitMQ sends it to one of the subscribed/listening consumers. By the time a consumer receives a message, it now only has one part: a payload. The labels attached to the message don't get passed along with the payload when the message is routed. RabbitMQ doesn't even tell you who the producer/sender was. It would be like picking up your mail but all of the envelopes are blank. The only way to know a

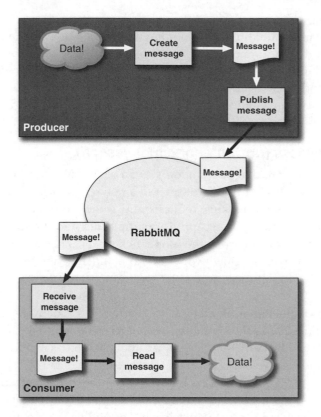

**Figure 2.1   Message flow
from producers to consumers**

message is from your Aunt Millie is if she signed the letter inside. Similarly, if you need to know specifically who produced an AMQP message, it's up to the producer to include that information as a part of the message payload.

From the outside it's simple: producers create messages and consumers receive them. Your app can be a producer when it needs to send a message to another app, or it can be a consumer when it needs to receive. It can also switch between the two. But before it can do either it has to set up a channel. Wait a minute … what's a channel?

Before you consume from or publish to Rabbit, you first have to connect to it. By connecting, you're creating a TCP connection between your app and the Rabbit broker. Once the TCP connection is open (and you're authenticated), your app then creates an AMQP channel. This channel is a virtual connection inside the "real" TCP connection, and it's over the channel that you issue AMQP commands. Every channel has a unique ID assigned to it (your AMQP library of choice will handle remembering the ID for you). Whether you're publishing a message, subscribing to a queue, or receiving a message, it's all done over a channel. Why do we need channels, you might ask? Why not just issue AMQP commands directly over the TCP connection? The main reason is because setting up and tearing down TCP sessions is expensive for an operating system. Let's say your app consumes messages from a queue and spins threads up or down based on service demand. If all you had were TCP connections,

each thread would need its own connection to Rabbit, which could mean
hundreds of connections per second
during high load periods. Not only
would this be a massive waste of TCP
connections, but an operating system
can only build so many per second. So
you could quickly hit a performance
wall. Wouldn't it be cool if you could

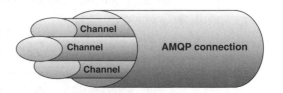

**Figure 2.2 Understanding AMQP channels and
connections**

use one TCP connection for all of your threads for performance, but get the same pri-
vacy as giving each thread its own connection? This is where a channel comes in. As
each thread spins up, it creates a channel on the existing connection and gets its own
private communication path to Rabbit without any additional load on your operating
system's TCP stack, as in figure 2.2. As a result, you can create a channel hundreds or
thousands of times a second without your operating system seeing so much as a blip.
There's no limit to how many AMQP channels you can have on one TCP connection.
Think of it like a bundle of fiber optic cable.

Each fiber strand in the cable can transmit (just like a channel). But the cable has
many fiber strands, allowing all the connected threads to transmit and receive simultaneously via multiple strands. A TCP connection is like the cable, and an AMQP channel
is like an individual fiber strand.

How about an example? Let's say you've written a service for keeping track of valet
parking, and everyone talks to it through RabbitMQ. Your service has to fulfill two
tasks:

1 Store valet ticket IDs and the associated parking space the car is in
2 Return the parking space for any particular valet ticket ID

For the first task, your service is a consumer. It's subscribed to a Rabbit queue waiting
for "store ticket" messages with ticket IDs and parking space numbers inside. With the
second task, your service is both a consumer *and* a producer. It needs to receive messages that tell it a particular valet ticket ID and then it needs to publish a response
message with the associated parking space number.

To fulfill the second task, your app is a producer. Once the connection to the
RabbitMQ broker is open, your app creates multiple channels: *chan_recv* for the receiving thread and a *chan_sendX* (*X* being the thread number) channel for each reply
thread. Using chan_recv, you set up a subscription to the queue that receives messages
containing "ticket retrieval" requests. When a ticket retrieval message is received by
your app over chan_recv, it looks up the ticket ID contained in the message. As soon as
the associated parking space number has been identified, your app then creates a
thread to send the response (letting the original thread continue to receive new
requests). The new reply thread then creates a message containing the parking space
number. Finally, the new thread labels the response message and publishes it to Rabbit
using its chan_sendX channel. If your app had only one channel, it wouldn't be

possible to share the TCP connection with the new reply threads. This would leave you with two choices. Either use one connection and one thread—meaning your app couldn't process new ticket retrieval requests until it sent a response to the current one—or spawn a TCP connection for each sending thread, wasting TCP resources. With multiple channels, many threads can share the same connection simultaneously, meaning that responding to requests doesn't block you from consuming new requests and you don't waste a TCP connection for each thread. Sometimes you may choose to use only one channel, but with AMQP you have the flexibility to use as many channels as your app needs without the overhead of multiple TCP connections.

The important thing to remember about consumers and producers is that they map to the ideas of sending and receiving rather than client and server. Messaging in general, and AMQP in particular, can be thought of as an enhanced transport layer. With channels, you have the ability to create as many parallel transport layers as your app needs without being limited by TCP connection restrictions. When you understand these concepts, you can begin thinking of RabbitMQ as a router for your software.

2.2   *Building from the bottom: queues*

You have consumers and producers under your belt, and now you're itching to get started eh? Not so fast. First, you need to understand queues. Conceptually, there are three parts to any successful routing of an AMQP message: exchanges, queues, and bindings. The exchanges are where producers publish their messages, queues are where the messages end up and are received by consumers, and bindings are how the messages get routed from the exchange to particular queues. Before you get to examine exchanges and bindings, you need to understand what a queue is and how it works. Take a look at figure 2.3.

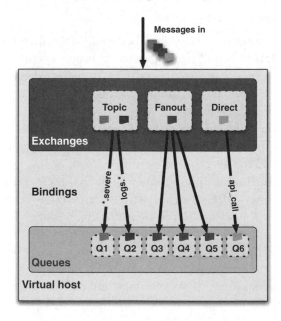

Figure 2.3   AMQP stack: exchanges, bindings, and queues

As we said when we were talking about producers and consumers, queues are like named mailboxes. They're where messages end up and wait to be consumed. Consumers receive messages from a particular queue in one of two ways:

1   By subscribing to it via the `basic.consume` AMQP command. This will place the channel being used into a receive mode until unsubscribed from the queue. While subscribed, your consumer will automatically receive another message from the queue (as available) after consuming (or rejecting) the last received message. You should use `basic.consume` if your consumer is processing many messages out of a queue and/or needs to automatically receive messages from a queue as soon as they arrive.

2   Sometimes, you just want a single message from a queue and don't need to be persistently subscribed. Requesting a single message from the queue is done by using the `basic.get` AMQP command. This will cause the consumer to receive the next message in the queue and then *not* receive further messages until the next `basic.get`. You shouldn't use `basic.get` in a loop as an alternative to `basic.consume`, because it's much more intensive on Rabbit. `basic.get` essentially subscribes to the queue, retrieves a single message, and then unsubscribes every time you issue the command. High-throughput consumers should always use `basic.consume`.

If one or more consumers are subscribed to a queue, messages are sent immediately to the subscribed consumers. But what if a message arrives at a queue with no subscribed consumers? In that case, the message waits in the queue. As soon as a consumer subscribes to the queue, the message will be sent to that consumer. A more interesting question is how messages in a queue are distributed when multiple consumers are subscribed to the same queue.

When a Rabbit queue has multiple consumers, messages received by the queue are served in a round-robin fashion to the consumers. Each message is sent to only one consumer subscribed to the queue. Let's say you had a queue named *seed_bin* and consumers Farmer Bob and Farmer Esmeralda subscribed to seed_bin. As messages arrive in seed_bin, the deliveries would look like this:

1   Message_A arrives in the seed_bin queue.
2   RabbitMQ sends Message_A to Farmer Bob.
3   Farmer Bob acknowledges receipt of Message_A.
4   RabbitMQ removes Message_A from the seed_bin queue.
5   Message_B arrives in the seed_bin queue.
6   RabbitMQ sends Message_B to Farmer Esmeralda.
7   Farmer Esmeralda acknowledges receipt of Message_B.
8   RabbitMQ removes Message_B from the seed_bin queue.

You may have noticed that Farmers Bob and Esmeralda did something we haven't talked about yet: they acknowledged receipt of the message. Every message that's received by a consumer is required to be acknowledged. Either the consumer must explicitly send an acknowledgement to RabbitMQ using the `basic.ack` AMQP command, or it can set the `auto_ack` parameter to true when it subscribes to the queue. When `auto_ack` is specified, RabbitMQ will automatically consider the message acknowledged by the consumer as soon as the consumer has received it. An important thing to remember is that message acknowledgements from the consumer have nothing to do with telling the producer of the message it was received. Instead, the acknowledgements are a way for the consumer to confirm to RabbitMQ that the consumer has correctly received the message and RabbitMQ can safely remove it from the queue.

If a consumer receives a message and then disconnects from Rabbit (or unsubscribes from the queue) before acknowledging, RabbitMQ will consider the message undelivered and redeliver it to the next subscribed consumer. If your app crashes, you can be assured the message will be sent to another consumer for processing. On the other hand, if your consumer app has a bug and forgets to acknowledge a message, Rabbit won't send the consumer any more messages. This is because Rabbit considers the consumer not ready to receive another message until it acknowledges the last one it received. You can use this behavior to your advantage. If processing the contents of a message is particularly intensive, your app can delay acknowledging the message until the processing has finished. This will keep Rabbit from overloading you with more messages than your app can handle.

What if you want to specifically reject a message rather than acknowledge it after you've received it? For example, let's say that when processing the message you encounter an uncorrectable error, but it only affects this consumer due to a hardware issue (this is a good reason to never acknowledge a message until it's processed). As long as the message hasn't been acknowledged yet, you have two options:

1 Have your consumer disconnect from the RabbitMQ server. This will cause RabbitMQ to automatically requeue the message and deliver it to another consumer. The advantage to this method is that it works across all versions of RabbitMQ. The disadvantage is the extra load put on the RabbitMQ server from the connecting and disconnecting of your consumer (a potentially significant load if your consumer is encountering errors on every message).

2 If you're running RabbitMQ 2.0.0 or newer, use the `basic.reject` AMQP command. `basic.reject` does exactly what it sounds like: it allows your consumer to reject a message RabbitMQ has sent it. If you set the `requeue` parameter of the `reject` command to true, RabbitMQ will redeliver the message to the next subscribed consumer. Setting `requeue` to false will cause RabbitMQ to remove the message from the queue immediately without resending it to a new consumer. You can also discard a message simply by acknowledging it (this method of discarding has the advantage of working with all versions of RabbitMQ). This is useful if you detect a malformed message you know none of your consumers will be able to process.

NOTE When discarding a message, why would you want to use the `basic.reject` command with the `requeue` parameter set to false instead of acknowledging the message? Future versions of RabbitMQ will support a special "dead letter" queue where messages that are rejected without requeuing will be placed. A dead letter queue lets you inspect rejected/undeliverable messages for issues. If you want your app to automatically take advantage of the dead letter queue feature when it's added to Rabbit, use the `reject` command with `requeue` set to false.

There's one more important thing you need to know about queues: how to create them. Both consumers and producers can create queues by using the `queue.declare` AMQP command. But consumers can't declare a queue while subscribed to another one on the same channel. They must first unsubscribe in order to place the channel in a "transmit" mode. When creating a queue, you usually want to specify its name. The name is used by consumers to subscribe to it, and is how you specify the queue when creating a binding. If you don't specify a name, Rabbit will assign a random name for you and return it in the response to the `queue.declare` command (this is useful when using temporary "anonymous" queues for RPC-over-AMQP applications, as you'll see in chapter 4). Here are some other useful properties you can set for the queue:

- `exclusive`—When set to true, your queue becomes private and can only be consumed by your app. This is useful when you need to limit a queue to only one consumer.

- `auto-delete`—The queue is automatically deleted when the last consumer unsubscribes. If you need a temporary queue used only by one consumer, combine `auto-delete` with `exclusive`. When the consumer disconnects, the queue will be removed.

What happens if you try to declare a queue that already exists? As long as the declaration parameters match the existing queue exactly, Rabbit will do nothing and return successfully as though the queue had been created (if the parameters don't match, the declaration attempt will fail). If you just want to check whether a queue exists, you can set the `passive` option of `queue.declare` to true. With `passive` set to true, `queue.declare` will return successfully if the queue exists, and return an error without creating the queue if it doesn't exist.

When you're designing your apps, you'll most likely ask yourself whether your producers or consumers should create the queues you need. It might seem that the most natural answer is that your consumers should create your queues. After all, they're the ones that need to subscribe, and you can't subscribe to a queue that doesn't exist, right? Not so fast. You need to first ask yourself whether the messages your producers create can afford to disappear. Messages that get published into an exchange but have no queue to be routed to are discarded by Rabbit. So if you can't afford for your messages to be black-holed, *both* your producers and your consumers should attempt to create the queues that will be needed. On the other hand, if you can afford to lose messages or have implemented a way to republish messages that don't get processed (we'll show you how to do this) you can have only your consumers declare the queues.

Queues are the foundational block of AMQP messaging:

- They give you a place for your messages to wait to be consumed.
- Queues are perfect for load balancing. Just attach a bunch of consumers and let RabbitMQ round-robin incoming messages evenly among them.
- They're the final endpoint for any messages in Rabbit (unless they get black-holed).

With queues under your belt, you're ready to move to the next building block of Rabbit: exchanges and bindings!

2.3   *Getting together: exchanges and bindings*

As you saw in the previous sections, you want to have consumers fetching messages from your queues. Now the question, is how does a message reach a queue? Meet AMQP bindings and exchanges. Whenever you want to deliver a message to a queue, you do it by sending it to an exchange. Then, based on certain rules, RabbitMQ will decide to which queue it should deliver the message. Those rules are called *routing keys*. A queue is said to be *bound* to an exchange by a routing key. When you send a message to the broker, it'll have a routing key—even a blank one—which RabbitMQ will try to match to the routing keys used in the bindings. If they match, then the message will be delivered to the queue. If the routing message doesn't match any of binding patterns, it'll be black-holed.

Why do you need such indirection? "I just want my messages on the queue," you might be saying. Let's look at an example to understand the advantages of such concept.

You can compare this scenario with email: if you want to send a message to any of your contacts, you send it to his address, and the SMTP server will check whom the message is addressed to and will take care of delivering it to that user's inbox. But what happens if your contact wants every message sent from you to be filed into the business folder? Then they have to set up certain rules based on the content of the message in order to achieve such a goal. They may also want rules that send the message to the same folder, for example, based on the hostname of some business providers. With the concepts of exchanges, bindings, and queues, AMQP can accommodate such use cases and many more, so you can bind a queue to an exchange with no routing key and then every message with no routing key that you send to that exchange will be delivered to said queue, in a fashion similar to email. If you require complex use cases, like publish/subscribe or multicast, you can achieve that too. You'll see that in a moment.

Besides the different use cases that you can handle with exchanges and bindings, there's another advantage: the publisher—the process that is sending messages to the broker—doesn't have to care about the logic on the other side of the broker (the queues and consumers involved in processing the messages). As you'll see, this can lead to interesting messaging scenarios that aren't possible—or are very hard to accomplish—with a broker that only allows you to publish directly to queues.

As you've seen, the broker will route messages from exchanges to queues based on routing keys, but how does it handle delivery to multiple queues? Here come into play the different types of exchanges provided by the protocol. There are four: direct, fanout, topic, and headers. Each implements a different routing algorithm. We'll go over all of them except the headers exchange, which allows you to match against a header in the AMQP message instead of the routing key. Other than that, it operates identically to the direct exchange but with much worse performance. As a result, it doesn't provide much real-world benefit and is almost never used. Let's see each of the other exchange types in detail.

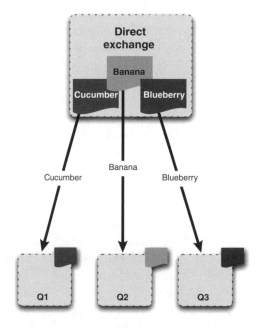

Figure 2.4   Direct exchange message flow

The direct exchange is pretty simple: if the routing key matches, then the message is delivered to the corresponding queue. You can see a representation of this in figure 2.4.

The broker must implement the direct exchange, including a default exchange with an empty string as its name. When a queue is declared, it'll be automatically bound to that exchange using the queue name as routing key. This means that you can use code like the following to send messages to a previously declared queue, provided that you obtained a channel instance:

```
$channel->basic_publish($msg, '', 'queue-name');
```

The first parameter is the message that you want to send, the second one is an empty string to specify the default exchange, and the third one will be the routing key, which is the name you used to declare the queue. Later you'll see how to achieve the RPC messaging pattern using the default exchange and temporary queues.

When the default direct exchange isn't enough for your application's needs, you can declare your own exchanges. You can issue the `exchange.declare` command with appropriate parameters to accomplish that.

The next type of exchange that we'll discuss is the fanout exchange. As you can see from figure 2.5, this exchange will multicast the received message to the bound queues. The messaging pattern is simple: when you send a message to a fanout exchange, it'll be delivered to all the queues attached to this exchange. This allows you to react in different ways based on only one message. For example, a web application may require that when a user uploads a new picture, the user's own image gallery cache must be cleared and also they should be rewarded with some points. You can have two queues bound to the upload-pictures exchange, one with consumers clearing the cache and the other one for increasing user points. Also from this scenario, you can see the advantage of using exchanges, bindings, and queues over publishing messages directly to queues. Let's say that the first requirement of the application was that after a picture was uploaded to the website, the user gallery cache was cleared. You can easily implement that by using just one queue, but what happens when the product owner comes to you with the new feature of giving awards to users for their actions? If you're sending messages directly to queues, then you have to modify the publisher's code to send message to the new *points* queue. If you've been using fanout exchanges, the only thing that you have to do is to write the code for your new consumer and then declare and bind a new queue to the fanout exchange. As we said earlier, the publisher's code is completely decoupled from the consumer's code, allowing you to increase your application functionality with ease.

Last but not least, we'll discuss the topic exchange. This exchange allows you to achieve interesting messaging scenarios, where messages can arrive to the same queue coming from different sources. Let's take as an example a logging system for your web application. You have several logging levels, like error, info, and warning, and at the same time your application is separated into modules like *user-profile*, *image-gallery*, *msg-inbox*, and so forth. As you can see in figure 2.6, if you want to report an error when the send message action failed, you can do so with the following code:

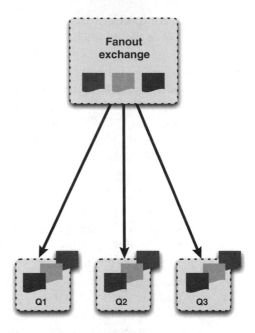

Figure 2.5   Fanout exchange message flow

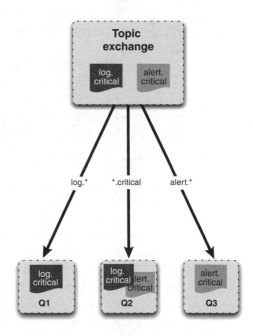

Figure 2.6   Topic exchange message flow

```
$channel->basic_publish($msg, 'logs-exchange', 'error.msg-inbox');
```

Then, provided that you've declared a queue msg-inbox-errors, you can bind it to the exchange to receive the messages like this:

```
$channel->queue_bind('msg-inbox-errors',
                'logs-exchange',
                'error.msg-inbox');
```

So far this looks very similar to a direct exchange. You've used the same string error.msg-inbox as the binding rule for the queue-binding operation and for the message publication routing key. That will ensure that your message is routed into the msg-inbox-errors queue, nothing fancy. But what if you want to have a queue *listening* to all kinds of error levels that happen in the *msg-inbox* module? You can do so using the same exchange that you already have by binding a new queue like this:

```
$channel->queue_bind('msg-inbox-logs',
                'logs-exchange',
                '*.msg-inbox');
```

The *msg-inbox-logs* queue will receive all the error, warning, and info log messages from the *msg-inbox* module. What about receiving all the logs? That's easy to accomplish too. You can use a wildcard while binding the queue to the exchange. As you can see from the previous examples, a single . delimits the routing key into parts, and the * matches any text in that particular part position. To perform a *match-all* rule you can use the # character:

```
$channel->queue_bind('all-logs', 'logs-exchange', '#');
```

With that binding, the *all-logs* queue will receive all the logs published by your web application. Of course for all the previous examples to work you must have declared the queues in advance before performing the bindings. Unlike the * operator, which considers . in the routing key as a part delimiter, the # operator has no concept of parts and considers any . characters as part of the key to match.

Now that you know about these three exchange types, you can see the power offered by AMQP. You can program the broker behavior to work in the way you want. It can be used *just* as a queue server, in a publish/subscribe setup, or as an RPC server. It just depends on how you wire the pieces together.

Let's recap what you've learned in this section:

- The key components in the AMQP architecture are exchanges, queues, and bindings.
- You bind queues to exchanges based on binding rules.
- Messages are sent to exchanges.
- There are three exchange types: direct, fanout, and topic.
- Based on the message routing key and the exchange type, the broker will decide to which queue it has to deliver the message.

2.4   *Multiple tenants: virtual hosts and separation*

With exchanges, bindings, and queues under your belt, you might think you have all the coolness that is Rabbit figured out. But if you've played around much with Rabbit, you know there's one nagging concept we haven't talked about yet: the vhost. Within every RabbitMQ server is the ability to create virtual message brokers called *virtual hosts* (*vhosts*). Each one is essentially a mini-RabbitMQ server with its own queues, exchanges, and bindings ... and, more important, its own permissions. This lets you safely use one RabbitMQ server for multiple applications without worrying that your Sudoku app might delete queues used by your lost Fido tracker. Vhosts are to Rabbit what virtual machines are to physical servers: they allow you to run data for multiple applications safely and securely by providing logical separation between instances. This is useful for anything from separating multiple customers on the same Rabbit to avoiding naming collisions on queues and exchanges. Where otherwise you might have to run multiple Rabbits and gain all the management headaches that come with that, you can instead run one Rabbit and build up or tear down vhosts on demand.

Vhosts are so fundamental to the concept of AMQP that you have to specify one when you connect. RabbitMQ makes it easy to get started by including a default vhost called / right out of the box. If you don't need multiple vhosts, just use the default one. It's accessible using the default *guest* username with password *guest*, though you should change the password for security (more on this in chapter 3). An interesting property of AMQP is that it doesn't specify whether permissions are per vhost or server-wide. This is left up to the broker developer and in RabbitMQ's case *permissions are per vhost*.

When you create a user in Rabbit, it's usually assigned to at least one vhost and will only be able to access queues, exchanges, and bindings on those assigned vhosts. Also, when you're designing your messaging architecture, keep in mind that separation between vhosts is absolute. You can't bind an exchange on vhost banana_tree to a queue on vhost oak_tree. This is actually a good thing, not only for security, but also for portability. Imagine for a second that you've designed the check cashing tier of your magnificent banking app to use its own vhost. You might initially put this vhost on the same Rabbit that houses the vhosts for other tiers of your app. But one day your customers start cashing millions of checks—good for you but bad for the Rabbit server. Check cashing needs to be on a Rabbit server with less load. If the check cashing tier had used the default vhost, you would have to worry about naming collisions (queues and exchanges) when you point it to the new Rabbit server. But since it has its own vhost, you can safely move everything to any other Rabbit server and instantly start handling the new load without any name collisions. Hence, we highly recommend identifying the common functionality groups in your infrastructure (such as web logging) and giving each one its own vhost. Also, keep in mind that when you create a vhost on a RabbitMQ cluster, it's created across the entire cluster. Just as vhosts eliminate needing to run a RabbitMQ server for every tier in your infrastructure, they also avoid making you create different clusters for each tier.

We've talked about all of the great benefits of vhosts, but how do you create them? Vhosts and permissions are unique in that they're the only primitives in AMQP (unlike queues, exchanges, and bindings) that can't be created using the AMQP protocol. For RabbitMQ they're created using the `rabbitmqctl` utility found in the ./sbin/ directory of your RabbitMQ installation. To create a vhost simply run `rabbitmqctl add_vhost [vhost_name]`, where *[vhost_name]* is the vhost you want to create. Deleting a vhost is similarly simple: `rabbitmqctl delete_vhost [vhost_name]`. Once a vhost has been created, you can connect to it and start adding your queues and exchanges. If you need to find out what vhosts are running on a particular Rabbit server, run `rabbitmqctl list_vhosts` and voila! There they are:

```
$ ./sbin/rabbitmqctl list_vhosts
Listing vhosts ...
/
oak
sycamore
...done.
```

> **NOTE** Typically you'll run `rabbitmqctl` directly on the server with the RabbitMQ node you want to manage. But you can also pass the `-n rabbit@[server_name]` option before any command to manage a remote RabbitMQ node. The node identifier (rabbit@[server_name]) is split into two parts at the @: the left half is the Erlang application name and will almost always be *rabbit*, and the right half is the server hostname or IP address. You need to make sure the server running the Rabbit node and the workstation you're running `rabbitmqctl` on have the same Erlang cookie installed. For more info on Erlang cookies, check out section 3.4.1.

Now that you've secured your queues and exchanges with vhosts, it's time to talk about making sure critical messages don't disappear when Rabbit crashes or reboots.

2.5 *Where's my message? Durability and you*

There's a dirty secret about creating queues and exchanges in Rabbit: by default they don't survive reboot. That's right; restart your RabbitMQ server and watch those queues and exchanges go poof (along with the messages inside). The reason is because of a property on every queue and exchange called `durable`. It defaults to false, and tells RabbitMQ whether the queue (or exchange) should be re-created after a crash or restart of Rabbit. Set it to true and you won't have to re-create those queues and exchanges when the power supply in your server dies. You might also think that setting `durable` to true on the exchanges and queues is all you need to do to make your messages survive a reboot, but you'd be wrong. Whereas queues and exchanges *must* be durable to allow messages to survive reboot, it isn't enough on its own.

A message that can survive a crash of the AMQP broker is called *persistent*. You flag a message as persistent by setting the *delivery mode* option of the message to 2 (your AMQP client may use a human-friendly constant instead) before publishing it. At this point, the message is indicated as persistent, but it must be published to an exchange that's durable and arrive in a queue that's durable to survive. If this weren't the case, the queue (or exchange) a persistent message was sitting in when Rabbit crashed wouldn't exist when Rabbit restarted, thereby orphaning the message. So, for a message that's in flight inside Rabbit to survive a crash, the message must

- Have its delivery mode option set to 2 (persistent)
- Be published into a durable exchange
- Arrive in a durable queue

Do these three things and you won't have to play Where's Waldo with your critical messages.

The way that RabbitMQ ensures persistent messages survive a restart is by writing them to the disk inside of a persistency log file. When you publish a persistent message to a durable exchange, Rabbit won't send the response until the message is committed to the log file. Keep in mind, though, that if it gets routed to a nondurable queue after that, it's automatically removed from the persistency log and won't survive a restart. When you use persistent messages it's crucial that you make sure *all* three elements required for a message to persist are in place (we can't stress this enough). Once you consume a persistent message from a durable queue (and acknowledge it), RabbitMQ flags it in the persistency log for garbage collection. If Rabbit restarts anytime before you consume a persistent message, it'll automatically re-create the exchanges and queues (and bindings) and replay any messages in the persistency log into the appropriate queues or exchanges (depending on where in the routing process the messages were when Rabbit died).

You might be thinking that you should use persistent messaging for all of your messages. You could do that, but you'd pay a price for ensuring your messages survive Rabbit restarts: performance. The act of writing messages to disk is much slower than just storing them in RAM, and will significantly decrease the number of messages per second your RabbitMQ server can process. It's not uncommon to see a 10x or more decrease in message throughput when using persistency.[1] There's also the issue that persistent messages don't play well with RabbitMQ's built-in clustering. Though RabbitMQ clustering allows you to talk to any queue present in the cluster from any node, those queues are actually evenly distributed among the nodes *without redundancy* (there's no backup copy of any queue on a second node in the cluster). If the cluster node hosting your seed_bin queue crashes, the queue disappears from the cluster until the node is restored … if the queue was durable. More important, while the node is down its queues aren't available and the durable ones can't be re-created. This can lead to black-holing of messages. We'll cover the behavior in more detail and show alternate clustering approaches to get around this in chapter 5.

Given the trade-offs, when should you use persistent/durable messaging? First, you need to analyze (and test) your performance needs. Do you need to process 100,000

---

[1] Placing your RabbitMQ's message store on an SSD can greatly improve the performance of persistent messaging.

messages per second on a single Rabbit server? If so, you should probably look at other ways of ensuring message delivery (or get a *very* fast storage system). For example, your producer could listen to a reply queue on a separate channel. Every time it publishes a message, it includes the name of the reply queue so that the consumer can send a reply back to confirm receipt. If a message isn't replied to within a reasonable amount of time, the producer can republish the message. That said, the critical nature of messages requiring guaranteed delivery generally means they're lower in volume than other types of messages (such as logging messages). So if persistent messaging meets your performance needs, it's an excellent way to help ensure delivery. We use it a lot for critical messages. We're just selective about what types of content use persistent messaging. For example, we run two types of Rabbit clusters: traditional RabbitMQ clustering for nonpersistent messaging, and pairs of active/hot-standby nonclustered Rabbit servers for persistent messaging (using load balancers). This ensures the processing load for persistent messaging doesn't slow down nonpersistent messages. It also means Rabbit's built-in clustering won't black-hole persistent messages when a node dies. Do keep in mind that while Rabbit can help ensure delivery, it can never absolutely guarantee it. Hard drive corruption, buggy behavior by a consumer, or other extreme events can trash/black-hole persistent messages. It's ultimately up to you to ensure your messages arrive where they need to go, and persistent messaging is a great tool to help you get there.

A concept that's related to the durability of a message is the AMQP *transaction*. So far we've talked about marking messages, queues, and exchanges as durable. That's all well and good for keeping a message safe once RabbitMQ has it in its custody, but since a publish operation returns no response to the producer, how do you know if the broker has persisted the durable message to disk? Should the broker die before it can write the message to disk, the message would be lost and you wouldn't know. That's where transactions come in. When you absolutely need to be sure the broker has the message in custody (and has routed the message to all matching subscribed queues) before you move on to another task, you need to wrap it in a transaction. If you come from a database background, it's important not to confuse AMQP transactions with what "transaction" means in most databases. In AMQP, after you place a channel into transaction mode, you send it the publish you want to confirm, followed by zero or more other AMQP commands that should be executed or ignored depending on whether the initial publish succeeded. Once you've sent all of the commands, you *commit* the transaction. If the transaction's initial publish succeeds, then the channel will complete the other AMQP commands in the transaction. If the publish fails, none of the other AMQP commands will be executed. Transactions close the "last mile" gap between producers publishing messages and RabbitMQ committing them to disk, but there's a better way to close that gap.

Though transactions are a part of the formal AMQP 0-9-1 specification, they have an Achilles heel in that they're huge drains on Rabbit performance. Not only can using transactions drop your message throughput by a factor of 2–10x, but they also make your producer app synchronous, which is one of the things you're trying to get rid of with messaging. Knowing all of this, the guys at RabbitMQ decided to come up with a better way to ensure message delivery: *publisher confirms.*[2] Similar to transactions, you have to tell Rabbit to place the channel into confirm mode, and you can't turn it off without re-creating the channel. Once a channel is in confirm mode, every message published on the channel will be assigned a unique ID number (starting at 1). Once the message has been delivered to all queues that have bindings matching the message's routing key, the channel will issue a publisher confirm to the producer app (containing the message's unique ID). This lets the producer know the message has been safely queued at all of its destinations. If the message and the queues are durable, the confirm is issued only after the queues have written the message to disk. The major benefit of publisher confirms is that they're asynchronous. Once a message has been published, the producer app can go on to the next message while waiting for the confirm. When the confirm for that message is finally received, a callback function in the producer app will be fired so it can wake up and handle the confirmation. If an internal error occurs inside Rabbit that causes a message to be lost, Rabbit will send a message *nack* (not acknowledged) that's like a publisher confirm (it has the message's unique ID) but indicates the message was lost. Also, since there's no concept of message rollback (as with transactions), publisher confirms are much lighter weight and have an almost negligible performance hit on the Rabbit broker.

Now you have the individual parts of RabbitMQ down, from consumers and producers to durable messaging, but how do they all fit together? What does the lifecycle of an actual message look like from beginning to end? The best way to answer that is to look at the life of a message in code.

2.6 *Putting it all together: a day in the life of a message*

We've talked about the history of RabbitMQ, we've discussed AMQP and its details, and we have the broker installed; now it's time we get our hands dirty and write some code. We'll illustrate how a message is created, published, and then consumed on the other side of the wire. We don't want to break the tradition of the initial Hello World example, so let's do that.

In this book we write code in PHP and Python, but—as you'll see when you compare the Python code with the PHP code—thanks to AMQP the examples are easy to port to other libraries and languages. For our first program, we'll use Python since the code is easy to understand and read even for people new to Python.

Let's get started by going over what you're going to need to build your Hello World.

- *Python 2.6 or higher*—You'll need a recent version of the Python interpreter. The version (2.6.1) installed with Mac OS X 10.6 is what we'll use. You can install Python on your Linux of choice by telling your package manager to install the `python` package.

---

[2] Publisher confirms are a RabbitMQ-only extension to AMQP (though other brokers are free to add it to their AMQP implementation). They're only available in version 2.3.1 or higher of RabbitMQ.

- *easy_install*—This handy program is part of the `setuptools` Python package and will help you install the extra packages you need for your framework.
- *Pika 0.9.6 or higher*—Besides being a cute member of the rabbit family, *Pika* is also the official Python AMQP library produced by the guys at Rabbit.

To set up your environment, you first need to install *easy_install* (you may need to run these commands under *sudo* depending on your OS):

```
$ wget http://peak.telecommunity.com/dist/ez_setup.py
...
 (25.9 KB/s) - ez_setup.py saved [10285/10285]

$ python ez_setup.py
...
Installed /Library/Python/2.6/site-packages/setuptools-0.6...
```

With easy_install ready to do your bidding, next get Pika installed:

```
$ easy_install pika
...
Installed /Library/Python/2.6/site-packages/pika-0.9.6-py2.6.egg
Processing dependencies for pika
Finished processing dependencies for pika
```

The next step is to create a folder to store your sample code:

```
$ mkdir chapter-2
$ cd chapter-2
```

Let's start with the code for the publisher. It has to perform the following tasks:

- Connect to RabbitMQ
- Obtain a channel
- Declare an exchange
- Create a message
- Publish the message
- Close the channel
- Close the connection

Now that you're all set up, open the file hello_world_producer.py in your text editor and type code from the following listing.

Listing 2.1 Hello World producer

```
import pika, sys

credentials = pika.PlainCredentials("guest", "guest")          ❶ Establish connection
conn_params = pika.ConnectionParameters("localhost",              to broker
                                  credentials = credentials)
conn_broker = pika.BlockingConnection(conn_params)

channel = conn_broker.channel()                                ❷ Obtain channel

channel.exchange_declare(exchange="hello-exchange",            ❸ Declare exchange
                  type="direct",
```

```
                              passive=False,
                              durable=True,
                              auto_delete=False)

msg = sys.argv[1]
msg_props = pika.BasicProperties()                              ❹ Create plaintext
msg_props.content_type = "text/plain"                              message

channel.basic_publish(body=msg,
                      exchange="hello-exchange",
                      properties=msg_props,
                      routing_key="hola")              ◁─❺ Publish message
```

That's a bunch of code; let's see what's happening. First at ❶ you have boilerplate code to set up your connection to RabbitMQ (by not specifying the virtual host, you're using the default one at /). You'll connect to a RabbitMQ server running on port 5672 on your local machine. You'll use the default *guest* user and password. Then you obtain a channel ❷ to communicate with RabbitMQ.

The next step is to declare an exchange ❸ where your message will be sent to. The first parameter is the exchange name, `hello-exchange`; the second one is the exchange type, *direct*. The first Boolean flag tells RabbitMQ that you're issuing the `declare` command in nonpassive mode—you want to declare the exchange, not just obtain information about it. The last two flags will tell RabbitMQ that you want your exchange to be durable and to not be automatically deleted.

Then at ❹ you proceed to create a message whose content will be the first argument passed to your hello_world_consumer.py script. The content type of the message will be `text/plain`.

Once you get the message, you'll publish it to the `hello-exchange` ❺ issuing the `basic_publish` command.

You don't have to close the connection right away every time. You can send several messages through one channel/connection and then close them when you're done.

You have your publisher ready; now let's create the message consumer. It has to do the following tasks:

- Connect to RabbitMQ
- Obtain a channel
- Declare an exchange
- Declare a queue
- Bind the queue with the exchange
- Consume the messages
- Close the channel
- Close the connection

That seems like a lot, but it's not really. You already wrote the first three steps and the last two in the previous code example. What will be new is how to declare a queue, bind it to an exchange, and start consuming new messages.

Create a file called *hello_world_consumer.py* and add the code from the following listing.

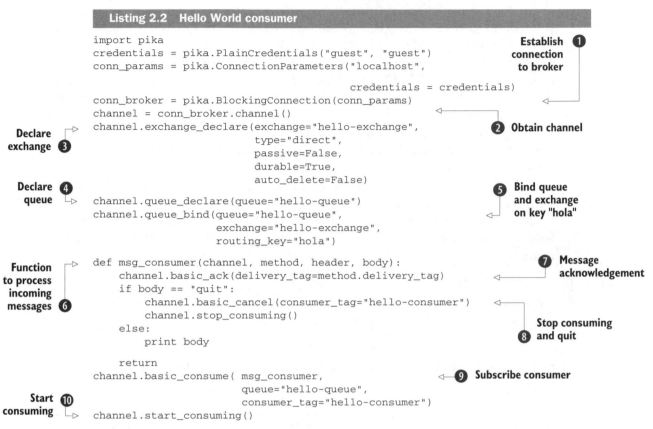

Listing 2.2   Hello World consumer

```
import pika
credentials = pika.PlainCredentials("guest", "guest")
conn_params = pika.ConnectionParameters("localhost",
                                        credentials = credentials)
conn_broker = pika.BlockingConnection(conn_params)
channel = conn_broker.channel()
channel.exchange_declare(exchange="hello-exchange",
                         type="direct",
                         passive=False,
                         durable=True,
                         auto_delete=False)
channel.queue_declare(queue="hello-queue")
channel.queue_bind(queue="hello-queue",
                   exchange="hello-exchange",
                   routing_key="hola")
def msg_consumer(channel, method, header, body):
    channel.basic_ack(delivery_tag=method.delivery_tag)
    if body == "quit":
        channel.basic_cancel(consumer_tag="hello-consumer")
        channel.stop_consuming()
    else:
        print body

    return
channel.basic_consume( msg_consumer,
                       queue="hello-queue",
                       consumer_tag="hello-consumer")
channel.start_consuming()
```

❶ Establish connection to broker

❷ Obtain channel

❸ Declare exchange

❹ Declare queue

❺ Bind queue and exchange on key "hola"

❻ Function to process incoming messages

❼ Message acknowledgement

❽ Stop consuming and quit

❾ Subscribe consumer

❿ Start consuming

As you can see, you have the same code as before for including the library and defining some constants for your connection parameters. You could move those definitions to a config.py file and avoid duplicated code. We leave that as an exercise for you.

At point ❶ you set up your connection to the broker and then ❷ create your channel. After you have the connection ❸, you declare the exchange again. Since the semantics for the declare commands mean "create if not present; otherwise continue," nothing will break. You do that to avoid errors when you later issue the queue_bind command in case the exchange hasn't been created in advance.

At ❹ you declare a queue with the name hello-queue using AMQP default options. Then you bind the queue to hello-exchange ❺. You're using the routing key hola, which will work for this simple example.

You're almost ready to start consuming messages, but you need a callback function where you'll process the message. At point ❻ you create such a function that will acknowledge ❼ the message so RabbitMQ can delete it and send a new one to your consumer. At the end of your callback function you echo the body of the message. Soon you'll see what the code at point ❽ is doing.

Once you have your callback function you can issue the ❾ basic_consume command to subscribe to the queue. The first parameter will be the callback that you just wrote. Next you pass as parameters the name of the queue and the consumer tag that you want to use to identify your process. Every message that RabbitMQ sends to your consumer will be passed to your callback function.

With the previous command you're ready to receive messages. Now you have to actually do it. For that you ❿ start a blocking loop waiting for incoming data through the channel. If RabbitMQ sends you a message, `pika` will take care of passing it to the callback function.

The last bit of the puzzle is point ❽. `start_consuming()` is a blocking `while` loop that will never end. To make it end, you inserted a condition inside your callback stating that if a message has the text `'quit'` as body, then you'll issue the `basic_cancel` command to stop consuming (and then close the channel and connection). You have to provide the consumer tag as parameter for `basic_cancel`.

Now let's test the code. First you have to start RabbitMQ, so open a new terminal window, move to the folder where you installed RabbitMQ and type the following command:

```
$ sbin/rabbitmq-server
```

Once RabbitMQ is running, switch to the previous terminal window and start the consumer with the following command (see figure 2.7):

```
$ python ./hello_world_consumer.py
```

Open a new terminal window, move to the chapter-2 folder and type the following:

```
$ python ./hello_world_producer.py 'Hello World!'
```

If everything went okay, you should see the text `"Hello World!"` in the terminal window where you're running the consumer. Congratulations, everything is working fine!

Now try sending other messages like this:

```
$ python ./hello_world_producer.py 'Hello Mundo!'
```

And you should see this text: `"Hello Mundo!"`

And finally you stop the consumer with

```
$ python ./hello_world_producer.py 'quit'
```

Let's see what you just did. You wanted to send messages over the wire and consume them, so you declared your exchange in order to have a place to publish your messages. You also created a queue and bound it to the `hello-exchange`. Then based on text that you input at the command line, you created your message instances and send them over RabbitMQ. Based on your `direct` exchange type, RabbitMQ routed your message to the `hello-queue`. Since you had a consumer on the other side of the wire, RabbitMQ delivered the message and it was processed by your callback function. You can see that no routing key was provided; that's because AMQP can be as simple or complex as you want it to be. For our example the empty routing key sufficed.

```
Terminal — tmux — 80×24
mrhyde:chapter-2 mrhyde$ python ./hello_world_producer.py 'Hello World!'
mrhyde:chapter-2 mrhyde$ python ./hello_world_producer.py 'Hello Mundo!'
mrhyde:chapter-2 mrhyde$ python ./hello_world_producer.py 'quit'
mrhyde:chapter-2 mrhyde$



mrhyde:chapter-2 mrhyde$ python ./hello_world_consumer.py
Hello World!
Hello Mundo!
mrhyde:chapter-2 mrhyde$




[1] 0:bash*                                        "mrhyde" 20:51 18-Dec-11
```

Figure 2.7   Rabbit MQ Hello World

2.7   Using publisher confirms to verify delivery

So now you know how to write a basic consumer and producer, but you might be wondering how publisher confirms and transactions fit into the mix. Let's take a look at how you can upgrade your Hello World producer to take advantage of publisher confirms to track message delivery.[3] Before we dive into updating the Hello World producer to use publisher confirms, look at figure 2.8, which is an illustration of how message IDs are assigned.

We said that every message published gets a unique ID if the channel is in confirm mode. This might make you think that `basic _publish` will suddenly start returning a message ID, but that's not how message IDs work. Since a channel can only be used by a single thread, you can be assured that all publishes using that channel are sequential. As a result, RabbitMQ makes a simple assumption: the first message published on any channel

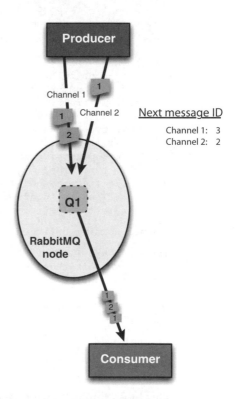

Figure 2.8   Publisher confirm message IDs

---

[3] Since transactions kill performance, we focus on publisher confirms as the preferred way to add delivery confirmation to your producers. If you really need to learn how to add transactions to your producers, don't worry. We've included a version of the Hello World producer that uses transactions in the *RabbitMQ in Action* examples online: https://github.com/rabbitinaction/sourcecode.

will have an ID of 1, and every subsequent message on the channel will increment that
ID by 1. So the second published message on the channel will have an ID of 2, the
third message an ID of 3, and so on. The message IDs are unique to the channel, so
once the channel is closed you won't be able to track the status of any outstanding
publisher confirms for messages published on that channel. What this means is that
RabbitMQ doesn't have to tell you the ID of the message you just published; you keep
track of it yourself in a counter internal to your app and increment that counter every
time your app's channel publishes. Also, since every channel starts its message IDs at 1,
if you have multiple channels open in parallel, you need to maintain a separate internal message ID counter for each channel. Now that you understand how message IDs
are assigned, let's take a look at the following version of your Hello World producer,
now updated to use publisher confirms.

Listing 2.3   Hello World producer with confirms

```
import pika, sys
from pika import spec
credentials = pika.PlainCredentials("guest", "guest")
conn_params = pika.ConnectionParameters("localhost",
                                        credentials = credentials)
conn_broker = pika.BlockingConnection(conn_params)
channel = conn_broker.channel()
def confirm_handler(frame):                              ❶ Publisher
    if type(frame.method) == spec.Confirm.SelectOk:        confirm handler
        print "Channel in 'confirm' mode."
    elif type(frame.method) == spec.Basic.Nack:
        if frame.method.delivery_tag in msg_ids:
            print "Message lost!"
    elif type(frame.method) == spec.Basic.Ack:
        if frame.method.delivery_tag in msg_ids:
            print "Confirm received!"
            msg_ids.remove(frame.method.delivery_tag)
                                                         ❷ Put channel in
channel.confirm_delivery(callback=confirm_handler)         confirm mode

msg = sys.argv[1]
msg_props = pika.BasicProperties()
msg_props.content_type = "text/plain"                    ❸ Reset message
msg_ids = []                                               ID tracker
channel.basic_publish(body=msg,
                      exchange="hello-exchange",         ❹ Publish message
                      properties=msg_props,
                      routing_key="hola")                ❺ Add ID to
msg_ids.append(len(msg_ids) + 1)                           tracking list
channel.close()
```

This looks similar to your original Hello World producer, but you've now added a callback function ❶ confirm_handler that will be called when the app receives a publisher confirm. You then tell Pika to put the channel into confirm mode ❷ and use
confirm_handler as the callback that will receive publisher confirms as they arrive.
Once your channel is set up to handle publisher confirms, you then set up your

internal list (msg_ids) for tracking message IDs on the channel ❸, and publish the message ❹. Finally, once the publish completes you increment msg_id_no to indicate the message's ID of 1 ❺. Inside confirm_handler is where all the interesting magic with confirms happens.

When confirm_handler receives a publisher confirm, it first checks whether the confirmation type is Confirm.SelectOk:

```
if type(frame.method) == spec.Confirm.SelectOk:
    print "Channel in 'confirm' mode."
```

RabbitMQ sends a confirmation of type Confirm.SelectOk when you first put the channel into confirm mode. It's not a confirmation of a message, but rather a notification that your channel is now set to receive publisher confirms. If the confirmation isn't Confirm.SelectOk, then confirm_handler checks whether it's a Basic.Nack confirmation:

```
elif type(frame.method) == spec.Basic.Nack:
    if frame.method.delivery_tag in msg_ids:
        print "Message lost!"
```

You might remember from our explanation of publisher confirms that Basic.Nack indicates the message was lost due to an internal RabbitMQ error. But before you treat the message as lost, you check frame.method.delivery_tag for the message ID of the message being "nacked." If the message ID matches the ID of the message you published, then you tell the user that the message was lost. In a more sophisticated application, this is where you'd put code that republishes the lost message. Finally, if the confirmation isn't Confirm.SelectOk or Basic.Nack, you check whether it's Basic.Ack:

```
elif type(frame.method) == spec.Basic.Ack:
```

Providing the message is a publisher confirm acknowledgement (Basic.Ack), you need to make sure that the message ID is in your list of published message IDs:

```
if frame.method.delivery_tag in msg_ids:
    print "Confirm received!"
    msg_ids.remove(frame.method.delivery_tag)
```

If the message ID of the confirmation is one you're tracking in msg_ids, you confirm to the user that the message was successfully queued and then remove the message ID from your list of IDs awaiting delivery acknowledgement. It's slightly more complicated than your original Hello World producer, but in only 12 lines of code you've added the ability to track delivery of your published messages. Even more impressive is that this simple code can track delivery of millions of published messages per minute! That's how much better publisher confirms perform than AMQP transactions.

2.8 *Summary*

We've covered a lot of territory in this chapter. Not only do you have the foundation you need to build nearly any messaging app you can dream up, but you also have a real-live running producer and consumer, including a producer that can track message delivery! In future chapters we'll cover specific patterns for building messaging applications that will make your apps elegant, efficient, and powerful. But with what you've learned so far you can start coding right away on that distributed Twitter clone you've been dying to build. Before we dive into more coding, let's take a look at how to manage your RabbitMQ server more expertly. For example, it's probably not a great idea that anyone can connect to your virtual hosts and publish messages into any exchange they like. That's exactly the type of problem we'll show you how to avoid next by setting permissions. So let's take a look at how to start, stop, and generally manage RabbitMQ!

Running and
administering Rabbit

3

This chapter covers

- Server management—starting and stopping nodes
- Permission configuration
- Usage statistics
- Troubleshooting problems with RabbitMQ and Erlang

We've spent the majority of our time so far on the concepts of AMQP messaging and how to get a basic install of RabbitMQ running. Now we're ready to more deeply explore what it takes to administer RabbitMQ on a day-to-day basis. Knowing how to get RabbitMQ started on your workstation is one thing, but how do you get it stopped cleanly? How do you limit the amount of RAM it can consume so it doesn't starve other applications on the same server? These are the kinds of things you'll run into when it comes time to move RabbitMQ out of development and into production. We'll use this chapter to show you how to run a top-notch production RabbitMQ environment so you can avoid the big gotchas.

Among the different things we'll cover are

- Some background on how Erlang operates, including those mysterious Erlang cookies
- Controlling user access via RabbitMQ's permissions system
- Using the command-line tools to view the status of your vhosts, queues, exchanges, and bindings
- What to do when you see scary Erlang error messages like `"badrpc,nodedown"`
- How to interpret RabbitMQ's various log files

By the time we're done, you'll be a top-notch RabbitMQ admin and ready to tackle your production Rabbit environment. Let's get started with the basics and dive into how to manage a RabbitMQ server.

3.1 Server management

Running a RabbitMQ server effectively can be different from other products you've used. This is primarily because RabbitMQ is written in Erlang and Erlang does things its own way. For the most part this is a good thing. Erlang was designed from day one to let apps talk to each other without having to know whether they're on the same machine or different machines. For RabbitMQ, this makes clustering and reliable routing of messages a breeze. But accomplishing this "easy distribution" requires two concepts you might be unfamiliar with: the Erlang node and the Erlang application. Not to worry; these concepts aren't as alien as they may sound. If you're familiar with Java Virtual Machines (JVM), these ideas are very similar to the ideas behind the JVM. As we move through this section, you'll learn how to start and stop RabbitMQ nodes and how to work with the RabbitMQ config file. Without further ado, we'll begin by looking at what a node is and how to start it.

3.1.1 Starting nodes

Up to this point, we've frequently used the term *node* to refer to a RabbitMQ server instance. In reality, what a node really describes is an Erlang node running an Erlang application. Don't get scared off by the mention of Erlang—you don't need to be an Erlang aficionado to understand what's going on. It's very similar to what happens with the JVM.

When you run a Java application, an instance of the JVM is spun up and begins executing the specified Java application. Similarly, Erlang has a virtual machine and each instance of it is referred to as a *node*. Nodes are special. Unlike the JVM, multiple Erlang applications can run inside the same node, and more important, nodes can talk natively to each other (whether they're on the same server or not). For example, due to the magic of Erlang, an application on node `asparagus` can call functions in applications running on node `artichoke` as though those functions were local. Also, if an application crashes for any reason (say, RabbitMQ crashing) the Erlang node will automatically attempt to restart the application (providing Erlang itself didn't crash).

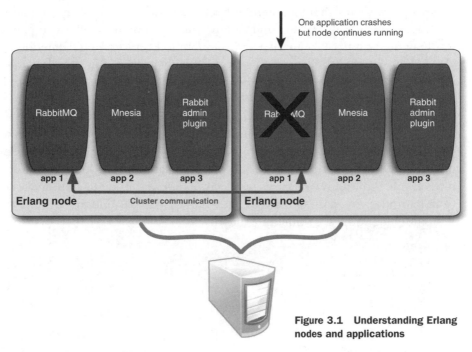

Figure 3.1 Understanding Erlang nodes and applications

This has some interesting benefits when we start talking about plugins and clustering. The important thing to remember right now is that when we talk about RabbitMQ nodes, we're referring to the RabbitMQ application *and* the Erlang node it runs on.

Luckily for us, RabbitMQ makes it easy to start the Erlang node and the Rabbit application in one step. Find the `./sbin` directory in your RabbitMQ installation and run `./rabbitmq-server`.[1] As you watch the console, you'll see the different RabbitMQ subsystems come online and become ready to process your messages. If you encounter any errors during startup, take a look at the RabbitMQ log. Normally, it's found in `/var/log/rabbitmq/` and is named `rabbit@[hostname].log` (the "rabbit" part of the filename is the default Erlang node name running RabbitMQ). You can also start the Rabbit node in the background as a daemon by adding the `-detached` flag: `./rabbitmq-server -detached`. That's all there is to getting a single RabbitMQ node started. Now that it's started though, how do you stop it?

3.1.2 Stopping nodes

When it comes to stopping RabbitMQ, there are two ways of doing it: the clean way and dirty way. If you run RabbitMQ attached to the console, you might be confused when you punch CTRL-C and see something like this:

```
BREAK: (a)bort (c)ontinue (p)roc info (i)nfo (l)oaded
       (v)ersion (k)ill (D)b-tables (d)istribution
```

---

[1] If you installed RabbitMQ from packages specific to your OS (say, RPMs), it's a good idea to use the start/stop init.d scripts installed by the package.

Holey moley, what's that all about? All you wanted to do was stop RabbitMQ. What you're looking at is the Erlang node asking you if you want to kill the application, the whole node, or if it's all a mistake and you want to keep running. Generally speaking, you want to kill the whole node, so abort is what you want. But there's a much better way to stop RabbitMQ—a way that will tell RabbitMQ to cleanly shut down and protect all those persistent queues.

rabbitmqctl is the one-stop shop for almost all of your RabbitMQ management needs. You've already seen how it can help you create and list vhosts. It can also help you stop RabbitMQ. When you run `./sbin/rabbitmqctl stop` from your RabbitMQ installation directory, rabbitmqctl will communicate with the local node and instruct it to cleanly shut down. You can also specify a different node to shut down, including remote nodes, by passing the `-n rabbit@[hostname]` option. If you watch the RabbitMQ log you'll see something like this:

```
=INFO REPORT====
    application: rabbit
    exited: stopped
    type: permanent

=INFO REPORT====
    application: mnesia
    exited: stopped
    type: permanent

=INFO REPORT====
    application: os_mon
    exited: stopped
    type: permanent
```

When you see that rabbit, mnesia, and os_mon are stopped, the Rabbit node is completely shut down. If you installed RabbitMQ from a packaging system like APT on Ubuntu, you might also have a RabbitMQ startup/shutdown script installed in `/etc/init.d/`. You can use that script to accomplish the same shutdown task. At this point the entire RabbitMQ node is shut down, including its Erlang parent. Sometimes, though, you want to just stop the RabbitMQ application and leave the Erlang parent running. Let's take a look at how to do that.

3.1.3 *Stopping and restarting the application: what's the difference?*

So far we've talked about stopping the entire RabbitMQ node (application and Erlang node together). But sometimes you just want to restart the RabbitMQ application and keep the Erlang node running. What's the advantage? For clustering, it's required. Since rabbitmq-server starts both the node and the application, it preconfigures the RabbitMQ application for standalone mode. To add the node to an existing cluster, what you need to do is stop the application and reset the node to a pristine state so it can be prepared for clustering. If you were to use `./rabbitmqctl stop` you'd shut down both the application and the node, forcing you to start both in standalone mode again via `./rabbitmq-server`. There's also the use case where you're running other Erlang applications besides RabbitMQ on the same node, making stopping the whole node undesirable.

Stopping just the RabbitMQ application is a lot simpler than the reasons for wanting to. Just run `./rabbitmqctl stop_app`. The Rabbit logs will show the same shutdown messages as when shutting down the whole node.

Starting and stopping RabbitMQ is great, but what about when your problem is configuring RabbitMQ so it doesn't gobble up all the RAM on your server? Or maybe you need to change the port RabbitMQ listens on. That's where the RabbitMQ configuration files come into play.

3.1.4 *Rabbit configuration files*

Like most server applications, RabbitMQ allows you to set systemwide tunables and settings via a configuration file. Typically, this file is located at /etc/rabbitmq/ rabbitmq.config, but its location can be changed via the CONFIG_FILE environment variable set in the rabbitmq-server script. Within rabbitmq.config you'll find a scary-looking file format:

```
[ {mnesia, [{dump_log_write_threshold, 1000}]},
  {rabbit, [{vm_memory_high_watermark, 0.4}]} ].
```

What you're looking at is essentially a raw Erlang data structure. But if you're familiar with Python, JavaScript, or any other modern programming language, it's easy to understand once you break it down. Let's reformat the configuration to be more human friendly:

```
1) [
2)    {mnesia, [{dump_log_write_threshold, 1000}]},
3)    {rabbit, [{vm_memory_high_watermark, 0.4}]}
4) ].
```

That's better. You can see that a RabbitMQ configuration file is really an array containing *nested hashtables* (dictionaries or named arrays). Lines 1 and 4 open and close the configuration array. Within the outer config array, each Erlang application gets its own hashtable for its configuration options (here we have two applications). mnesia specifies configuration options for the Mnesia database (Mnesia is what RabbitMQ uses for storing exchange and queue metadata). rabbit specifies RabbitMQ-specific configuration options. Each option is expressed in the format: *{[option_name], [option_value]}*. For example, {dump_log_write_threshold, 1000} changes how often Mnesia flushes entries from its append-only log file into the actual database files. To add another Mnesia configuration option, just add another {[option_name], [option_value]} term separated from the last one by a comma.

> **NOTE** The metadata for every queue, exchange, and binding in RabbitMQ (but not message content) is written to Mnesia, which is a non-SQL database built right into Erlang. Mnesia ensures RabbitMQ metadata integrity through crashes by writing first to an append-only log file. It then regularly dumps the contents of the log into the actual Mnesia database files. If you're familiar with

the way a logging database like MySQL's InnoDB or a logging filesystem like XFS works, it's the same concept. The Mnesia `dump_log_write_threshold` option controls how often the dumping occurs. A setting of 1000 tells Mnesia to dump the log contents into the database files every 1000 entries.

With the Rabbit configuration file format squared away, what are the actual options you can change? Some are related to the Mnesia database, and some are directly for Rabbit, as shown in tables 3.1 and 3.2.

Table 3.1   Mnesia configuration options

Option name Value type	Default	Description
`dump_log_write_threshold`		
Integer	100	How often to flush/dump the contents of the append-only log into the actual database files. It's specified in terms of how many entries must be in the log before a dump operation occurs. Setting this to a higher number can reduce I/O load and increase performance for persistent messages.

Table 3.2   Rabbit configuration options

Option name Value type	Default	Description
`tcp_listeners`		
Array of {"ip_address", port_number}	`[{"0.0.0.0", 5672},]`	Defines which IP addresses and ports RabbitMQ should listen on for non-SSL-encrypted traffic.
`ssl_listeners`		
Array of {"ip_address", port_number}	NONE	Defines which IP addresses and ports RabbitMQ should listen on for SSL-encrypted traffic.
`ssl_options`		
Array of {"key", value}	NONE	Specifies SSL-related options. Valid options are `cacertfile` (CA certificate file), `certfile` (server certificate file), `keyfile` (server key file) and `fail_if_no_peer_cert` (require client to have a valid certificate: True/False).
`vm_memory_high_watermark`		
Decimal percentage	0.4	Controls how much memory RAM RabbitMQ is allowed to consume. It's specified in terms of a decimal number representing the percentage of installed memory Rabbit is allowed to use (0.4 = 40%).

Table 3.2 Rabbit configuration options *(continued)*

Option name Value type	Default	Description
`msg_store_file_size_limit` Integer (bytes)	16777216	The maximum size of the message store DB before RabbitMQ garbage collects the contents of the store.
`queue_index_max_journal_entries` Integer	262144	The maximum number of entries in the message store journal before they're flushed into the message store DB and committed.

Though the configuration files allow you to change a lot of different aspects about how RabbitMQ operates, one thing they don't do is control access to RabbitMQ itself. For that RabbitMQ has an entire specialized subsystem dedicated to permissions. Let's start getting familiar with permissions by learning how to create a user.

3.2   Asking permission

If you're familiar with access control lists on various operating systems, understanding RabbitMQ's permission system will come readily to you. Like most permission systems, it starts with users who are then granted rights, as shown in figure 3.2.

The nice thing about the RabbitMQ permission system is that a single user can be granted permissions across multiple vhosts. This can greatly simplify the management of access control for an application that needs to talk across multiple security domains (using virtual hosts for separation). Enough talk; let's create a user!

3.2.1   Managing users

Within RabbitMQ, users are the basic unit of access control. They can be granted different levels of access to one or more vhosts, and use a standard username/password pair to authenticate the user. Adding, deleting, and listing them is simple and is accomplished using `rabbitmqctl`. Let's create a new user for the check-cashing app.

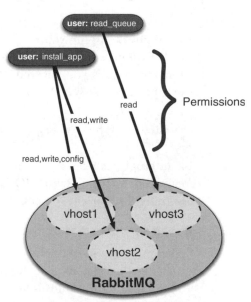

Figure 3.2   How RabbitMQ permissions work: your users get varying levels of permissions (read, write, and/or config) for their applications connected to RabbitMQ hosts

From the ./sbin directory of your RabbitMQ installation run

```
$ ./rabbitmqctl add_user cashing-tier cashMe1
Creating user "cashing-tier" ...
...done.
```

This will create a new Rabbit user with the username cashing-tier and give it the password cashMe1. If you wanted to remove the user, you'd simply run

```
$ ./rabbitmqctl delete_user cashing-tier
Deleting user "cashing-tier" ...
...done.
```

Please note that when you delete a user, any access control entries referencing that user will be deleted automatically from the Rabbit permissions database. rabbitmqctl *will not* warn you that related access control entries are being removed when you delete the user. So be careful when removing users; otherwise you may find yourself re-creating a bunch of access control entries.

Frequently, what you need to know is which users currently exist on your Rabbit server. You do this by passing the list_users command to rabbitmqctl:

```
$ ./rabbitmqctl list_users
Listing users ...
cashing-tier
guest
...done.
```

You might be asking yourself, "Great. But how do I change an existing user's password? Do I have to re-create the user and lose all my access control entries?" Fear not; rabbitmqctl has you covered. Simply run the change_password command, specify the user whose password you want to change, and what the new password should be:

```
$ ./rabbitmqctl change_password cashing-tier compl3xPassword
Changing password for user "cashing-tier" ...
...done.
```

Ba-da bing! cashing-tier's new password is now compl3xPassword. As you can see, managing users in RabbitMQ is simple. The complexity comes in when you start assigning those users to access control entries.

3.2.2   *Rabbit's permissions system*

Starting with version 1.6.0, RabbitMQ implemented an access control list (ACL) style of permissions system. Prior to this, users could only be granted or denied access to entire vhosts (within those vhosts, they could do anything). The new system allows for a great deal of granularity, and gives the ability to grant users read, write, and configure permissions. What's the difference between the three?

- *Read*—Any operation related to consuming messages, including "purging" an entire queue (also required for binding operations to succeed)
- *Write*—Publishing messages (also required for binding operations to succeed)
- *Configure*—Creation and deletion of queues and exchanges

Table 3.3 AMQP operations-to-RabbitMQ permissions map

AMQP command	Configure	Write	Read
exchange.declare	exchange		
exchange.delete	exchange		
queue.declare	queue		
queue.delete	queue		
queue.bind		queue	exchange
basic.publish		exchange	
basic.get			queue
basic.consume			queue
queue.purge			queue

Table 3.3 shows a list of the different AMQP commands and the permissions they require (current as of RabbitMQ 2.0.0).

An access control entry consists of four parts:

- The user being granted access.
- The vhost on which the permissions apply.
- The combination of read/write/configure permissions to grant.
- The permission scope—whether the permissions apply only to client-named queues/exchanges, server-named queues/exchanges, or both. Client-named means your app set the name of the exchange/queue; server-named means your app didn't supply a name and let the server assign a random one for you.

It's important to remember that access control entries can't span vhosts. For example, if you wanted to grant the same permissions to the user cashing-tier on vhost oak and vhost sycamore, you'd need to create two access control entries (one for each vhost). Enough theory though. Let's create an access control entry!

For this example, assume you have a vhost named sycamore, and you want to grant cashing-tier full access (configure, write and read permissions). To do this you want rabbitmqctl's set_permissions command:

```
$ ./rabbitmqctl set_permissions -p sycamore \
cashing-tier ".*" ".*" ".*"
Setting permissions for user "cashing-tier" in vhost "sycamore" ...
...done.
```

Let's take the set_permissions command apart, piece by piece:

- -p sycamore—This tells set_permissions which vhost the entry should apply to.
- cashing-tier—The user being granted the permissions.
- ".*" ".*" ".*"—These are the granted permissions. The values map to configure, write, and read respectively.

The permission values are the most interesting part of the command. Each of the three values is a regular expression. In this case, you used `".*"` for every permission (configure, write, and read). `".*"` means match any queue or exchange name, which allows `cashing-tier` to execute any configure, write, or read commands against any queue or exchange. Another example may help clear this up.

Let's say for a minute that you need to grant `cashing-tier` access to the oak vhost. You want to allow the user to be able to execute a read command against any queue or exchange, while restricting writes only to queues or exchanges whose names starts with *checks-*. Also, you want to prevent configure operations entirely. To do this you'll want to craft three regular expressions:[2]

- `".*"` to match any queue or exchange
- `"checks-.*"` to match only queues and exchanges starting with *checks-*
- `""` to match *no* queues or exchanges (this is how you deny a specific permission type to a user)

Putting it all together, you'd execute a `set_permissions` that looks like this:

```
$ ./rabbitmqctl set_permissions -p oak \
-s all cashing-tier "" "checks-.*" ".*"
Setting permissions for user "cashing-tier" in vhost "oak" ...
...done.
```

You can verify that the permissions have correctly applied to the oak vhost by using rabbitmqctl's `list_permissions` command:

```
$ ./rabbitmqctl list_permissions -p oak
Listing permissions in vhost "oak" ...
cashing-tier              checks-.*        .*        all
...done.
```

The empty column between `cashing-tier` and `"checks-.*"` on the output indicates the empty (`""`) value you passed for configure permissions. As you can see, the permissions did correctly apply to the oak vhost and your queues/exchanges are secured as you want. What if you wanted to remove these permissions? You can remove a user's permissions on any vhost by using rabbitmqctl's `clear_permissions` command:

```
$ ./rabbitmqctl clear_permissions -p oak cashing-tier
Clearing permissions for user "cashing-tier" in vhost "oak" ...
...done.
```

By running `list_permissions` you can see that the permissions are now gone:

```
$ ./rabbitmqctl list_permissions -p oak
Listing permissions in vhost "oak" ...
...done.
```

It's important to note that `clear_permissions` will remove *all* permissions for the user on the specified vhost. If you only want to modify the existing permissions for a user,

---

[2] RabbitMQ permissions accept standard Perl-compatible regular expression (PCRE) syntax.

just execute `set_permissions` with the new permission values. If you want to see what permissions a user has across *all* vhosts on your RabbitMQ server, use `rabbitmqctl`'s `list_user_permissions` command:

```
$ ./rabbitmqctl list_user_permissions cashing-tier
Listing permissions for user "cashing-tier" ...
oak             checks-.*      .*       all
sycamore        .*      .*      .*       all
...done.
```

Permissions in RabbitMQ are simple to create and very flexible. The flexibility allows you to create complex permission structures for your vhosts, which can be a benefit when you need it, but can be difficult to interpret if they become too complex. Where possible, try to use vhost separation as your primary method of securing one app from another, and keep the number of access control entries per vhost to a minimum. This will help you to avoid unexpected permission behavior that can be difficult to debug.

Now that you can connect and secure your Rabbit server, maybe you'd like to see what's going on inside. Perhaps you need to know how many provisioning messages are in your user creation queue. Maybe you'd like to see if your exchanges are on the right vhost. One of the most important parts of a healthy RabbitMQ server is being able to monitor its internals. So let's find out how to check up on our Rabbits!

3.3   Checking up

So far you've learned about RabbitMQ management—how to start and stop the server, add users, manage permissions, and so forth—but what if you want to check what's there on the server, or how many queues you have? That `logs-exchange` you created in the previous chapter: was it topic or fanout? Are there any messages left to be consumed in the `msg-inbox-logs` queue? All these questions can be answered by the mighty `rabbitmqctl`!

3.3.1   Viewing statistics

As you might've noticed when we played with the `rabbitmqctl` script before, it accepts many options and commands. One that you'll see often is the `-p` option. It specifies the *virtual host* or *path* for which you want information. If you omit that option, `rabbitmqctl` will take / as the default path.

To prepare the ground for experimenting with `rabbitmqctl`, let's create an exchange and bind it to a couple of queues so you can have some sample data to play with. As you know, most of the examples in this book will be in PHP or Python. You already set up Python, so now it's time to code this simple script in PHP. Let's see what you need to install to get your development environment ready. First you need to get a PHP package that suits your operating system. Since PHP is popular, you shouldn't have problems there and chances are that your operating system already comes with PHP preinstalled. If you still need to install it, we recommend that you pick up one of the 5.3.x versions because PHP got a lot of improvements related to memory management and garbage collection since the 5.3 release. Once you get PHP set up, it's time to download the PHP AMQP library that we'll use during the course of this book. The library is called `php-amqplib` and can be obtained at https://github.com/videlalvaro/php-amqplib. Create a folder for your PHP examples and then download the library there:

```
$ mkdir php
$ cd php
$ wget https://github.com/videlalvaro/php-amqplib/tarball/v1.0 \
 --no-check-certificate
$ tar -xzvf v1.0
$ mv videlalvaro-php-amqplib-b0b8696 php-amqplib
```

First you created a folder called `php` and then *changed directory* into that folder. Then you obtained the library tarball by using `wget` and decompressed the file that you got from GitHub. Finally you moved the library to a most suitable location to save some typing later.

Now that you have `php-amqplib` downloaded, create the PHP script to initialize your queues and exchanges. Create a new file called `rabbitmqctl-examples.php` and add the code from the following listing.

Listing 3.1   rabbitmqctl examples

```php
<?php

require_once('./php-amqplib/amqp.inc');

define('HOST', 'localhost');
define('PORT', 5672);
define('USER', 'guest');
define('PASS', 'guest');

$conn = new AMQPConnection(HOST, PORT, USER, PASS);    ← ❶ Obtain connection and channel
$channel = $conn->channel();

$channel->exchange_declare('logs-exchange',    ← ❷ Declare exchange
 'topic', false, true, false);

$channel->queue_declare('msg-inbox-errors',
  false, true, false, false);

$channel->queue_declare('msg-inbox-logs',    ← ❸ Declare queues
  false, true, false, false);

$channel->queue_declare('all-logs', false,
  true, false, false);
                                               ← ❹ Bind queues to exchange
$channel->queue_bind('msg-inbox-errors',
 'logs-exchange', 'error.msg-inbox');

$channel->queue_bind('msg-inbox-logs',
 'logs-exchange', '*.msg-inbox');

?>
```

This script is fairly simple and we won't go into detail about the AMQP methods that we call here because we have a whole chapter dedicated to AMQP usage. For now let's try to understand the basics of this script. First you connect to the broker and obtain a channel ❶ so you have a way to communicate with RabbitMQ. Once you have the channel, you declare an exchange called `logs-exchange` ❷ and then create three queues: `msg-inbox-errors`, `msg-inbox-logs`, and `all-logs` ❸. Finally you bind only two of the three queues to the `logs-exchange` using the `error.msg-inbox` binding rule in the first case and `*.msg-inbox` as the binding rule in the second example ❹. The goal of the script is to have something to display when you run the `rabbitmqctl` commands for listing exchanges, queues, and bindings. Just make sure that the path in the `require_once` line points to the place where you have the `amqp.inc` library installed. Execute the code with the following command:

```
$ php ./rabbitmqctl-examples.php
```

If everything went well then you're ready to keep experimenting with `rabbitmqctl`.

LISTING QUEUES AND MESSAGE COUNTS

Let's start with the `list_queues` command. On the terminal, change to the `sbin` folder (or the folder where `rabbitmqctl` is located) and type

```
$ ./rabbitmqctl list_queues
```

The output of this command will depend on the queues that you have declared on your server, but you should see something similar to this:

```
Listing queues ...
msg-inbox-logs  0
msg-inbox-errors  0
all-logs 3
...done.
```

There you see the queue name and the number of messages in each queue. As we said, this information is for the default vhost. If you want to get it for a different vhost, try adding the `-p` option like this:

```
$ ./rabbitmqctl list_queues -p sycamore
```

The queues for the sycamore vhost should be displayed.

Now let's see which other options you have for this command. If you run the `rabbitmqctl` command with no options, the usage help will be displayed. Among all the help text, you'll see this:

```
list_queues    [-p <VHostPath>] [<QueueInfoItem> ...]
```

You already saw what *VHostPath* means. Scroll down a bit and you'll see what options are accepted as `QueueInfoItem`:

```
<QueueInfoItem> must be a member of the list [name, durable,
auto_delete, arguments, pid, owner_pid, exclusive_consumer_pid,
exclusive_consumer_tag, messages_ready, messages_unacknowledged,
messages_uncommitted, messages, acks_uncommitted, consumers,
transactions, memory]. The default is to display name and (number of)
messages.
```

This means that if you want to know more information about the queues, like the name, number of messages, or number of consumers and memory used, you can issue this command:

```
$ ./rabbitmqctl list_queues name messages consumers memory
Listing queues ...
msg-inbox-logs  0 2 34632
msg-inbox-errors  0 1 34632
all-logs 3 0 43664
...done.
```

As expected, `rabbitmqctl` returned the name of the queue, *msg-inbox-logs*; the number of messages, *0*; the number of attached consumers, *0*; and memory used, 43664 bytes.

You can also check the properties used to declare the queue:

```
$ ./rabbitmqctl list_queues name durable auto_delete
Listing queues ...
msg-inbox-logs  true false
msg-inbox-errors  true false
all-logs true false
...done.
```

There you can see that the queues are `durable` and the `auto_delete` property was set to false.

Of course nothing can stop you from playing with the other command options. You can experiment by yourself on the command line.

VIEWING EXCHANGES AND BINDINGS

It's time to get information about the exchanges. In this case the command to obtain the default information is

```
$ ./rabbitmqctl list_exchanges
Listing exchanges ...
logs-exchange     topic
amq.rabbitmq.log     topic
amq.match     headers
amq.headers     headers
amq.topic     topic
amq.direct     direct
amq.fanout     fanout
     direct
...done.
```

By default, this command returns the exchange name and the exchange type. You can see that several exchanges are declared already, such as `amq.topic`, `amq.direct` and `amq.fanout`. Those exchanges are mandated by the AMQP specification. On top of the list you see your own `logs-exchanges` and the type is `topic`. If you look carefully at the bottom of the results, you'll see that it says *direct* but there's no exchange name. That's the anonymous exchange that we mentioned in chapter 1. As you'll soon see, every queue is bound by default to that exchange.

Let's run the `rabbitmqctl` command with no arguments and find out the expected options for `list_exchanges`:

```
$ ./rabbitmqctl

    ...

<ExchangeInfoItem> must be a member of the list [name, type,
durable, auto_delete, arguments]. The default is to display name
and type.

    ...
```

The information that you can get is related to the options that you used to declare the exchanges. Let's take a look at those:

```
$ ./rabbitmqctl list_exchanges name type durable auto_delete
logs-exchange    topic      true     false
amq.topic      topic      true     false
amq.direct     direct     true     false
amq.fanout     fanout     true     false
      direct      true     false
```

You can tell by the options passed to this command that the `logs-exchange` exchange is `durable` and that it won't be automatically deleted by the server.

After checking information about queues and exchanges, you naturally may want to see their bindings. Type this at the command line:

```
$ ./rabbitmqctl list_bindings
Listing bindings ...
    all-logs      all-logs    []
    msg-inbox-errors    msg-inbox-errors    []
    msg-inbox-logs    msg-inbox-logs    []
logs-exchange    all-logs    #    []
logs-exchange    msg-inbox-logs    *.msg-inbox    []
logs-exchange    msg-inbox-errors    error.msg-inbox    []
...done.
```

This command doesn't accept extra options except for -p, which specifies the vhost path. The output consists of rows containing the exchange name, queue name, routing key, and arguments. The first three rows look special, like something is missing... That's the anonymous exchange again. Those rows are showing that each queue is bound to the anonymous exchange using the queue name as the routing key. You also have the `logs-exchange`—a topic exchange—with three queues bound to it. The first one, `all-logs`, is bound using the # routing key—the wildcard. The other two queues are bound using `*.msg-inbox` and `error.msg-inbox` as routing keys respectively.

We've covered many commands from `rabbitmqctl` and—as you could see when running it without options—many more commands are available. You'll see some of them when we talk about clustering and monitoring RabbitMQ.

3.3.2   *Understanding RabbitMQ's logs*

In the previous section you learned how to use the `rabbitmqctl` script to get information about what's on the server, so let's see how can you check what's actually going on in the server—what kinds of events are happening. RabbitMQ logs events for many reasons, such as connections attempts, user creation, and errors when decoding requests. The cool thing about RabbitMQ is that you can get all this data and react to it in real time, using AMQP exchanges, queues, and bindings. If you want to go the classic way, then you can also see the log files on the filesystem. Let's do that first and then you can build an AMQP consumer that will display RabbitMQ logs; later you could tweak it and set up a monitoring system for RabbitMQ.

READING THE LOGS ON THE FILESYSTEM

The setting that you care when checking the logs is the `LOG_BASE` environment variable. The default value, as it appears in the `rabbitmq-server` script, is this:

```
LOG_BASE=/var/log/rabbitmq
```

Inside that folder RabbitMQ will create two log files: `RABBITMQ_NODENAME-sasl.log` and `RABBITMQ_NODENAME.log`, where *RABBITMQ_NODENAME* will be something like *_rabbit@localhost_* or just *rabbit* depending on how you configured your system.

What's the difference between the *sasl* log and the other one? *SASL (System Application Support Libraries)* is a set of libraries that are part of the Erlang-OTP distribution. They help the developer to have a set of standards when developing their Erlang apps. One of those is the logging format. So, when RabbitMQ logs Erlang-related information, it'll go to the `rabbit-sasl.log` files. For example, there you can find Erlang's crash reports that can be helpful when debugging a RabbitMQ node that doesn't want to start.

Now if you want to see the events happening at the server, you could `tail -f` the rabbit.log file. There you can see things like this:

```
=INFO REPORT==== 10-Sep-2010::13:50:58 ===
accepted TCP connection on 0.0.0.0:5672 from 192.168.1.253:44550

=INFO REPORT==== 10-Sep-2010::13:50:58 ===
starting TCP connection <0.29749.52> from 192.168.1.253:44550

=INFO REPORT==== 10-Sep-2010::13:50:58 ===
closing TCP connection <0.29749.52> from 192.168.1.253:44550

=INFO REPORT==== 10-Sep-2010::13:51:08 ===
Rolling persister log to
"/var/lib/rabbitmq/mnesia/rabbit/rabbit_persister.LOG.previous"
```

This information can be useful to debug your consumers/producers; you can see if they got connected, if the connection got closed abruptly, and so forth. Also you can find out if someone is connecting to your broker from an IP address that shouldn't be allowed.

Apart from network traffic information, in the `rabbit.log` file you'll see events like operations on users, exchanges, queues, and so on. So if for some reason your

AMQP client fails to encode a request, or there are some conflicts when declaring a queue, you could see those events logged here.

ROTATING THE LOGS

The last bit of information to know about the log files is how to rotate them. First you need to know that whenever the broker starts, it'll create them afresh and will append a number to the old ones. You'll get files like `rabbit.log.1`. If you want to rotate the logs manually or via cronjob, you can do it using—you guessed right—`rabbitmqctl`. There's a command that you can run like this,

```
$ ./rabbitmqctl rotate_logs suffix
```

where *suffix* is a word, usually a number, that you want to append to the end of the rotated log files. You can try something like this:

```
$ ./rabbitmqctl rotate_logs .1
```

And then you should see the following files in the log folder:

```
$ ls /var/log/rabbitmq
    rabbit@mrhyde-sasl.log
    rabbit@mrhyde-sasl.log.1
    rabbit@mrhyde.log
    rabbit@mrhyde.log.1
```

ACCESSING THE LOGS IN REAL TIME VIA AMQP

Now let's see how can you get all this information in real time using AMQP. Perhaps when you were listing exchanges using `rabbitmqctl` you spotted an exchange called `amq.rabbitmq.log` whose type is `topic`. RabbitMQ will publish its logs to that exchange using the severity level as a routing key—you'll get `error`, `warning`, and `info`. Based on what you learned from the previous chapter, you can create a consumer to listen to those logs and react accordingly. For the sake of the example you'll just output the logs to the console.

Before coding the consumer, let's do some refactoring. Create a file called `config` `.php` in a folder called `config` and put the code from the following listing inside.

Listing 3.2 Default configuration file

```php
<?php
define('HOST', 'localhost');
define('PORT', 5672);
define('USER', 'guest');
define('PASS', 'guest');
define('VHOST', '/');
?>
```

From now on we'll assume that the file `config.php` and the `amqp.inc` library are already included, so we won't mention them on future code examples. We'll also assume that you initialized the connection and you obtained a communication channel. With that in mind, the code for the PHP consumers is shown in the following listing.

Listing 3.3   Log listeners

```
list($errors_queue, , ) = $ch->queue_declare();          ◁—┐  Declare three
list($warnings_queue, , ) = $ch->queue_declare();          ❶  listening queues
list($info_queue, , ) = $ch->queue_declare();

$exchange = 'amq.rabbitmq.log';

$ch->queue_bind($errors_queue, $exchange, "error");      ◁—┐  Bind queues to
$ch->queue_bind($warnings_queue, $exchange, "warning");    ❷  log exchange
$ch->queue_bind($info_queue, $exchange, "info");

$error_callback = function($msg){                        ◁—┐  Create callback
  echo 'error: ',  $msg->body, "\n";                       ❸  functions
  $msg->delivery_info['channel']->basic_ack(
                   $msg->delivery_info['delivery_tag']);
};

$warning_callback = function($msg){
  echo 'warning: ',  $msg->body, "\n";
  $msg->delivery_info['channel']->basic_ack(
                   $msg->delivery_info['delivery_tag']);
};

$info_callback = function($msg){
  echo 'info: ',  $msg->body, "\n";
  $msg->delivery_info['channel']->basic_ack(
                   $msg->delivery_info['delivery_tag']);
};

$ch->basic_consume($errors_queue, "", false,
                           false, false, false,
                           $error_callback);
$ch->basic_consume($warnings_queue, "", false,          ◁—┐  Prepare
                           false, false, false,            ❹  consumers
                           $warning_callback);
$ch->basic_consume($info_queue, "", false,
                           false, false, false,
                           $info_callback);

while(count($ch->callbacks)) {
  $ch->wait();                                           ◁—❺  Wait for messages
}
```

Let's see what's going on this script. At ❶ you declare three queues. As you can see, you didn't provide any options to the declare command, so RabbitMQ will assign a random name to your queue. Besides that, the queue will be *exclusive* to your consumer, and it'll be *auto_deleted* when you kill the script. In this way you can attach your consumer to RabbitMQ at any time, spy what's going on, and then detach, and everything will be cleaned up for you. You won't need to delete the queues later. Also you get the return value from this command and keep the queue name under the variables $errors_queue, $warnings_queue, and $info_queue.

You use those variables at ❷ to bind the queues to the amq.rabbitmq.log exchange. You use different routing keys depending on which logs you want to route to your queues. Then at ❸ you define three callback functions to process your messages. They do basically the same thing: output the log with the log warning as prefix. You could modify them to perform more advanced tasks.

Then at ❹ you send the `basic_consume` commands and set up your callbacks to start receiving messages form the server. Finally at ❺ you loop, waiting for incoming messages. If you run this script you should start seeing logs like this:

```
info: closing TCP connection <0.25403.2> from 127.0.0.1:54197
info: accepted TCP connection on 0.0.0.0:5672 from 127.0.0.1:54204
```

If you were wondering what was the name of the queues that you just created, go to another terminal window and list the queues with `rabbitmqctl`. You'll see something like this:

```
Listing queues ...
amq.gen-kkcRbifmFzl4cVI6FLA4fQ==     0
amq.gen-4dngVZQA3QZOUf1obu391w==     0
amq.gen-NeTS98PHQygG3S2ciSzOww==     0
...done.
```

The nice thing about this approach for creating queues is that you don't have to worry about your queue names.

As you saw in this section, RabbitMQ is pretty informative about what's going on in the server. You have two ways of checking what's happening; one way is by the traditional file logs, and the other is using the more advanced AMQP exchanges, which can give you flexibility when reacting to events and can make it easier for you to filter logs.

3.4 Fixing a bad Rabbit: troubleshooting

So far everything has been going fine, but what happens when your Rabbit doesn't want to get domesticated? No matter what you try, it just doesn't want to start, or is running but doesn't want to reply to your messages. Let's see what you can do to troubleshoot those problems.

3.4.1 badrpc,nodedown and other Erlang-induced problems

One thing that puts RabbitMQ neophytes away are the weird error messages that it returns when something fails. What we learned over time is that most of those cryptic messages come from the underlying system RabbitMQ runs on: Erlang. We're not saying here that Erlang is a problem (far from it); our point is that messages like `badrpc,nodedown` are generated on the Erlang virtual machine, and with a little knowledge of how things work on the Erlang side, we can easily overcome these kinds of problems.

ERLANG COOKIES

One common error that you can get when you start working with RabbitMQ is `badrpc,nodedown`. It usually happens when you try to use the `rabbitmqctl` command, but instead of getting the expected result, you get that error message as a reply. At first you might think that RabbitMQ isn't running, but executing the following commands will prove that wrong:

```
$ ps ax | grep rabbit
34373 ?? S 0:01.67 /usr/local/lib/erlang/erts-5.8.5/bin/beam.smp -W
... omitted output ...
dir "/var/lib/rabbitmq/mnesia/rabbit@mrhyde" -noshell -noinput
```

A server process is running, so what's going on? Let's try to understand how the `rabbitmqctl` command works. `rabbitmqctl` will start up an Erlang node, and from there it'll try to communicate with the RabbitMQ node using the Erlang distribution system. For this to work, you need two things: the proper *Erlang cookie* and the proper *node name*. So what's an Erlang cookie? An Erlang cookie acts as a secret token that two Erlang nodes exchange in order to authenticate themselves. Since you can execute commands on the remote node once you're connected to it, there's a need to make sure that the peer is trusted. Erlang stores such tokens in a file called `.erlang.cookie`, which is usually located in the user's home directory. You can execute this command to see its contents:

```
$ cat ~/.erlang.cookie
```

In order for `rabbitmqctl` to communicate with the RabbitMQ node, it needs to share the same cookie. If you're running RabbitMQ as the same user that you use to execute the `rabbitmqctl` command, then you won't have any problem, but in production you'll probably want to create a `rabbitmq` user and run the server with that user. This means that you must share the cookie with the `rabbitmq` user or you have to switch to that user to be able to execute `rabbitmqctl` successfully. When we talk about *clustering* several RabbitMQ servers, we'll discuss Erlang cookies again.

ERLANG NODES

What about *nodes*; what's the problem with them? When you start an Erlang node, you can give it two mutually exclusive options, `name` and `sname`, which will specify the node name. That node name can be long or short, hence the *s* in `sname`. If you start your node with a long name, it will get something like `rabbit@hostname.network.tld`. If you use short names, you'll see something similar to this: `rabbit@hostname`. The latter is the default way of starting RabbitMQ. When you want `rabbitmqctl` to be able to communicate with RabbitMQ, you have to get those options to match on both sides. Just for an experiment, see what happens if you edit your `rabbitmqctl` and change where it says `-sname rabbitmqctl$` to `-name rabbitmqctl$`. Save and run the following:

```
./rabbitmqctl  list_queues
Listing queues ...
```

You'll get a nice error message like this:

```
=ERROR REPORT==== 21-Sep-2010::16:01:46 ===
** System running to use fully qualified hostnames **
** Hostname mrhyde is illegal **
Error: unable to connect to node rabbit@mrhyde: nodedown
diagnostics:
- nodes and their ports on mrhyde: [{rabbit,54174}...]
- current node: 'rabbitmqctl1027@mrhyde.network.tld'
- current node home dir: /Users/mrhyde
- current node cookie hash: oNANSQ6MP0092ATN9U7Hcc==
```

Change the option back to read sname and everything should work as normal. Again, later when we talk about clustering, we'll have to tweak this option.

MNESIA AND HOST NAMES

Next we have to take care of Mnesia, the Erlang database that was there even before NoSQL was cool. RabbitMQ uses Mnesia to store information about queues, exchanges, bindings, and so on. One of the things that RabbitMQ does at startup time is launch the Mnesia database. Since this step is essential for the server to behave correctly, if Mnesia fails to start, then RabbitMQ will fail too.

There are a couple of reasons why Mnesia may fail to start. The first and most common is a permission problem on the MNESIA_BASE directory. The user that's running the RabbitMQ server needs write permissions on that folder. Another common problem is when you see an error message like this:

```
starting database              ...{"init terminating in
do_boot",{{nocatch,{error,
    {cannot_start_application,rabbit,
        {{timeout_waiting_for_tables [...]
```

Here Mnesia failed to load the tables, as you can see from the message. This happens if the hostname has changed or if the server is running in clustered mode and the other peer is unreachable during startup. Why do you have to care about the hostname? Mnesia creates a database schema based on the machine hostname. If you list the contents of the MNESIA_BASE folder, you'll see a folder called rabbit@hostname. If *hostname* changes due to some network reconfiguration, then Mnesia won't be able to load the old schema. Also keep in mind that RabbitMQ uses the word *rabbit* as node name. If you changed it using the Erlang sname option, then Mnesia will encounter the same problem again.

For the same reason you can see that if you rename the rabbit@hostname folder, then Mnesia won't be able to find the old database files. It'll create the rabbit@hostname folder again and start a database from scratch. Keep in mind that you still can find the old database files in the folder that you renamed.

Mnesia deserves a book for itself, so if you want to learn more about it, you can read the user guide at http://www.erlang.org/doc/apps/mnesia/users_guide.html.

ERLANG TROUBLESHOOTING TIPS

To end this section, let's do a simple exercise in Erlang that will help you understand what we just talked about. You'll connect an Erlang node to your running RabbitMQ server. You could use this knowledge to monitor a running broker, execute Erlang functions on it remotely, and much more.

Providing that you started RabbitMQ using *short names*, run the following command:

```
$ erl -sname test
```

Depending on your hostname and Erlang version, you should see something like this:

```
Erlang R13B04 (erts-5.7.5) [source] [64-bit] [smp:2:2] ...
Eshell V5.7.5  (abort with ^G)
(test@mrhyde)1>
```

This means you started your Erlang node using `test` as node name. What you're seeing is the Erlang Read Eval Print Loop or *REPL* for short. There you can input commands, execute Erlang code, and so forth. Let's find out your node name:

```
(test@mrhyde)1> node().
test@mrhyde
```

There you typed `node()` at the REPL and got back `test@mrhyde` as a result. Your Erlang node will be known to other Erlang applications by that name. As an example, if you start your own Mnesia database, that will be the name used for the schema folder.

Now let's check which other nodes are running on your machine:

```
(test@mrhyde)2> net_adm:names().
{ok,[{"rabbit",59106},{"test",59127}]}
```

There you called the `names` function from the `net_adm` module. As you can see, RabbitMQ is running on your machine, using `rabbit` as the node name and `59106` as the port. Wait … that's not the port you use to connect to RabbitMQ from an AMQP client. What's going on? Here's when another piece comes into play: the Erlang Port Mapper Daemon (`epmd`). Whenever you start a distributed Erlang node, it'll register with the `epmd` process, giving it the address and port assigned to it by the OS kernel. Then when another Erlang node comes to life, it'll do the same. Finally if the latter wants to connect to your first node, it'll go through `epmd` to obtain the other node address. In that way you don't need to track that information yourself. Then, that port number (`59106` in the example) is the one assigned by the OS to the Erlang VM where RabbitMQ is running.

Now that you know that you can *see* the RabbitMQ node, let's try to establish a connection to it:

```
(test@mrhyde)3> net_adm:ping('rabbit@mrhyde').
pong
```

You use the `ping` function to try to reach the other node, giving as argument the `'node@hostname'` that you want to connect to. If the answer is `pong`, then you succeeded; if you get `pang` as reply, that means you couldn't connect to the other node. Keep in mind that for all this to work you have to share the same Erlang cookie.

Let's confirm that you're connected to the `rabbit` node:

```
(test@mrhyde)4> nodes().
[rabbit@mrhyde]
```

Executing the function `nodes()` will display a list—those square brackets delimit lists in Erlang—with the nodes that you're connected to.

Finally, let's execute a function on the remote `rabbit` node:

```
(test@mrhyde)8> rpc:call('rabbit@mrhyde',
                         erlang,
                         system_info,
                         [process_count]).
```

There you used Erlang's `rpc` module to call a function on the `rabbit@mrhyde` node. The function is `erlang:system_info` and you use it to obtain the number of Erlang processes running on that node. You could use this to monitor the health of your RabbitMQ system. If the `process_count` goes above the value `process_limit`, then your server will crash. This is unlikely to happen—on some machines the limit is 1048576—but it's nice to keep this in mind when things goes wrong.

Using `rpc:call` and providing the node, module, function, and arguments as parameters, you can execute other functions on the remote `rabbit` and obtain different information. For a final example, let's gather information about the running Mnesia system on the remote `rabbit` node:

```
rpc:call('rabbit@mrhyde', mnesia, info, []).
```

The REPL will print out several lines of information regarding Mnesia, such as the tables created by RabbitMQ, the memory used to hold the information, and more.

Finally, to close the Erlang REPL, execute the q function and you should be back on the terminal command prompt:

```
(test@mrhyde)11> q().
ok
```

Keeping aside the fact that Erlang deserves a book on its own, you can use the techniques described here to troubleshoot your RabbitMQ installation. To name an example, if you start up the Erlang VM with the same parameters as the `rabbitmqctl` script, then you should be able to connect to the `rabbit` node. If that's not the case, you can start finding out what hostname your machine is getting. Then you can continue by listing the names of the nodes registered with the `epmd` daemon, and so on. With such simple tools you can be troubleshooting and monitoring your RabbitMQ servers in no time.

3.5 Summary

In this chapter we covered a lot of practical techniques that help you with your everyday working with RabbitMQ. You saw how to perform server management tasks, such as working with the RabbitMQ permission system to add and remove users. We went through RabbitMQ configuration files and we covered how to work with the `rabbitmqctl` command—the Swiss army knife for working with the server. Then you saw how to get statistics out of the server to see the queues and exchanges that you've created and the relationships between them. Last but not least, we went through some of the strange Erlang errors that RabbitMQ may throw at you from time to time. Since Erlang is a fundamental piece in the server structure, you learned a bit about the language in order to perform more advanced management tasks, giving you a solid foundation of *what means what* in RabbitMQ and Erlang parlance. With all this knowledge in place, let's go to chapter 4 to see some real-world examples of how to power your applications with messaging.

Solving problems with Rabbit: coding and patterns

This chapter covers

- Designing applications toward messaging
- Messaging patterns
- Fire-and-forget models
- RPC with RabbitMQ

At this point you know how to install, configure, and even run Rabbit in production. It's about time we got to some coding. First, you need to understand problems you're trying to solve when you code messaging into your apps. Like a lot of people who discover RabbitMQ, your lovable authors weren't looking for a message queue; we were looking to solve a decoupling problem. How do you take a time-intensive task and move it out of the app that triggers it (thereby freeing that app to service other requests)? Also, how do you glue together applications written in different languages like PHP and Erlang so that they act as a single system? These seem like two different problems but they have a common kernel: decoupling the request from the action. Or put another way, both problems demand moving from a synchronous programming model to an asynchronous one.

Normally, when programmers hear *asynchronous programming* they either go running for the hills or think "Cool. Like Node.js right?" Sometimes both. The problem with normal approaches to asynchronous programming is that they're all-or-nothing propositions. You rewrite all of your code so none of it blocks or you're just wasting your time. RabbitMQ gives you a different path. It allows you to fire off a request for processing elsewhere so that your synchronous application can go back to what it was doing. When you start using messaging, you can achieve most of the benefits of pure asynchronous programming without throwing your existing code or knowledge away. In this chapter, we'll show you what asynchronous coding means in the Rabbit world. In particular, we'll show you how to use Rabbit to solve a number of real-world problems from picture processing (parallel processing) and alerting (notifications) to using RabbitMQ for distributed remote procedure calls (APIs) that are as simple as pie. We'll start by teaching some fundamental messaging paradigms and then diving into the code. Let's get decoupling!

4.1 A decoupling story: what pushes us to messaging

You do it all the time. You write your latest and greatest web app (scheduling Chihuahua walking), and decide the fastest way to go is to take web orders and stuff them directly into a database. It makes sense. How much time can stuffing a small record into a database take? Not to mention, it's so simple to code. The problem is, what happens when you go nationwide and you're now scheduling 100,000 Chihuahuas an hour? Or better yet, you decide you want to store your data in two places (gotta archive those requests). Guess what? It's time to rip out all of that carefully debugged code. Coupling an app directly to storage is usually a recipe for rip-and-replace later, and that's where messaging can help you.

4.1.1 An asynchronous state of mind (separating requests and actions)

How often do you operate in a synchronous fashion? If you order a pizza, do you wait for it to show up before you do anything else? Of course not. You watch TV or read a book, or maybe give your sweetie some quality conversation time. Rarely do you put your life on hold waiting for a response to your requests. You multitask, so your lives can scale and you can get more done. Your apps need the same approach.

Why do you design your apps to be synchronous in the first place? Mostly, because you think about the whole job instead of the smaller tasks that make it up. You think "my app needs to schedule a Chihuahua appointment." Instead the reality is that your app needs to receive a scheduling request; then it needs to store that request in a database; then it has to alert the closest dog walker; and finally it needs to let the customer know they're scheduled. Even if you make your app multithreaded, you've severely limited the rate at which you can take orders because each thread has to wait for the record to be stored and the dog walker to be alerted. Rather, you should look at those four steps as falling into two separate apps: an app that takes the request, and an app that processes the request. To hijack a great analogy from Gregor Hohpe, we could call it the Coffee Bean model (Coffee Bean & Tea Leaf is a chain of coffee houses in California).

When you place an order for your chai latte, you don't wait at the cash register until your order is ready. Instead, Coffee Bean splits the order taking operation from the order preparation operation. The order taker collects your request (and your dinero), and transmits a message to the baristas telling them what you ordered. You then wait for your order to be prepared, freeing up the order taker to take another order. The most important part of the operation is getting your money collected, and so by separating order taking from order processing, Coffee Bean has maximized the number of orders they can take per minute. Similarly, if the backlog of coffee waiting to be prepared gets too high, they can add more baristas to reduce the backlog without changing the number of order takers. By decoupling the process (separating requests and actions), they've increased the amount of work they can accomplish with the same number of workers and made it easy to scale up when they need to. Messaging does the same thing for your app.

So let's reanalyze your Chihuahua app with decoupling in mind. Figure 4.1 shows the steps in completing a dog walking order.

If you want to increase the scalability and flexibility of your app, you need to split it into two different apps: *dog _walk_order* and *dog_walk_process*, as in figure 4.2. dog_walk_order sits on the internet and receives web requests to schedule walkings. When it receives a request, dog_walk_order creates a new AMQP message and publishes that into the chihuahua_scheduling exchange on Rabbit. dog_walk_order can then put Customer A on hold and go receive other requests. Meanwhile, dog_walk_process listens to a Rabbit queue and receives the message containing customer A's scheduling order. It then gets to work creating the required database entry for the order and firing off a text message to your main dog walker, Gustav. Once Gustav has been sent his text message, dog _walk_process sends a message back

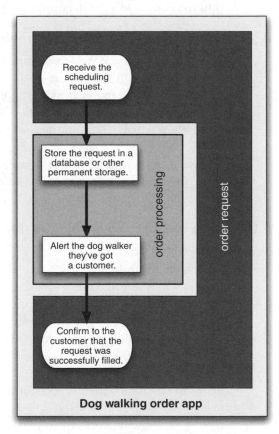

Figure 4.1 Steps for completing a dog walking order

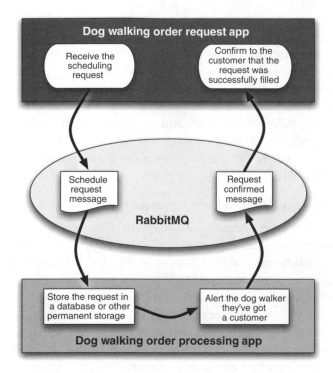

Figure 4.2   Splitting the dog walking program into two apps

to dog_walk_order that customer A's request was successfully processed. During the whole time that dog_walk_process was dealing with Customer A's order, dog_walk _order was able to receive 100 new walking requests. Had they still been one app, you would've received only one walking request during that whole interval.

By putting RabbitMQ between two parts of your app that were once tightly coupled, you've made it possible to continually receive requests, where before you could only process one at a time. But you've also opened up a whole other world of benefits. What if you get so much load that one order processing server is no longer enough?

4.1.2   Affording scale: a world without load balancers

One of the great things about using messaging is that it's simple to add processing capacity to your apps. Let's say you've just expanded your service to Japan, and now you're receiving 1,000,000 walking orders a second. Though your frontend order taker is more than able to keep up with the load, your order processor is keeling over. Taking a customer's order no longer keeps you from taking other orders, but those customers are getting fed up waiting for you to confirm their reservations. You need more order processors. Just like at Coffee Bean, you can add more baristas. In your case, you spool up additional dog_walk_process servers and attach them to the queue that receives the orders. Presto! Without one line of code change, you added 10x processing capacity by spooling up 10 new dog_walk_process servers. The best part is that RabbitMQ will evenly distribute the requests among the processing servers due to the automatic round-robin behavior we talked about in section 2.2. No expensive load balancers required.

That's important for any organization, not just cash-conscious startups. Load balancing hardware is expensive, which means you're normally limited to how many places you can use it to decouple and scale your apps. If instead you can use AMQP and Rabbit, then you can add decoupling and load balancing anywhere you want for free. Not to mention, you can do more complex routing, such as send a message to more than one destination in addition to round-robin load balancing. Load balancers will always have a place on the frontend distributing requests coming in from the internet, but if you can heavily leverage messaging, you can reduce your reliance on them inside the firewall and greatly increase the number of places you decouple your apps. Decoupled apps are scalable apps.

4.1.3   *Zero-effort APIs: why be locked into just one language?*

We've skipped over one of the best benefits of using AMQP to decouple your apps: APIs for free. Today everyone is talking about web APIs that allow you to integrate an app's functionality into any other app. Generally, this takes a bit of effort because you end up writing a lot of code to translate incoming HTTP requests into your app's function calls. If you write your app using AMQP to connect the parts, you actually get an API for no additional effort—an API that uses messaging.

Let's say you've expanded your Chihuahua walking business into dog washing. You have two new apps to support the new service: *dog_wash_request* and *dog_wash_process*. Then you get a great idea: offer a free dog walk with every wash. Since both the washing and walking scheduling apps use AMQP, all you need to do is update dog_wash _request to generate an additional AMQP message that contains the dog walk scheduling information. dog_wash_request can instantly take advantage of dog_walk_process. This means no recoding of the scheduling code and no need to duplicate that code inside the dog washing apps. Equally important, there's no requirement that the walking and washing apps be written in the same language.

When you wrote the dog walking apps, you may have chosen Erlang as the best language for the job. But in the months since, you've discovered how much you like Clojure for building high-concurrency applications. So you wrote the dog washing apps in Clojure. If you were using Erlang's built-in communication protocol for connecting dog_walk_request to dog_walk_process, it'd be difficult for the dog washing apps to talk to dog_walk_process since they're not written in Erlang. But because AMQP is language-agnostic and has native language bindings for dozens of languages, you can easily connect a Clojure request receiver to an Erlang request processor over Rabbit. Using AMQP to connect your applications gives you the flexibility to use the right language for each part of the job, and even to change your mind later and connect in new applications written in completely different languages. RabbitMQ makes it easy to connect any and all parts of your infrastructure in any way you want.

So, the first thing you should always ask is, how can break you apps apart? Or rather, which parts of your app are order takers and which parts are order processors? With that in mind, let's dive into some real-world examples of using Rabbit and messaging to solve real problems and answer those questions.

4.2 Fire-and-forget models

When we look at the types of problems messaging can solve, one of the main areas that messaging fits is fire-and-forget processing. Whether you need to add contacts to a mailing list or convert 1,000 pictures into thumbnails, you're interested in the jobs getting done but there's no reason they need to be done in real-time. In fact, you usually want to avoid blocking the user who triggered the jobs. We describe these types of jobs as *fire-and-forget*: you create the job, put it on the exchange, and let your app get back to what it was doing. Depending on your requirements, you may not even need to notify the user when the jobs complete.

Two general types of jobs fit into this pattern:

- *Batch processing*—Work and transformations that need be completed on a large data set. This can be structured as a single job request or many jobs operating on individual parts of the data set.
- *Notifications*—A description of an event that has occurred. This can be anything from a message to be logged, to an actual alert that should be sent to another program or an administrator.

We're going to show you two different real-world examples of fire-and-forget apps that fit into these two categories. The first is an alerting framework that will allow the apps in your infrastructure to generate administrator alerts without worrying about where they need to go or how to get them there. The second example is a perfect demonstration of batch processing: taking a single image upload and converting into multiple image sizes and formats. When you're done with this section you'll have the most fundamental type of RabbitMQ programming under your belt: triggering work with messages that need no reply. Let's start generating some alerts!

4.2.1 Sending alerts

No matter what type of apps you write, getting notifications when things go awry is critical. Typically you run some sort of service monitor like Nagios to let you know when your app is down or services that it relies upon are unavailable. But what about getting notified when your app is experiencing an unusual number of requests for user logins, all from a single IP? Or perhaps you'd like to allow your customers to be notified when unusual events occur to their data? What you need is for your app to generate alerts, but this opens up a whole new set of questions and adds a lot of complexity to your app. What events do you alert on, and more important, how do you alert? SMS? IM? No matter how you slice it, you're looking at adding a lot of new surface area to your code for bugs to hide in. For example, what happens when the SMS gateway is down? All of your web apps that need to alert now need error-handling code to deal with the SMS server being unavailable.

Worry not, for RabbitMQ is riding to your rescue. The only thing about alerting that inherently needs to be done in your web apps is generating the contents of the alert. There's no reason why your web app needs to know whom the alert should go to, how to get it there, or what to do when the alert deliveries go awry. All you need to do is write a new alerting server app that receives alert messages via Rabbit, and then enhance your web app to publish these alert messages where appropriate.

How should you design this new alerting framework? Particularly, what type of AMQP exchange should you use? You could use a fanout exchange and then create a queue for each alert transmission type (IM, Twitter, SMS, and so on). The advantage is that your web app doesn't have to know anything about how the alerts will be delivered to the ultimate receiver. It just publishes and moves on. The disadvantage is that *every* alert transmitter gets a copy, so you get flooded with an IM, a text message, and a Twitter direct message every time an alert happens.

A better way to organize your alerting system would be to create three severity levels for your alerts: info, warning, and critical. But with the fanout exchange, any alert published would get sent to all three severity level queues. You could instead create your exchange as a direct exchange, which would allow your web app to tag the alert messages with the severity level as the routing key. But what would happen if you chose a topic exchange? Topic exchanges let you create flexible tags for your messages that target them to multiple queues, but only the queues providing the services you want (unlike the fanout exchange). If you were to use a topic exchange for your alerting framework, you wouldn't be limited to just one severity level per alert. In fact, you could now tag your messages not only with a severity level, but also the type of alert it is. For example, let's say Joe Don Hacker is hitting your statistics server with 10,000 requests per second for map data on your dog walking reservations. In your organization, you need an alert about this to go both to the infrastructure admins (who get all alerts flagged as `critical`), and to your API dev team (who get all alerts tagged `rate_limiting`). Since you've chosen a topic exchange for the alerting framework, your web app can tag the alert about such underhanded activity with `critical.rate_limiting`. Presto! The alert message is automatically routed by RabbitMQ to the `critical` and `rate_limiting` queues, because of the exchange bindings you've created: `critical.*` and `*.rate_limiting`. Figure 4.3 shows how the flow of your alerting system will work.

To build this alerting framework you'll need the Pika library you installed as a part of your Hello World in chapter 2. If you skipped that part, here are some quick steps to get Pika installed (assuming you don't have easy_install yet either):

```
$ wget http://peak.telecommunity.com/dist/ez_setup.py
...
  (25.9 KB/s) - ez_setup.py saved [10285/10285]

$ python ez_setup.py
...
Installed /Library/Python/2.6/site-packages/setuptools-0.6...
$ easy_install pika
...
Installed /Library/Python/2.6/site-packages/pika-0.9.6-py2.6.egg
Processing dependencies for pika
Finished processing dependencies for pika
```

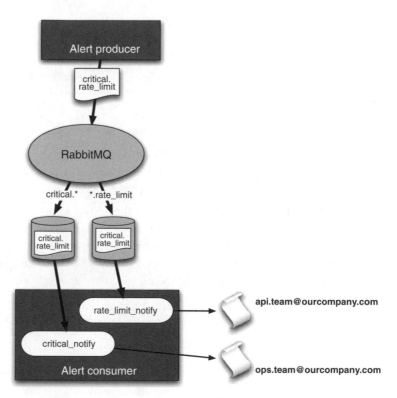

**Figure 4.3
Alerting system flow**

Next you need to set up the RabbitMQ user and password the applications will use to publish and receive alert messages. Let's call the user `alert_user` and give it the password `alertme`. Let's also grant `alert_user` read/write/configure permissions on the default vhost /.

From the `./sbin` directory of your RabbitMQ install, run the following:

```
$ ./rabbitmqctl add_user alert_user alertme
Creating user "alert_user" ...
...done.
$ ./rabbitmqctl set_permissions alert_user ".*" ".*" ".*"
Setting permissions for user "alert_user" in vhost "/" ...
...done.
```

With the setup out of the way, you're ready to work on the most important part of your alerting system: the AMQP consumer that will receive the alert messages and transmit them to their destinations. Create a file called `alert_consumer.py` and put the code in the following listing inside.

Listing 4.1 Connect to the broker

```
import json, smtplib
import pika

if __name__ == "__main__":              Broker
    AMQP_SERVER = "localhost"           settings
```

```
AMQP_USER = "alert_user"
AMQP_PASS = "alertme"
AMQP_VHOST = "/"                                      Establish
AMQP_EXCHANGE = "alerts"                              connection
                                                      to broker
creds_broker = pika.PlainCredentials(AMQP_USER, AMQP_PASS)
conn_params = pika.ConnectionParameters(AMQP_SERVER,
                                    virtual_host = AMQP_VHOST,
                                    credentials = creds_broker)
conn_broker = pika.BlockingConnection(conn_params)

channel = conn_broker.channel()
```

The first thing this code does is import the libraries you'll need to make the consumer tick, and tell Python where the main body of your program is (if __name__ == "__main__":). Next, you establish the settings you need to make a successful connection to your broker (user, name, password, virtual host, and so forth). The settings assume you have RabbitMQ running locally on your development workstation and are using the username and password you just created. For simplicity, let's use the default virtual host / where you're going to create an exchange called alerts. Here's where the real action starts:

```
channel.exchange_declare( exchange=AMQP_EXCHANGE,
                          type="topic",
                          auto_delete=False)
```

You're declaring the alerts exchange as a topic exchange with the type="topic" parameter that's passed to channel.exchange_declare. The auto_delete parameter you're also passing to the exchange and queue declarations ensures they'll stick around when the last consumer disconnects from them.

Remember that we talked about two tagging patterns for alerts:

- .* for tagging alerts with their severity level (say, critical)
- *. for tagging alerts with a specific alert type such as rate_limiting

What you need to do is create bindings that implement these rules so that the alert messages go to the queues you want. For your example, let's create a binding that routes any messages with tags starting with critical. to the critical queue. Let's also create a different binding that routes any messages with tags ending in .rate _limit to the rate_limit queue. Go ahead and create the critical and rate_limit queues and bind them, as shown in the following listing.

Listing 4.2   Declare and bind queues and exchanges for the alert topics

```
channel.queue_declare(queue="critical", auto_delete=False)    critical queue
channel.queue_bind(queue="critical",                          and critical.*
               exchange="alerts",                             topic binding
               routing_key="critical.*")

channel.queue_declare(queue="rate_limit", auto_delete=False)
channel.queue_bind(queue="rate_limit",                        rate_limit queue
               exchange="alerts",                             and *.rate_limit
               routing_key="*.rate_limit")                    topic binding
```

You'll notice that the binding rule created for critical alerts is `critical.*` and not `critical*`. This is because RabbitMQ uses `.` as a separator for different parts of a tag. If you were to use `critical*` as the rule, only messages tagged exactly `critical*` would match. What you want is to match `critical.mywebapp`, `critical.rate_limit`, or anything that starts with `critical.`; hence the binding rule should be `critical.*`. When using topic exchanges, it's important to be careful to design your tagging patterns to use `.` to separate the parts of the tag you want to match separately on.

You could've also passed `durable=True` to the queue declarations and bindings, which would ensure that they survived a restart of RabbitMQ. Since restarting your consumer will automatically create the exchange, queues, and bindings it needs, you don't need to worry about durability for your alerting system. The other reason you're not concerned about making the queues durable is because you're not going to flag your alert messages as durable either. Your system could be handling very high volumes of alerts, so you want to ensure the highest performance and not use durable messaging, which is persisted to relatively slow disk.

You might be thinking, "We have exchanges, queues, and bindings ... where do we turn an alert message into an actual alert?" You do that by setting up your consumer subscriptions and starting the listener loop, as in the following listing.

Listing 4.3 Attach the alert processors

```
channel.basic_consume( critical_notify,
                       queue="critical",
                       no_ack=False,
                       consumer_tag="critical")

channel.basic_consume( rate_limit_notify,
                       queue="rate_limit",
                       no_ack=False,
                       consumer_tag="rate_limit")

print "Ready for alerts!"
channel.start_consuming()
```

Let's take the `channel.basic_consume` call apart and explain what each parameter does:

- `critical_notify` is the callback. It's the function that will be called when a message is received for your subscription to the `critical` queue. The Pika library will call `critical_notify` when a message is received on this subscription, passing in the channel, message headers, message body, and message method from the message.
- `queue="critical"` specifies the queue you want to receive messages from.
- `no_ack=False` tells RabbitMQ you want to explicitly acknowledge received messages. This will keep Rabbit from sending new messages from the queue until you've processed and acknowledged the last one you received.
- `consumer_tag` is an identifier that will identify this subscription uniquely on the AMQP channel you created with `channel = conn_broker.channel()`. The

consumer tag is what you'd pass to RabbitMQ if you wanted to cancel your subscription.

Once you've established the consumer subscriptions, you only need to call `channel` `.start_consuming()` to start your consumer listening for messages. You may have noticed that the callback functions (`critical_notify` and `rate_limit_notify`) you specified for your subscriptions haven't been defined yet. Let's go ahead and specify one of those in the following listing.

Listing 4.4 Critical alerts processor

```
def critical_notify(channel, method, header, body):
    """Sends CRITICAL alerts to administrators via e-mail."""

    EMAIL_RECIPS = ["ops.team@ourcompany.com",]

    message = json.loads(body)

    send_mail(EMAIL_RECIPS, "CRITICAL ALERT", message)
    print ("Sent alert via e-mail! Alert Text: %s  " + \
            "Recipients: %s") % (str(message), str(EMAIL_RECIPS))

    channel.basic_ack(delivery_tag=method.delivery_tag)
```

Decode message from JSON (annotation pointing to `message = json.loads(body)`)

Transmit email to SMTP server (annotation pointing to `send_mail(...)`)

Acknowledge message (annotation pointing to `channel.basic_ack(...)`)

When a consumer callback is called, Pika passes in four parameters related to the message:

- `channel`—The channel object you're communicating on with Rabbit. If you have multiple channels open, it'll be the one associated with the subscription the message was received on.
- `method`—A method frame object that carries the consumer tag for the related subscription and the delivery tag for the message itself.
- `header`—An object representing the headers of the AMQP message. These carry optional metadata about the message.
- `body`—The actual message contents.

In `critical_notify` the first thing to check is the `content_type` header. Your alerts will be JSON encoded, so you'll check the content type to make sure it's `application/json`. The `content_type` is optional, but it's useful when you want to communicate encoding information about the message between producer and consumer. After you've verified the content type, you decode the message body from JSON to text and construct an email to the Ops Team (ops.team@ourcompany.com) containing the alert text. Once the email alert has been successfully sent, you send an acknowledgement back to RabbitMQ that you've received the message. The acknowledgement is important because RabbitMQ won't give you another message from the queue until you've acknowledged the last one you received. By putting the acknowledgement as the last operation, you ensure that if your consumer were to crash, RabbitMQ would assign the message to another consumer.

With all of the pieces of your consumer explained, let's look at the whole thing put together in the following listing.

Listing 4.5   Alert consumer—alert_consumer.py, start to finish

```python
import json, smtplib
import pika

def send_mail(recipients, subject, message):
    """E-mail generator for received alerts."""
    headers = ("From: %s\r\nTo: \r\nDate: \r\n" + \
               "Subject: %s\r\n\r\n") % ("alerts@ourcompany.com",
                                              subject)

    smtp_server = smtplib.SMTP()
    smtp_server.connect("mail.ourcompany.com", 25)
    smtp_server.sendmail("alerts@ourcompany.com",
                         recipients,
                         headers + str(message))
    smtp_server.close()

def critical_notify(channel, method, header, body):
    """Sends CRITICAL alerts to administrators via e-mail."""

    EMAIL_RECIPS = ["ops.team@ourcompany.com",]

    message = json.loads(body)

    send_mail(EMAIL_RECIPS, "CRITICAL ALERT", message)
    print ("Sent alert via e-mail! Alert Text: %s  " + \
           "Recipients: %s") % (str(message), str(EMAIL_RECIPS))

    channel.basic_ack(delivery_tag=method.delivery_tag)

def rate_limit_notify(channel, method, header, body):
    """Sends the message to the administrators via e-mail."""

    EMAIL_RECIPS = ["api.team@ourcompany.com",]

    message = json.loads(body)

    #(f-asc_10) Transmit e-mail to SMTP server
    send_mail(EMAIL_RECIPS, "RATE LIMIT ALERT!", message)

    print ("Sent alert via e-mail! Alert Text: %s  " + \
           "Recipients: %s") % (str(message), str(EMAIL_RECIPS))

    channel.basic_ack(delivery_tag=method.delivery_tag)

if __name__ == "__main__":
    AMQP_SERVER = "localhost"
    AMQP_USER = "alert_user"
    AMQP_PASS = "alertme"
    AMQP_VHOST = "/"
    AMQP_EXCHANGE = "alerts"

    creds_broker = pika.PlainCredentials(AMQP_USER, AMQP_PASS)
    conn_params = pika.ConnectionParameters(AMQP_SERVER,
                                            virtual_host = AMQP_VHOST,
                                            credentials = creds_broker)
    conn_broker = pika.BlockingConnection(conn_params)

    channel = conn_broker.channel()

    channel.exchange_declare( exchange=AMQP_EXCHANGE,
```

Annotations:
- Notify processors
- Decode message from JSON
- Transmit email to SMTP server
- Acknowledge message
- Decode message from JSON
- Acknowledge message
- Broker settings
- Establish connection to broker
- Declare the exchange

**Build queues
and bindings
for topics**

```
                                     type="topic",
                                     auto_delete=False)
        channel.queue_declare(queue="critical", auto_delete=False)
        channel.queue_bind(queue="critical",
                           exchange="alerts",
                           routing_key="critical.*")
        channel.queue_declare(queue="rate_limit", auto_delete=False)
        channel.queue_bind(queue="rate_limit",
                           exchange="alerts",
                           routing_key="*.rate_limit")

        channel.basic_consume( critical_notify,                    Make alert
                               queue="critical",                   processors
                               no_ack=False,
                               consumer_tag="critical")

        channel.basic_consume( rate_limit_notify,
                               queue="rate_limit",
                               no_ack=False,
                               consumer_tag="rate_limit")

        print "Ready for alerts!"
        channel.start_consuming()
```

You now have an elegant consumer that will translate alert AMQP messages into email
alerts targeted at different groups simply by manipulating the message tag. Adding
additional alert types and transmission methods is simple. All you need to do is create
a consumer callback to provide the new alert processing and connect it to a queue
that's populated via a binding rule for the new alert type. Your consumer wouldn't be
very useful without alerts for it to process. So let's see what it takes to produce alerts
that your consumer can act on.

Our goal when we started this section was to make producing alerts simple and
uncomplicated for existing apps. If you look at the following listing, you'll see that,
though the consumer takes some 90 lines of code to process an alert, the alert itself
can be generated in less than 20 lines.

> **Listing 4.6   Alert generator example—alert_producer.py**

```
import json, pika
from optparse import OptionParser
                                                        Read in command-
opt_parser = OptionParser()                             line arguments
opt_parser.add_option("-r",
                      "--routing-key",
                      dest="routing_key",
                      help="Routing key for message " + \
                      " (e.g. myalert.im)")
opt_parser.add_option("-m",
                      "--message",
                      dest="message",
                      help="Message text for alert.")
                                                        Establish
args = opt_parser.parse_args()[0]                        connection
                                                        to broker
creds_broker = pika.PlainCredentials("alert_user", "alertme")
```

```
conn_params = pika.ConnectionParameters("localhost",
                                        virtual_host = "/",
                                        credentials = creds_broker)
conn_broker = pika.BlockingConnection(conn_params)

channel = conn_broker.channel()

msg = json.dumps(args.message)
msg_props = pika.BasicProperties()
msg_props.content_type = "application/json"
msg_props.durable = False

channel.basic_publish(body=msg,
                      exchange="alerts",
                      properties=msg_props,
                      routing_key=args.routing_key)
print ("Sent message %s tagged with routing key '%s' to " + \
       "exchange '/'.") % (json.dumps(args.message),
                           args.routing_key)
```

Publish alert
message to
broker

The sample producer can be run from the command line to generate alerts with any contents and routing tags you like. The first part of the program simply extracts the message and the routing key from the command line. From there you're connecting to the RabbitMQ broker identically to the way you did in the alert consumer. Where things get interesting is when you publish the message:

```
msg = json.dumps(args.message)
msg_props = pika.BasicProperties()
msg_props.content_type = "application/json"
msg_props.durable = False

channel.basic_publish(body=msg,
                      exchange="alerts",
                      properties=msg_props,
                      routing_key=args.routing_key)
```

Five lines of code is all it takes for you to create the alert message and tag it with the appropriate routing key (say, `critical.mywebapp`). After you JSON-encode the alert's message text, you create a `BasicProperties` object called `msg_props`. This is where you can set the AMQP message's optional content type header, and also where you'd make the message durable if you wanted persistency. Finally, in one line of code you publish the message to the `alerts` exchange with the routing key that classifies what type of alert it is. Since messages with routing keys that don't match any bindings will be discarded, you can even tag alerts with routing keys for alert types you don't support yet. As soon as you do support those alert types, any alert messages with those routing keys will be routed to the right consumer. The last bit to note about the consumer is the `block_on_flow_control` flag you're passing to `channel.basic_publish`. This tells Pika to hold off on returning from `basic_publish` if RabbitMQ's flow control mechanism tells it to stop publishing. When RabbitMQ tells Pika it's okay to proceed, it'll finally return, allowing more publishing to occur. This makes your producer play nicely with RabbitMQ so that if Rabbit becomes overloaded, it can throttle the producer to slow it down. If you're publishing alerts from another program that can't afford to be blocked, be sure to set block_on_flow_control to false.

In only 100 lines of code total, you've given your web apps a flexible and scalable way to issue alerts that then get transmitted asynchronously to their recipients. You've also seen how beneficial the fire-and-forget messaging pattern can be when you need to transmit information to be processed quickly but don't need to know the result of the processing. For example, you could easily extend the alert consumer to add an additional processor that uses the binding pattern *.* to log a copy of all alerts to a database. But alerting and logging are far from the only uses of the fire-and-forget messaging pattern. Let's look at an example where you need to perform CPU-intensive processing on the contents of the message, and how RabbitMQ can help you move that into an asynchronous operation.

4.2.2   *Parallel processing*

Say you started running your own social network website and you just deployed a shiny new feature: picture uploads. People want to share their holiday pictures with friends and family—perhaps you've seen this somewhere. Also, to improve the interaction among users, you want to notify their friends when one of their contacts has uploaded a new picture. A week after the new feature release, the marketing guys come to your desk asking you to give some *points* to the users, a reward for the pictures they upload to encourage them to keep submitting pictures and improve the activity on the site. You agree and add a few lines of code, and now you hook a *reward system* into the upload picture process. It looks a bit nasty for your coder eyes, but it's working as expected and the boss is happy with the results.

Next month the bandwidth bill arrives and the ops guy is angry because the bandwidth usage has doubled. The external API offered to clients is displaying full-size images when it should be offering links to small thumbnails. So you'd better get your uploading code generating those thumbnails too. What to do? The easy way would be to add one more hook in there and execute the thumbnail generation directly from the upload controller, but wait … If for every picture upload you have to execute a picture resize operation, this means the frontend web servers will get overloaded, so you can't just do that. And users of your website don't want to wait for your picture processing script to get a confirmation that their upload is okay. This means you need a smarter solution, something that allows you to run tasks in parallel and in a different machine than the one serving requests to the users.

You can see that resizing a picture, rewarding the user, and notifying friends are three separate tasks. Those tasks are independent in that they don't have to wait for each other's results to be able to run, which means that you can refactor your code not only to process the image resize separately, but also to do those other things in parallel. Also, if you achieve such design, you can cope with new requirements easily. You need to log every picture upload? You just add a new worker to do the logging, and so on.

This sounds nice, almost like a dream, but all this parallelization stuff seems hard to accomplish. How much do you have to code to achieve message multicast? Not much; enter the *fanout* exchange.

As we said when we described the exchange types, the *fanout* exchange will put a copy of the message into the bound queues, as simple as that, and that's what you need for your upload picture module. Every time the user uploads a picture, instead of doing all the processing work right away, you'll publish a message with the picture metainformation and then let your asynchronous workers do the rest in parallel. RabbitMQ will ensure that each consumer gets a copy of the message. It's the worker's duty to process it accordingly.

The messages will contain the following metainformation about the picture: the *image ID* of the picture, the *user ID*, and the *path* to locate the picture on the filesystem. You'll use JSON as the data exchange format. This will make it easier in the future if you need to support several languages for the different tasks. Your messages will look like this:

```
{
    'image_id': 123456,
    'user_id': 6543,
    'image_path': '/path/to/pic.jpg'
}
```

Figure 4.4 shows that you'll declare an upload-pictures exchange and will bind three queues to it: resize-picture, add-points, and notify-friends. From this design you can tell that adding a new *kind* of task, like logging, is just a matter of declaring a new queue and binding it to the upload-pictures exchange. Your focus as developers will be to code each of the workers and the publishing logic; RabbitMQ will do the rest.

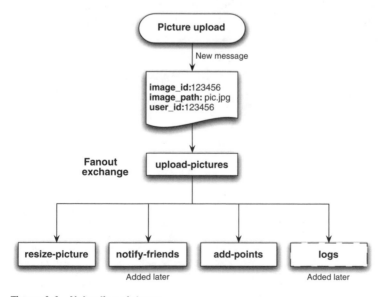

Figure 4.4 Uploading pictures

So, let's start by adding the publisher logic into the upload picture module, as in the following listing. You omit the logic for taking the picture from the POST request and moving it to some place on the filesystem.

Listing 4.7   Upload pictures publisher

```php
<?php

$channel->exchange_declare('upload-pictures',
  'fanout', false, true, false);

$metadata = json_encode(array(
     'image_id' => $image_id,
     'user_id' => $user_id,
     'image_path' => $image_path
     ));

$msg = new AMQPMessage($metadata,
               array('content_type' => 'application/json',
                     'delivery_mode' => 2));

$channel->basic_publish($msg, 'upload-pictures');
?>
```

❶ Declare exchange

❷ Encode image metadata as JSON

❸ Instantiate AMQP

Publish message ❹

Let's see what you did here. The code for obtaining an AMQP channel isn't present since we covered that in previous examples. At ❶ you declare the upload-pictures exchange, with a fanout type and with *durable* properties. Then at ❷ you create the message metadata encoded as JSON. The $image_id, _$user_id, and $image_path were initialized during the upload process. At ❸ you create a new instance of the message specifying the deliver_mode as 2 to make it persistent. Finally at ❹ you publish the message to the upload-pictures exchange. You don't need to provide a routing key since the messages will be fanned-out to all the bound queues.

Next let's create one of the consumers, the one for adding points to the users after each upload. Check inside add-points-consumer.php for the complete code, since the following listing omits bits that we've covered before, like including the AMQP libraries or instantiating the connection and the channel.

Listing 4.8   Add points consumer

```php
<?php

$channel->exchange_declare('upload-pictures',
    'fanout', false, true, false);

$channel->queue_declare('add-points',
    false, true, false, false);

$channel->queue_bind('add-points', 'upload-pictures');

$consumer = function($msg){};

$channel->basic_consume($queue,
                        $consumer_tag,
                        false,
```

❶ Declare exchange

Declare ❷ queue

❸ Bind queue

❹ Code omitted

```
                                    false,
                                    false,                          ⑤ Start
                                    false,                            consuming
                                    $consumer);                       messages
    ?>
```

The code is straightforward. At ❶ you declare the *topic* exchange as when publishing the message; then at ❷ you create the `add-points` queue where the message will be delivered by RabbitMQ. You bind that queue at ❸ to the exchange using the empty routing key. At ❹ you omit the code for your callback function for now; at ❺ you send the `basic_consume` command to prepare the consumer. You also omit the wait loop and the channel and connection cleanup code. The following listing shows the callback function.

Listing 4.9   Add points callback function

```php
<?php
                                                              ❶ Add points to
function add_points_to_user($user_id){                          user function
    echo sprintf("Adding points to user: %s\n", $user_id);
}
                    ❷
Consumer
callback    $consumer = function($msg){
                                                              ❸ Stop
        if($msg->body == 'quit'){                               consuming
            $msg->delivery_info['channel']->                    messages
                basic_cancel($msg->delivery_info['consumer_tag']);
        }
Decode  ❹
JSON        $meta = json_decode($msg->body, true);
metadata
            add_points_to_user($meta['user_id']);             ❺ Process
                                                                data
        $msg->delivery_info['channel']->
            basic_ack($msg->delivery_info['delivery_tag']);   Acknowledge
};                                                            message

?>
```

In listing 4.9 you have the code for actually processing the message. At ❶ you add a dummy function that for now just echoes that it's giving points to the user. In a real-world application you'd include the logic for increasing the user points, say on a Redis database. Then at ❷ you define the consumer callback function. The tricky bit of code at ❸ is a hook to stop consuming messages. If the message body equals `quit`, then you stop the consumer. This simple trick is sure to close the channel and the connection in a clean way. Then at ❹ you pass the message body to the `json_decode` function to obtain the metadata. You give `true` as the second parameter to make sure PHP will decode the JSON object as an associative array. At ❺ you call the `add_points _to_user` function, passing as parameters the `user_id` that you obtained from the decoded message.

Let's test the implementation. You'll just copy the code from the publisher and modify the logic for creating the message to have a simple test script. In this case you'll take three arguments from the command line: *image ID, user ID,* and *image path.*

You'll encode them and send them over RabbitMQ to the consumer that you created before. We won't explain the following listing because it's the same as you saw before in listing 4.7.

> **Listing 4.10 Upload pictures test**

```php
<?php
require_once('../lib/php-amqplib/amqp.inc');
require_once('../config/config.php');

$conn = new AMQPConnection(HOST, PORT, USER, PASS, VHOST);
$channel = $conn->channel();

$channel->exchange_declare('upload-pictures',
  'fanout', false, true, false);

$metadata = json_encode(array(
      'image_id' => $argv[1],
      'user_id' => $argv[2],
      'image_path' => $argv[3]
));

$msg = new AMQPMessage($metadata, array(
      'content_type' => 'application/json',
      'delivery_mode' => 2));

$channel->basic_publish($msg, 'upload-pictures');

$channel->close();
$conn->close();
?>
```

Save this code in a file called `fanout-publisher.php` and open two terminal windows. In the first window, launch the `add-points-consumer.php` script:

```
$ php add-points-consumer.php
```

In the other window, execute the publisher, passing some random parameters to simulate a request:

```
$ php fanout-publisher.php 1 2 /path/to/pic.jpg
```

If everything went well, you can switch to the first terminal to see the following message:

```
Adding points to user: 2
```

So far nothing impressive. Let's add another consumer to see a fanout exchange and parallel processing in action. Put the code from the following listing in the file `resize-picture-consumer.php`.

> **Listing 4.11 Resize picture consumer**

```php
<?php

require_once('../lib/php-amqplib/amqp.inc');
require_once('../config/config.php');
```

```
$conn = new AMQPConnection(HOST, PORT, USER, PASS, VHOST);
$channel = $conn->channel();

$channel->exchange_declare('upload-pictures',
    'fanout', false, true, false);

$channel->queue_declare('resize-picture',
    false, true, false, false);

$channel->queue_bind('resize-picture', 'upload-pictures');

$consumer = function($msg){

    if($msg->body == 'quit'){
        $msg->delivery_info['channel']->
            basic_cancel($msg->delivery_info['consumer_tag']);
    }

    $meta = json_decode($msg->body, true);

    resize_picture($meta['image_id'], $meta['image_path']);

    $msg->delivery_info['channel']->
        basic_ack($msg->delivery_info['delivery_tag']);
};
function resize_picture($image_id, $image_path){
    echo sprintf("Resizing picture: %s %s\n",
        $image_id, $image_path);
}

$channel->basic_consume($queue,
                        $consumer_tag,
                        false,
                        false,
                        false,
                        false,
                        $consumer);

while(count($channel->callbacks)) {
    $channel->wait();
}

$channel->close();
$conn->close();
?>
```

1 Declare resize picture queue

2 Bind queue to exchange

3 Resize picture

4 Resize picture function

The code in listing 4.11 is basically the same from listing 4.8. The interesting bits are at **1** and **2** where you create and bind the `resize-picture` to the `upload-picture` exchange. You can see that this uses the same exchange as the previous example. As always with AMQP, the messages are published to *one* exchange and then, depending on the bindings, they can be routed to one or several queues (or none at all).

The code continues straightforwardly; inside the consumer callback you call the `resize_picture` **3** function passing the `image_id` and `image_path` that you got from the metadata. Finally the function `resize_picture` **4** echoes a message to tell you that it's resizing the image. As before, on a real setup, here you'd want to have the code to actually resize the image.

Now, open a third window on the terminal and type

```
$ php resize-picture-consumer.php
```

Then go back to the window where you have the publisher script and run it again:

```
$ php fanout-publisher.php 1 2 /path/to/pic.jpg
```

If everything went fine, then you should see on each consumer window the following messages:

```
Adding points to user: 2
```

and

```
Resizing picture: 1 /path/to/pic.jpg
```

Based on the examples from the *add points to user* consumer, you can see that if you integrate RabbitMQ into your solution, then scaling the code to new requirements is simple. To add the *image resize* consumer you just need a function that's based on the image ID and path, and is able to load the picture from the filesystem, resize it (probably using some tool like Imagemagick), and then update the record on the database based on the image ID. The same goes for notifying the user's friends. Taking the user ID as a parameter, you can retrieve the user's contacts from the database and then send a notification, perhaps in the form of an email, to each of those friends.

What you can learn from this example is that the power of messaging with RabbitMQ resides in how you combine exchanges and queues together. If you need some way to filter out messages, then you can use a topic exchange as in the previous section. Does one action in your application trigger several others that can run in parallel? Then use topic exchanges. If you want to "spy" on a flow of messages and then quit without leaving traces, then use anonymous queues set to be autodeleted. Once you get used to thinking about messaging patterns, you'll start seeing how simple some programming tasks can become.

But the advantages of this design over the one where everything happens in the same module don't stop here. Imagine now that the pictures are being resized too slowly; you need more computing power and you don't want to change the code. That's easy to solve. You can launch more consumer processes and RabbitMQ will take care of distributing the messages accordingly. Even if they're on different machines, it's no problem. Try to imagine now how you'd scale the original code, where everything happened sequentially while you were serving the request to the user. As you saw, parallel processing with RabbitMQ is simple.

4.3 Remember me: RPC over RabbitMQ and waiting for answers

There are many ways of doing remote procedure calls (RPC)—everything from UNIX RPC to REST APIs and SOAP. What all of these traditional methods of RPC have in common is a tight linkage between the client and server. The client directly connects to the server, makes a request, and then blocks, waiting for a response from the server. This model has a lot of benefits in that its point-to-point nature makes the topology simple at small scale. But that simple topology also limits its flexibility and increases its complexity when it becomes time to scale up. For example, how do your clients discover where to find servers with the services they want when there are multiple servers? SOAP and most enterprise RPCs have come up with complex supplementary protocols and service directories that layer on additional complexity and points of failure, all in the name of being able to serve APIs from multiple RPC servers without tight coupling between the clients and the server. Also, what happens if the RPC server your client is talking to crashes? It's up to the client to reconnect, and if the server is completely down, to rediscover a new server offering the same services—and the client still has to retry the API call once all that's done.

What if, instead of complex directories and multiple protocols, you could do RPC over one protocol? What if your client could issue an API call without worrying about which server was going to serve it, and what to do if the server failed? Using an MQ broker to do RPC can give you all of these things. When you use RabbitMQ for RPC, you're simply publishing a message. It's up to RabbitMQ to use bindings to route the message to the appropriate queue where it'll be consumed by the RPC server. RabbitMQ does all the hard work of getting the message to the right place, load balancing RPC messages across multiple RPC servers, and even retasking an RPC message to another server when the server it was assigned to crashes. All of this without complicated WS-* protocols, or any routing intelligence on the part of the client. The question is, how do you get replies back to the client? After all, your experience so far with RabbitMQ has been fire-and-forget.

4.3.1　Private queues and sending acknowledgements

Since AMQP messages are unidirectional, how can an RPC server reply back to the original client with a result? With RabbitMQ in the middle, the RPC server doesn't even know the identity of the calling client unless there's an application-specific ID in the message payload. Thankfully, the guys at RabbitMQ have an elegant solution: use messages to send replies back. On every AMQP message header is a field called `reply_to`. Within this field the producer of a message can specify the queue name they'll be listening to for a reply. The receiving RPC server can then inspect this `reply_to` field and create a new message containing the response with this queue name as the routing key.

You might be saying yourself, "That sounds like a lot of work to create a unique queue name every time. How do we keep other clients from reading the replies?" Once again, RabbitMQ rides to the rescue. You might remember from chapter 1 that if you declare a queue with no queue name, RabbitMQ will assign one for you. This name happens to be a unique queue name, and when declared with the `exclusive` parameter ensures that only you can read from the queue. All your RPC clients have to do is declare a temporary, exclusive, anonymous queue, and include the name of that queue in the `reply_to` header of their RPC message, and the server now has a place to send the response. Note that we didn't say anything about binding the reply queue to an exchange. This is because when the RPC server publishes its reply message to RabbitMQ without an exchange specified, RabbitMQ knows that it's targeted for a reply queue and that the routing key is the queue's name.

Enough talk; let's look at how you get RPC working with RabbitMQ in real code.

4.3.2 *Simple JSON RPC with reply_to*

The first thing you need is an RPC server. Before we dive into the code, it might help to take a look at the flow of your RPC client and server, shown in figure 4.5.

In the following listing you'll build a simple API server that implements a ping call. This call's only function is to receive the ping invocation from the client, and send a `Pong!` reply with the timestamp included by the client in the original call.

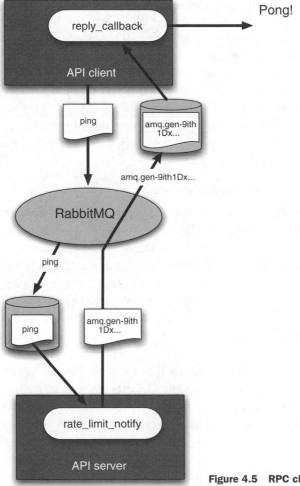

Figure 4.5   RPC client and server flow

Listing 4.12   API server—rpc_server.py

```python
import pika, json

creds_broker = pika.PlainCredentials("rpc_user", "rpcme")
conn_params = pika.ConnectionParameters("localhost",
                                        virtual_host = "/",
                                        credentials = creds_broker)
conn_broker = pika.BlockingConnection(conn_params)
channel = conn_broker.channel()

channel.exchange_declare(exchange="rpc",
                         type="direct",
                         auto_delete=False)
channel.queue_declare(queue="ping", auto_delete=False)
channel.queue_bind(queue="ping",
                   exchange="rpc",
                   routing_key="ping")

def api_ping(channel, method, header, body):
    """'ping' API call."""
    channel.basic_ack(delivery_tag=method.delivery_tag)
    msg_dict = json.loads(body)
    print "Received API call...replying..."
    channel.basic_publish(body="Pong!" + str(msg_dict["time"]),
                          exchange="",
                          routing_key=header.reply_to)

channel.basic_consume(api_ping,
                      queue="ping",
                      consumer_tag="ping")

print "Waiting for RPC calls..."
channel.start_consuming()
```

Establish connection to broker ▷

Declare exchange and ping call queue ◁

Wait for RPC calls and reply ◁

We've covered the setup and connection to RabbitMQ, so let's skip forward to the interesting part where the exchange and queues for receiving the API calls are created:

```python
channel.exchange_declare(exchange="rpc",
                         type="direct",
                         auto_delete=False)
channel.queue_declare(queue="ping", auto_delete=False)
channel.queue_bind(queue="ping",
                   exchange="rpc",
                   routing_key="ping")
```

What you've done here is set up a typical direct exchange and created a queue and binding. For the API, you're following a pattern where the name of the RPC function call is what you use as the binding pattern (and queue name for those calls). In this case, the ping API call is created by binding the ping queue to the rpc exchange using ping as the binding pattern. All your clients need to do is put ping as their routing key and their arguments into the message body. You could also use more complex routing of RPC requests by using a topic exchange. Next you need to set up your consumer subscription:

```
def api_ping(channel, method, header, body):
    """'ping' API call."""
    channel.basic_ack(delivery_tag=method.delivery_tag)
    msg_dict = json.loads(body)
    print "Received API call...replying..."
    channel.basic_publish(body="Pong!" + str(msg_dict["time"]),
                          exchange="",
                          routing_key=header.reply_to)

channel.basic_consume(api_ping,
                      queue="ping",
                      consumer_tag="ping")
```

api_ping will now be invoked every time a message is assigned to you by RabbitMQ via the ping queue. All of this is similar to what you've done so far in the book. What you'll notice is different is the basic_publish command you issue after acknowledging the call message. Wait a minute! How are you able to publish a reply on the same channel you were consuming on? Didn't we say that was impossible?! Actually, in this case it's possible because the Pika library won't start consuming again until your api_ping function returns. More important to focus on is the configuration of the basic_publish command. It's using the reply_to from the header as the routing key for the reply message. Also, unlike any other publish you'll ever do with RabbitMQ, there's no exchange you're publishing to. Those are the only two special components you need to know about making RPC work over Rabbit: publish the reply using the reply_to as the target, and publish without an exchange specification.

How about the RPC client? What does it look like and how do you set up your reply queue? Let's take a peek at the following listing.

Listing 4.13   API client—rpc_client.py

```
import time, json, pika
```

Establish
connection
to broker

```
creds_broker = pika.PlainCredentials("rpc_user", "rpcme")
conn_params = pika.ConnectionParameters("localhost",
                                        virtual_host = "/",
                                        credentials = creds_broker)
conn_broker = pika.BlockingConnection(conn_params)
channel = conn_broker.channel()

msg = json.dumps({"client_name": "RPC Client 1.0",
                  "time" : time.time()})
result = channel.queue_declare(exclusive=True, auto_delete=True)
msg_props = pika.BasicProperties()
msg_props.reply_to=result.method.queue

channel.basic_publish(body=msg,
                      exchange="rpc",
                      properties=msg_props,
                      routing_key="ping")

print "Sent 'ping' RPC call. Waiting for reply..."

def reply_callback(channel, method, header, body):
    """Receives RPC server replies."""
```

Issue RPC
call and
wait for
reply

```
    print "RPC Reply --- " + body
    channel.stop_consuming()

channel.basic_consume(reply_callback,
                      queue=result.method.queue,
                      consumer_tag=result.method.queue)

channel.start_consuming()
```

The heart of making RPC work on the client side is this bit here:

```
result = channel.queue_declare(exclusive=True, auto_delete=True)
msg_props = pika.BasicProperties()
msg_props.reply_to=result.queue
```

In those three lines you create your reply queue and set the `reply_to` header on the message to the name of the new queue. When you declare the reply queue, make sure to set `exclusive=True` and `auto_delete=True`. This ensures that no one else can pilfer your messages (though the queue name created by Rabbit *is* unique), and that when you disconnect from the queue after receiving your reply, the queue will be automatically deleted by Rabbit. All that's left is to publish the API call message and subscribe your callback function to the reply queue:

```
channel.basic_publish(body=msg,
                      exchange="rpc",
                      properties=msg_props,
                      routing_key="ping")

print "Sent 'ping' RPC call. Waiting for reply..."

def reply_callback(channel, method, header, body):
    """Receives RPC server replies."""
    print "RPC Reply --- " + body
    channel.stop_consuming()

channel.basic_consume(reply_callback,
                      queue=result.method.queue,
                      consumer_tag=result.method.queue)
```

There's nothing magical about that. Once you have the reply queue set up, you can consume from it like any other queue. Just be sure not to start consuming from the queue until after you publish your API call message. Otherwise, the channel will be in consume mode and you'll get an error when you try to publish. So what does it look like on the client and server sides when you run your RPC app?

```
Client) Sent 'ping' RPC call. Waiting for reply...
Server) Received API call...replying...
Client) RPC Reply --- Pong! (Client Name: RPC Client 1.0)
       (RPC Call Issued Time: 1288111236.43)
```

You can see that the server's reply really was based on the client's call because the timestamp included in the server's reply is the one that was in the body of the client's call message. From here you can easily extend the API by creating new queues and bindings for new API methods. The best part is there's no reason why any one RPC server needs to respond to all of the API calls. You could easily write a new RPC server that performs image processing, for example, and run it even on a different physical box than the ping API server. Your clients won't know the difference, and you're free to scale your APIs any way you see fit. RabbitMQ does the magic of making it all act like one API fabric. No special protocols. No service directories.

4.4   *Summary*

In this chapter we've covered the fundamental ways of writing apps that take advantage of RabbitMQ and the messaging patterns behind them. We've discussed everything from fire-and-forget patterns, like alerting and image processing, to true bidirectional communication powering RPC APIs. With these fundamental messaging architectures under your belt you're free to start designing your own sophisticated patterns that combine the fundamentals into unique solutions that accomplish your specific goals. Now that you're starting to build RabbitMQ into the heart of your application architecture, it's time we looked at how to run RabbitMQ in resilient configurations that ensure it's always available when your apps need it.

Clustering and dealing with failure

This chapter covers

- Architecture of a RabbitMQ cluster
- Setting up a cluster on your laptop
- Creating a cluster with physical servers
- Upgrading cluster nodes
- Working with mirrored queues

So you just finished your phenomenal new web app powered by RabbitMQ's queuing magic. The user interface displays real-time notifications fed from your backend API, and Rabbit is routing to each API client only the notifications they're interested in. Everything looks great, and Rabbit has made you look like a programming guru to your boss. Time to deploy to production; you can just throw up a RabbitMQ instance on a production server and call it a day, right? Not so fast. Your real-time magic may look great to your customers now, but what happens when your RabbitMQ server has its memory corrupted, or the server loses a power supply? Your high-performance app just became the company's black eye—and your problem. Guess it's time we talked about making RabbitMQ resilient to failure, so when

Murphy's Law wreaks havoc with your apps, you can trust RabbitMQ to keep chugging as the heart of your application.

There are two sides to making RabbitMQ highly available. One is setting up your Rabbits so that you can survive the failure of any one Rabbit and your applications can keep functioning without a hiccup. The other side is dealing with performance as your application scales. A single RabbitMQ instance maybe able to handle the message throughput generated by your Chihuahua walking service today, but what happens when you hit 1,000,000 dog walking requests a second? You're going to need a cluster of Rabbits to keep your applications humming along. Luckily, RabbitMQ comes with built-in clustering that can satisfy both problems and make sure your app always has a Rabbit to talk to, no matter whether server failure or massive success hits you. We're going to cover RabbitMQ's amazing clustering in this chapter. By the time we're done you'll understand how a cluster works under the hood, and how to create them in environments ranging from a small cluster on your development laptop to a real multi-server cluster in production. You'll even know how to upgrade your cluster when new versions of Rabbit come out. Enough talking about it; let's dive in and see how you can take a few Rabbits and turn them into a fire-breathing, message-passing cluster!

5.1 *Batteries included: RabbitMQ clustering*

One of RabbitMQ's best features is its built-in clustering. This sets it apart from almost every other open source messaging broker, and the fact that you can have a cluster up and running in 5 minutes sets it apart from every broker period. Start with one Rabbit today and add more Rabbits on-the-fly with zero downtime to add high availability or more performance. But RabbitMQ clustering isn't a complete panacea. So what does RabbitMQ clustering give you?

The clustering built in to RabbitMQ was designed with two goals in mind: allowing consumers and producers to keep running in the event one Rabbit node dies, and linearly scaling messaging throughput by adding more nodes. RabbitMQ adeptly satisfies both requirements by leveraging the *Open Telecom Platform (OTP)* distributed communication framework provided by Erlang. You can lose a RabbitMQ node and your applications can reconnect to any other node in the cluster and continue producing and consuming as if nothing had happened. Similarly, if your Rabbit cluster is straining under the load of your messaging volume, adding more nodes will linearly add capacity to add more performance. What RabbitMQ clustering *doesn't* necessarily do is provide guarantees against message loss.

Even if you do everything right (set your messages, queues, and exchanges to durable, and so forth), when a Rabbit cluster node dies, the messages in queues on that node can disappear. This is because RabbitMQ doesn't replicate the contents of queues throughout the cluster by default. Without specific configuration, they live only on the node that owns the queue. Wait a minute … you mean queues only live on one node in the cluster? Yes and no. To get a better understanding, let's take a look at the architecture of a RabbitMQ cluster.

5.2   *Architecture of a cluster*

Up to this point we've been vague about the internals of RabbitMQ. Sure, you know what queues and exchanges are—how to bind them together and why you'd want to use the various types. But what's really going on under the covers? How does RabbitMQ keep track of all the various primitives you're using and how they fit together to give you a messaging broker?

At all times RabbitMQ is keeping track of four kinds of internal metadata:

- *Queue metadata*—Queue names and their properties (are they durable or auto-delete?)
- *Exchange metadata*—The exchange's name, the type of exchange it is, and what the properties are (durable and so on)
- *Binding metadata*—A simple table showing how to route messages to queues
- *Vhost metadata*—Namespacing and security attributes for the queues, exchanges, and bindings within a vhost

With a single node, RabbitMQ stores all of this information in memory while writing it to disk for any queues and exchanges (and their bindings) marked durable. Writing it to disk is what ensures that your queues and exchanges will be re-created when you restart a RabbitMQ node. When you add clustering into the mix, RabbitMQ now has to keep track of a new type of metadata: cluster node location and the nodes' relationships to the other types of metadata already being tracked. Clustering also adds the choice about whether to store metadata on disk (the default in a standalone node) or in RAM only. But before we dive into cluster nodes and how they store their metadata, you should first understand how queues and exchanges behave in a cluster.

5.2.1   *Queues in a cluster*

The minute you join one node to another to form a cluster, something dramatically changes: not every node has a full copy of every queue. In a single node setup, all of the information about a queue (metadata, state, and contents) is fully stored in that node (see figure 5.1). But in a cluster when you create queues, the cluster only creates the full information about the queue (metadata, state, contents) on a single node in the cluster[1] rather than on all of them (queues are created on the node to which the client declaring the queue is connected). The result is that only the owner node for a queue knows the full information about that queue. All of the non-owner nodes only know the queue's metadata and a pointer to the node where the queue actually lives. So when a cluster node dies, that node's queues and associated bindings disappear. Consumers attached to those queues lose their subscriptions, and any new messages that would've matched that queue's bindings become black-holed.

---

[1] RabbitMQ 2.6.0 and newer provide *mirrored queues* that allow queue contents to survive cluster node failure. We'll cover mirrored queues in their own section in this chapter.

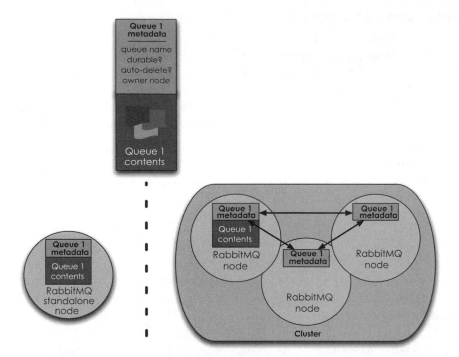

Figure 5.1   Queue behavior in standalone and cluster configurations

Not to worry: you can have your consumers reconnect to the cluster and recreate the queues, right? Only if the queues weren't originally marked durable. If the queues being re-created were marked as durable, redeclaring them from another node will get you an ugly 404 NOT_FOUND error. This ensures messages in that queue on the failed node don't disappear when you restore it to the cluster. The only way to get that specific queue name back into the cluster is to actually restore the failed node. But if the queues your consumers try to re-create are *not* durable, the redeclarations will succeed and you're ready to rebind them and keep trucking. The nagging question is, why *doesn't* RabbitMQ replicate queue contents and state across all nodes by default? There are two reasons:

1 *Storage space*—If every cluster node had a full copy of every queue, adding nodes wouldn't give you more storage capacity. For example, if one node could store 1 GB of messages, adding two more nodes would just give you two more copies of the same 1 GB of messages.

2 *Performance*—Publishing messages would require replicating those messages to *every* cluster node. For durable messages, that would require triggering disk activity on all nodes for every message. Your network and disk load would increase every time you added a node, keeping the performance of the cluster the same (or possibly worse).

By making only one node in a cluster responsible for any particular queue, only the responsible node experiences disk activity for that queue's messages. All of the other nodes need to pass the messages they receive for that queue to its owner node. As a result, adding more nodes to a Rabbit cluster means you have more nodes across which to spread queues, giving you an increase in performance for every node you add. This makes RabbitMQ clustering excellent for scaling up as your load increases. You might be wondering whether exchanges play by the same rules. They don't, and the reason is because exchanges are a figment of your imagination.

5.2.2 *Distributing exchanges*

Up to now we've always described exchanges as if they were a living entity like queues. The truth is that, unlike queues which get their own process, exchanges are just a name and a list of queue bindings. When you publish a message "into" an exchange, what really happens is the channel you're connected to compares the routing key on the message to the list of bindings for that exchange, and then routes it. The *channel* does the actual routing of the message to the queue as specified by the matching binding. Why does this matter? It's important to understand that the channel is the actual router because that explains why exchanges don't suffer from the same limitations as queues in a cluster.

> **NOTE** The way to understand how message routing works under the hood in RabbitMQ is to think of every queue being a running process on a node where each process has its own process ID (PID). Exchanges are simply a list of routing patterns and the queue process IDs where matching messages should be sent. When you publish a message that matches a binding in an exchange, the channel is actually what does the matching, and once matched establishes a connection to the queue PID and transfers the message to it. The process ID of the queue is essentially its Erlang address in the cluster.

Since an exchange is simply a lookup table rather than the actual router of messages, it's much easier to replicate exchanges throughout the cluster (see figure 5.2). For example, when you create a new exchange, all RabbitMQ has to do is add that lookup table to all of the nodes in the cluster. Every channel on every node then has access to the new exchange. So where the full information about a queue is by default on a single node in the cluster, every node in the cluster has all of the information about every exchange. For availability this is great, because it means you don't have to worry about redeclaring an exchange when a node goes down. Just have your producers on the failed node reconnect to the cluster and they can begin publishing immediately into the exchange. But what happens to messages that have been published into a channel but haven't finished routing yet when the node fails?

The basic.publish AMQP command doesn't return the status of the message. This means the channel might still be routing the message when the channel's node fails, though your producer has moved on to creating the next message. In this situation you risk losing those messages. The solution is to use an AMQP transaction, which

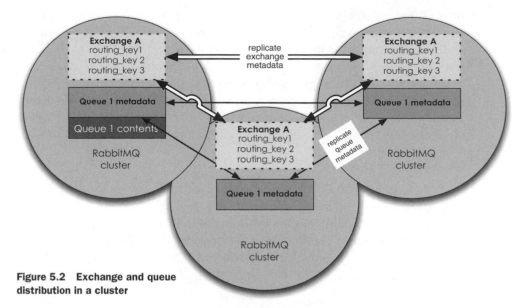

Figure 5.2   Exchange and queue distribution in a cluster

blocks until the message is routed to a queue, or to use *publisher confirms* to keep track of which messages are still unconfirmed when the connection to a node dies. Both solutions will also help you detect when a message is unroutable because a node has failed and the queue it's destined for no longer exists. When combined with the fact that exchanges are fully replicated throughout the cluster, transactions and publisher confirms can help ensure your apps can keep publishing and never lose a message.

Now that you understand how queues and exchanges behave in a cluster, it's time to look at how RabbitMQ keeps track of them all and the nodes powering them.

5.2.3   *Am I RAM or a disk?*

Every RabbitMQ node, whether it's a single node system or a part of a larger cluster, is either a *RAM node* or a *disk node*. A RAM node stores all of the metadata defining the queues, exchanges, bindings, users, permissions, and vhosts only in RAM, whereas a disk node also saves the metadata to disk (see figure 5.3). Single-node systems are only allowed to be disk nodes; otherwise every time you restarted RabbitMQ it would forget all of the configuration of the system. But in a cluster, you can choose to configure some of your nodes as RAM nodes. Why would you want to only store metadata in RAM? Because it makes operations like queue and exchange declarations faster.

When you declare a queue, exchange, or binding in a cluster, the operation won't return until all of the cluster nodes have successfully committed the metadata changes. For a RAM node, this means writing the changes into memory, but for a disk node this means an expensive disk write that must complete before the node can say "I've got it!" If you had a five-node cluster and all of the nodes were disk nodes, you'd have to wait for all five nodes to write the metadata to disk before a queue declaration could return. For a broker where the queues are long-lived that isn't a big deal. But

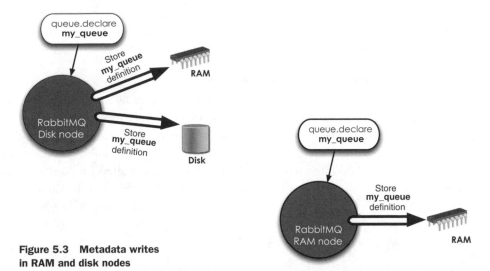

**Figure 5.3   Metadata writes
in RAM and disk nodes**

what if you're doing heavy RPC? If every RPC client is creating and destroying hundreds of reply queues every second, you start to see where disk nodes can kill performance. So how do you balance the performance of RAM nodes against the need to have some disk nodes that allow the cluster configuration to survive cluster restarts?

RabbitMQ only requires that one node in a cluster be a disk node. Every other node can be a RAM node. Keep in mind that when nodes join or leave a cluster, they need to be able to notify at least one disk node of the change. If you only have one disk node and that node happens to be down, your cluster can continue to route messages but you can't do any of the following:

- Create queues
- Create exchanges
- Create bindings
- Add users
- Change permissions
- Add or remove cluster nodes

In other words, your cluster can keep running if its sole disk node is down but you'll be unable to change anything until you can restore that node to the cluster. The solution is to make two disk nodes in your cluster so at least one of them is available to persist metadata changes at any given time. The only operation *all* of the disk nodes need to be online for is adding or removing cluster nodes. When RAM nodes restart, they connect to the disk nodes they're preconfigured with to download the current copy of the cluster's metadata. If you only tell a RAM node about one of your two disk nodes and that disk node is down when the RAM node's power cable gets knocked loose, the RAM node won't be able to find the cluster when it reboots. So when you join RAM nodes, make sure they're told about all of your disk nodes (the only metadata RAM nodes store to disk are the addresses of disk nodes in the cluster). As long as the RAM node can find at least one disk node, it can restart and happily rejoin the cluster.

Enough theory. Let's put a cluster together!

5.3   *Setting up a cluster on your laptop*

Understanding how RabbitMQ handles clustering internally is the hard part; setting a cluster up is easy! It's so easy that you can set up a fully functional cluster on your development system. This is great because it means that as you write your code, you can test failure scenarios and see how they'll actually be handled in production. From chapter 1 you should already have a RabbitMQ node installed on your development machine. Before you start configuring your cluster you first need to make sure that your existing Rabbit node is *not* running. To stop the node, change to your RabbitMQ installation's directory and run `sbin/rabbitmqctl stop`.[2] You should see a message like this to tell you that the node is stopped:

```
Stopping and halting node rabbit@Phantome ... ...done.
```

Now that the node is stopped, you can bootstrap the cluster. Normally you'd start a node using the `rabbitmq-server` command and call it a day. But without any additional arguments, this command will default the Rabbit node to use the node name `rabbit` and `5672` for the listener port. If you were to try to start three nodes on the same machine this way, the second and third nodes would crash on startup due to node name and port collisions. The way we'll work around this is by using the `RABBITMQ_NODENAME` and `RABBITMQ_NODE_PORT` environment variables to specify unique settings for the node name and port before every invocation of `rabbitmq-server`. In this case, you'll start the ports at `5672` and increment by one for every node you start. Similarly, the first node will be named `rabbit` but the second and third nodes will be named `rabbit_1` and `rabbit_2`. You can use different node names and ports as long as they're unique for each node. Let's spin up three nodes on your development system and get started, as in the following listing (make sure to remove [pre-2.7.0] or disable [2.7.0 and later] any plugins in your RabbitMQ install first).

> **NOTE** We haven't talked about RabbitMQ plugins yet, but it's possible that you've enabled a few by now. If you have, you'll want to disable those before starting the cluster nodes. This is because plugins like the RabbitMQ management plugin will listen on dedicated ports to provide their services (like a web UI for the management plugin). We haven't covered yet how to tell some plugins to listen on alternate ports, so when your second and subsequent nodes start their plugins, they'll clash with the ones running on the first node and the nodes will crash.

---

[2] It's also possible to configure cluster membership using the RabbitMQ central config file instead of `rabbitmqctl`. We won't cover this method as it can be error-prone and difficult to debug.

Listing 5.1   Starting a three-node cluster on your development system

```
$ RABBITMQ_NODE_PORT=5672 RABBITMQ_NODENAME=rabbit \
  ./sbin/rabbitmq-server -detached
Activating RabbitMQ plugins ...
0 plugins activated:

$ RABBITMQ_NODE_PORT=5673 RABBITMQ_NODENAME=rabbit_1 \
  ./sbin/rabbitmq-server -detached
Activating RabbitMQ plugins ...
0 plugins activated:

$ RABBITMQ_NODE_PORT=5674 RABBITMQ_NODENAME=rabbit_2 \
  ./sbin/rabbitmq-server -detached
Activating RabbitMQ plugins ...
0 plugins activated:
```

You'll now have three Rabbit nodes running on your development system called
rabbit, rabbit_1, and rabbit_2 (each will have the system's hostname appended at
the end with an @). But each is still a standalone node with its own metadata and no
idea that the others exist. The first node of a cluster is the one that brings the initial
metadata into the cluster and doesn't need to be told to join. Rather, the second and
subsequent nodes are joined to it and acquire its metadata. To join the second and third
nodes, you first need to stop the RabbitMQ app running on their Erlang nodes and
reset (empty) their metadata so they can be joined and acquire the metadata of the cluster. The rabbitmqctl utility will let you communicate with each node and accomplish
each of these tasks. Start by stopping the RabbitMQ app on the second node:

```
$ ./sbin/rabbitmqctl -n rabbit_1@Phantome stop_app
Stopping node rabbit_1@Phantome ...
...done.
```

Next, you need to reset the second node's metadata and state to be empty:

```
$ ./sbin/rabbitmqctl -n rabbit_1@Phantome reset
Resetting node rabbit_1@Phantome ...
...done.
```

Now that you have a stopped (and empty) Rabbit app, you're ready to join it to the
first cluster node:

```
$ ./sbin/rabbitmqctl -n rabbit_1@Phantome cluster rabbit@Phantome \
                                           rabbit_1@Phantome
Clustering node rabbit_1@Phantome with [rabbit@Phantome,
                                  rabbit_1@Phantome] ...
...done.
```

Finally you can start the second node's app again so it can start being a functioning
member of the cluster:

```
$ ./sbin/rabbitmqctl -n rabbit_1@Phantome start_app
Starting node rabbit_1@Phantome ...
...
broker running
...done.
```

You may have noticed that when you issued the cluster command to the second node you got the response Clustering node rabbit_1@Phantome with [rabbit@Phantome,rabbit_1@Phantome]. That's odd; besides the first node you're also clustering the second node with itself? That's right and the reason is because you want rabbit_1 to be a disk node. When you join a new node to a cluster, you have to list all of the disk nodes in the cluster as arguments to the cluster command. This is how a RAM node knows where to get its initial metadata and state if it reboots. If one of the disk nodes you're telling the new node about is itself, rabbitmqctl is smart enough to realize that you want the new node to also be a disk node. The other key piece of information you passed to rabbitmqctl is the -n rabbit_1@Phantome argument. This tells rabbitmqctl that you want it to execute the command you're specifying against a node other than the default node (rabbit@). You can use the -n argument to specify any RabbitMQ node either on your development system or on any other system reachable from your network.

> **NOTE**   Remember that the way Erlang nodes authenticate that they're allowed to talk to each other is via their Erlang cookie. Since rabbitmqctl uses the Erlang OTP communication mechanism to talk to the Rabbit nodes, the machine you're running rabbitmqctl on and the Rabbit nodes you want to talk to must be using the same Erlang cookie. Otherwise you'll get an error.

At this point you have a two-node Rabbit cluster running on your development system along with a third standalone Rabbit node waiting to be clustered. Let's not leave that third node standing out in the cold! Joining the third node, as shown in the following listing, is almost identical to joining the second node.

Listing 5.2   Joining the third node to the cluster

```
$ ./sbin/rabbitmqctl -n rabbit_2@Phantome stop_app
Stopping node rabbit_2@Phantome ...
...done.
$ ./sbin/rabbitmqctl -n rabbit_2@Phantome reset
Resetting node rabbit_2@Phantome ...
...done.
$ ./sbin/rabbitmqctl -n rabbit_2@Phantome cluster rabbit@Phantome \
                                          rabbit_1@Phantome
Clustering node rabbit_2@Phantome with [rabbit@Phantome,
                                        rabbit_1@Phantome] ...
...done.
$ ./sbin/rabbitmqctl -n rabbit_2@Phantome start_app
Starting node rabbit_2@Phantome ...
...
broker running
...done.
```

When you ran the same commands to join the third node, all that changed was the -n argument to specify the third node. You may also notice that you specified rabbit and rabbit_1 as arguments to the cluster command but not rabbit_2. As a result, rabbit_2 will know about the two disk nodes in your cluster, but won't be a disk node itself. Instead, by not specifying it as an argument, rabbit_2 will become a RAM node.

With all of your nodes running and successfully clustered, let's look at your handi-work and ask rabbitmqctl what your cluster looks like:

```
$ ./sbin/rabbitmqctl cluster_status
Cluster status of node rabbit@Phantome ...
[{nodes,[{disc,[rabbit2@Phantome,rabbit@Phantome]}]},
 {running_nodes,[rabbit2@Phantome,rabbit@Phantome]}]
...done.
```

The important part is the nodes section:

```
{nodes,[{disc,[rabbit_1@Phantome,rabbit@Phantome]},
        {ram,[rabbit_2@Phantome]}]},
```

rabbitmqctl is telling you that three nodes are joined to your cluster:

- Two disk ("disc") nodes: rabbit and rabbit_1
- One RAM node: rabbit_2

The running_nodes section tells you which of those cluster nodes is currently run-ning. Right now you could connect to any of the three running_nodes and start creat-ing queues, publishing messages, or performing any of the other AMQP tasks you've worked with up to this point. But before you start using the cluster to learn how to write programs that can reconnect and otherwise deal with node failure, you should take your newly acquired cluster-building skills and see how to apply them to create a cluster across more than one computer.

5.4 *Distributing the nodes to more machines*

Running a RabbitMQ cluster on more than one physical machine isn't much more difficult than building a cluster on your development system. The first thing you need to know is that RabbitMQ clustering is sensitive to latency and should only be used over a local area network. Using it to provide geographic availability/routing over a WAN will cause timeouts and strange cluster behavior, so it's ill-advised. With that in mind, we'll create a distributed cluster on a local area network that looks like this:

- Three nodes on three separate physical machines (Amazon EC2 micro instances/servers)
- Each node running RabbitMQ 2.7.0 on Ubuntu 10.04 LTS 64-bit
- Erlang R13B04

First you need to load your three machines with their operating systems and a running copy of RabbitMQ 2.7.0 (use the instructions from chapter 1 on each system). Though we're using Ubuntu here, this section should work on any UNIX-based oper-ating system. Also, in order to make setting up the three systems easy, we're creating the servers using Amazon Web Services EC2 servers (http://aws.amazon.com/ec2).

Our EC2 servers are micro instances with 613 MB of RAM and 8 GB of storage. So you can focus on the actual clustering instead of server setup, we've made our Amazon Machine Image (AMI) available that has Ubuntu and RabbitMQ already installed and ready to be clustered. To use it, launch three new servers in the EC2 US West - N. California region and search for AMI ID `ami-69ebb42c` when selecting the image for your new servers. Presto! You should have three shiny new micro EC2 servers running Ubuntu 10.04 LTS and a pristine copy of RabbitMQ 2.7.0.[3]

In our setup, our servers are called `ip-10-170-29-145`, `ip-10-170-30-18`, and `ip-10-170-29-88` (see figure 5.4). These are the hostnames that Amazon Web Services automatically assigned to our servers when we created them from our AMI. Yours will be different, so use the hostnames assigned to your servers instead.

At this point, what you need to do is copy the Erlang cookie from `ip-10-170-29-145` to the other nodes so that they can communicate. If the nodes don't have the same Erlang cookie string, then joining the cluster will fail when the Erlang nodes attempt to authenticate each other. If you're using our AMI, the Erlang cookie will be found in `/var/lib/rabbitmq/.erlang.cookie`. Copy the string contained in the cookie and paste it into `/var/lib/rabbitmq/.erlang.cookie` on the other two nodes. Then restart the RabbitMQ process on the other two nodes by running `sudo /etc/init.d/rabbitmq-server restart`. This is actually the hardest part of building the distributed cluster. Now you're ready to actually join the clusters together. First join `ip-10-170-30-18` to the cluster.

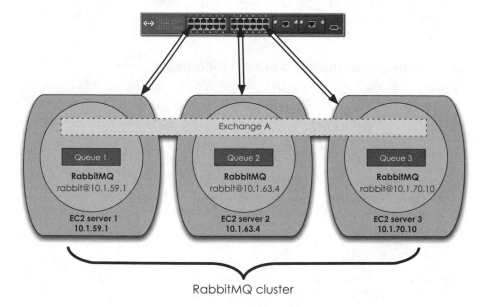

Figure 5.4   Distributing a Rabbit cluster on EC2 servers

---

[3]   If you build EC2 servers using our AMI, be sure to use `ubuntu` as the username when you SSH into the servers.

```
ubuntu@ip-10-170-30-18:~# sudo rabbitmqctl stop_app
Stopping node 'rabbit@ip-10-170-30-18' ...
...done.
ubuntu@ip-10-170-30-18:~# sudo rabbitmqctl reset
Resetting node 'rabbit@ip-10-170-30-18' ...
...done.
ubuntu@ip-10-170-30-18:~# sudo rabbitmqctl cluster \
                                    rabbit@ip-10-170-29-145 \
                                    rabbit@ip-10-170-30-18
Clustering node 'rabbit@ip-10-170-30-18' with
                            ['rabbit@ip-10-170-29-145',
                             'rabbit@ip-10-170-30-18'] ...
...done.
ubuntu@ip-10-170-30-18:~# sudo rabbitmqctl start_app
Starting node 'rabbit@ip-10-170-30-18' ...
...done.
```

You'll notice that you've made `rabbit@ip-10-170-30-18` a disk node, but also that the RabbitMQ node itself is called `rabbit` instead of `rabbit_1` like the second node was in the development machine cluster. On separate physical systems, the first RabbitMQ node on that system will always be called `rabbit`. Only when you have multiple Rabbit nodes on the *same* system will the nodes start to be named `rabbit_1`, `rabbit_2`, and so on. With the second node under your belt, let's add the third node, `ip-10-170-29-88`:

```
ubuntu@ip-10-170-29-88:~$ sudo rabbitmqctl stop_app
Stopping node 'rabbit@ip-10-170-29-88' ...
...done.
ubuntu@ip-10-170-29-88:~$ sudo rabbitmqctl reset
Resetting node 'rabbit@ip-10-170-29-88' ...
...done.
ubuntu@ip-10-170-29-88:~$ sudo rabbitmqctl cluster \
                                    rabbit@ip-10-170-29-145 \
                                    rabbit@ip-10-170-30-18
Clustering node 'rabbit@ip-10-170-29-88' with
                            ['rabbit@ip-10-170-29-145',
                             'rabbit@ip-10-170-30-18'] ...
...done.
ubuntu@ip-10-170-29-88:~$ sudo rabbitmqctl start_app
Starting node 'rabbit@ip-10-170-29-88' ...
...done.
```

If you run `sudo rabbitmqctl cluster_status` on any of the nodes you should see that you now have a three-node cluster:

```
Cluster status of node rabbit@ip-10-170-29-88 ...
 [{nodes,[{disc,['rabbit@ip-10-170-30-18','rabbit@ip-10-170-29-145']},
         {ram,['rabbit@ip-10-170-29-88']}]},
  {running_nodes,['rabbit@ip-10-170-29-145','rabbit@ip-10-170-30-18',
                  'rabbit@ip-10-170-29-88']}]
...done.
```

At this point you've built two different RabbitMQ clusters: one distributed across multiple servers, and one all on a single machine. But one thing we haven't covered is removing nodes from the cluster. What happens if you want to make a cluster smaller or replace a node with one that has better hardware? In either case what you need to do is tell the node to leave the cluster. It's similar to joining a node to the cluster, just without the `rabbitmqctl cluster` step. Let's remove `ip-10-170-29-88` from the cluster and turn it back into a standalone node:

```
ubuntu@ip-10-170-29-88:~$ sudo rabbitmqctl stop_app
Stopping node 'rabbit@ip-10-170-29-88' ...
...done.
ubuntu@ip-10-170-29-88:~$ sudo rabbitmqctl reset
Resetting node 'rabbit@ip-10-170-29-88' ...
...done.
ubuntu@ip-10-170-29-88:~$ sudo rabbitmqctl start_app
Starting node 'rabbit@ip-10-170-29-88' ...
...done.
```

The key command is `rabbitmqctl reset`. We've said before that `reset` empties the node of its metadata and restores it to an empty state. This is true, but when the node being reset is a part of a cluster, the command also communicates with the disk nodes in the cluster to tell them that the node is leaving. This is important because otherwise the cluster will consider the node failed and expect it to be eventually restored. It's particularly critical to formally leave the cluster when the node is a disk node. As you recall, disk nodes are required for every metadata change, but *all* the disk nodes are required for a node to join or leave the cluster. So if you don't formally remove a disk node, the cluster will consider it failed and will wait for it to be restored before it allows any new nodes to join the cluster. As a result, simply yanking a disk node from the cluster without formally removing it can render the cluster permanently unable to change. So be careful to always reset nodes when removing them from the cluster.

If you check the status of the cluster from the removed node you'll see that it now considers itself standalone:

```
Cluster status of node rabbit@ip-10-170-29-88 ...
  [{nodes,[{disc,['rabbit@ip-10-170-29-88']}]},
   {running_nodes,['rabbit@ip-10-170-29-88']}]
...done.
```

Also, if you check the cluster status from any of the other nodes remaining in the cluster, you'll see they no longer consider `ip-10-170-29-88` a part of the cluster:

```
Cluster status of node rabbit@ip-10-170-30-18 ...
  [{nodes,[{disc,['rabbit@ip-10-170-30-18','rabbit@ip-10-170-29-145']}]},
   {running_nodes,['rabbit@ip-10-170-29-145','rabbit@ip-10-170-30-18']}]
...done.
```

With building a distributed cluster and formally removing nodes under your belt, let's talk about what upgrading a cluster to a new version of RabbitMQ means.

5.5 *Upgrading cluster nodes*

Generally, upgrading to new versions of RabbitMQ on standalone systems is easy. You just unpack the new version and run it.[4] The old data will be retained and you'll be

---

[4] Upgrading from versions earlier than 2.1.0 is a manual upgrade procedure because the RabbitMQ storage formats changed between 1.x and 2.0 and then again between 2.1.0 and 2.1.1. If you move between versions of RabbitMQ that have incompatible storage formats, RabbitMQ will automatically copy the old storage files to a backup location and create new empty files.

running the latest and greatest version of RabbitMQ. But upgrading a cluster is less straightforward. Cluster upgrades are semi-automatic. Simply unpacking new versions of RabbitMQ on your cluster nodes and restarting them will kill any configuration and data in the cluster. If you don't have anything stored in the cluster that can't be re-created this isn't much of a problem. If you do, then upgrading is more of an involved process.

First you'll need to back up the current configuration via the RabbitMQ management plugin using the instructions in chapter 6. Then shut down any producers and wait for your consumers to drain all of the queues (use `rabbitmqctl` to watch queue statuses until all of them are empty).[5] Now, shut down the nodes and unpack the new version of RabbitMQ into your existing installation directories. At this point, select one of the disk nodes to be your upgrader node. When it starts, this node will upgrade the persisted cluster data to the new version. Then you can start the remaining cluster disk nodes, which will acquire the upgraded cluster data. Finally, start the cluster RAM nodes and you'll have your cluster running the shiny new version of RabbitMQ and all of your metadata/configuration will have been retained.

With upgrades and the operation of a traditional cluster under your belt, it's time to look at how to extend that cluster to preserve the contents of queues during node failure.

5.6 Mirrored queues and preserving messages

When we started talking about clustering, you may remember that we said queues only live on one node in the cluster by default. That's still true, and if you're using any version of RabbitMQ before 2.6.0, that's the only option you have. But with version 2.6.0, the folks at Rabbit gave us a built-in active-active redundancy option for queues: mirrored queues. Like a normal queue, the primary copy of a mirrored queue only lives on one node (the *master*), but unlike a normal queue, mirrored queues have *slave* copies on other nodes in the cluster. In the event that the queue's master node becomes unavailable, the oldest slave will be elected as the new master. This sounds like the high availability panacea we've been looking for since we ventured into clustering, but there are a few caveats you need to be aware of. Before we dive into the caveats, let's look at how you can write consumer apps that take advantage of mirrored queues.

5.6.1 Declaring and using mirrored queues

As with many aspects of AMQP, your application defines a queue as being *mirrored* rather than `rabbitmqctl`. Declaring a mirrored queue is just like declaring a normal queue; you pass an extra argument called `x-ha-policy` to the `queue.declare` call. To see how this looks in actual code, let's update the Hello World consumer program you wrote in chapter 2 to declare a mirrored queue instead of a normal one. Changing the

---

[5] Draining queues isn't required with versions of RabbitMQ newer than 2.6.0, as the broker will upgrade them automatically. But it's still a good safety measure, just in case something goes awry with the upgrade.

queue declaration to be mirrored instead of normal is as simple as replacing `channel.queue_declare(queue="hello-queue")` with this:

```
queue_args = {"x-ha-policy" : "all" }
channel.queue_declare(queue="hello-queue", arguments=queue_args)
```

`queue_args` is simply a dictionary (or hash) containing the additional arguments for the queue declaration. In this case, you're adding an argument called `x-ha-policy` and setting its value to `all`. When set to `all`, `x-ha-policy` tells Rabbit that you want the queue to be mirrored across all nodes in the cluster. This means that if a new node is added to the cluster after the queue is declared, it'll automatically begin hosting a slave copy of the queue. To test your new mirrored queue consumer, fire it up in one terminal and use `rabbitmqctl` in a separate terminal to see if the queue is really mirrored:

```
(terminal 1)> python hello_world_mirrored_queue_consumer.py

(terminal 2)> rabbitmqctl list_queues name pid slave_pids
Listing queues ...
hello-queue    <rabbit@Phantome.1.7429.1> [<rabbit2@Phantome.1.7...
...done.
```

This tells `rabbitmq` to show you the `name`, `pid`, and `slave_pids` fields when listing the queues in the cluster. When dealing with mirrored queues, `pid` is the Erlang process ID of the master copy of the queue, and `slave_pids` is a list of the slave copies and the nodes they're on. In this case, you have one master copy located at ID `1.7429.1` on node `rabbit@Phantome`, and one slave copy located at ID `1.7431.1` on node `rabbit2@Phantome`. Excellent; your Hello World consumer is now using a mirrored queue! But what do you do if you don't want your queue to be mirrored on every node in the cluster, but instead only a few?

This is where it gets trickier. Since the mirrored nature of a queue is specified by the application at runtime, the guys at Rabbit HQ decided that you'd specify which nodes your mirrored queue lives on at runtime as well. So, to make your mirrored queue live on a subset of nodes in the cluster, you have to specify in your application the exact node names of the cluster nodes you want the queue to live on (instead of specifying `all`). This is the tricky part, because it means you're hardcoding node names into your application. If any of those nodes are down (or have been removed from the cluster) when your application tries to declare the queue, the declaration will fail. There's no concept of an availability group in Rabbit that would abstract the set of nodes you want your mirrored queue to live on into a general name that won't change if your ops team decides to reshuffle your Rabbit cluster. As a result, we highly recommend you use the `all` setting for `x-ha-policy` whenever possible so that your mirrored queue declarations aren't hardcoded to specific node names that may change. But suppose you absolutely need to specify a subset of cluster nodes for your mirrored queue. How do you do it?

You only need to make two changes to your mirrored queue declaration to make it use a subset of nodes, instead of all the nodes in a cluster. First, you need to change x-ha-policy to nodes[6] instead of all. This tells RabbitMQ you're going to be giving it a specific list of cluster node names to mirror the queue on. Then you add another argument to the queue declaration called x-ha-policy-params, and set its value to the list of node names you want to mirror the queue across. In code it looks like this:

```
queue_args = {"x-ha-policy" : "nodes",
              "x-ha-policy-params" : ["rabbit@Phantome"]}
channel.queue_declare(queue="hello-queue", arguments=queue_args)
```

If you delete the mirrored queue (hello-queue) you created the first time you ran your updated Hello World consumer and re-run it, you should see that the mirrored queue now only lives on a single node in the cluster:

```
(terminal 1)> python hello_world_mirrored_queue_consumer.py

(terminal 2)> rabbitmqctl list_queues name pid slave_pids
Listing queues ...
hello-queue    <rabbit@Phantome.1.7429.1>    []
...done.
```

As expected, hello-queue only has a master copy and no slaves, even though there are two nodes in this cluster. What would happen if you were to add a new slave node to the queue at this point? The new slave copy would only contain messages received by the mirrored queue after the slave was added. RabbitMQ doesn't yet (as of 2.7.0) synchronize the existing contents of a mirrored queue to newly added slave copies. The theory goes that as messages are consumed from the existing master and slave copies, all of the old messages that the new slave doesn't know about will be removed and the new slave copy will eventually have the same state as the existing queue copies. But if you were to remove all of the nodes containing the existing master and slave copies before these old messages were consumed, and the new slave copy was promoted to be the master, you'd lose those old messages. As a result, until RabbitMQ provides synchronization of a mirrored queue's existing contents to new slaves, it's important to be able to tell whether all of the slaves have the same contents. To check the synchronization status of a mirrored queue, just ask rabbitmqctl to tell you the synchronised_slave_pids when listing queues:

```
> rabbitmqctl list_queues name pid slave_pids synchronised_slave_pids
Listing queues ...
hello-queue    <rabbit@Phantome.1.7429.1>    [<rabbit2@Phantome.1.74...
                                              [<rabbit2@Phantome.1.74...
...done.
```

If the list of PIDs in the first and second bracketed lists (say, [<rabbit2@Phantome.1.7431.1>]) are identical, then all of your slaves are synchronized. But if any of the PIDs in the first bracketed list aren't present in the second list, then the missing slave PIDs don't yet have identical contents to the older slave copies. If that's the case,

---

[6] In versions 2.6.0 and 2.6.1, the nodes queue copy distribution policy doesn't work. It works correctly in versions 2.7.0 and newer.

then you need to wait until the two bracketed lists become identical before you remove nodes from the cluster. This will ensure you don't lose any messages that are only present on the nodes you may be removing. This is one of the caveats that we alluded to when introducing mirrored queues. To get a better understanding of how mirrored queues work (and the rest of the caveats), let's dive into how mirrored queues operate under the covers.

So far you've learned how a cluster works (including mirrored queues) and how to deploy one either on a single development machine or distributed across a local area network. You even know how to upgrade a cluster without losing all of your configuration forever. What you don't know how to do is write code that can deal with cluster node failure and auto-reconnect to other nodes in the cluster.

5.6.2   *Under the hood with mirrored queues*

In a Rabbit cluster with nonmirrored queues, the channel does the job of routing messages to the appropriate queues in the cluster. When you add mirrored queues into the mix, the channel does the exact same thing, except instead of just delivering the messages to the appropriate queues specified by the routing bindings, it also delivers the messages to the slave copies of the mirrored queues (as shown in figure 5.5). In some ways you could view a mirrored queue as having a hidden fanout exchange that instructs the channel to also deliver to the queue's slave copies.

Understanding that the channel is what publishes the message in parallel to both the master and slave copies of a mirrored queue can also help you understand how transactions and publisher confirms are affected by mirrored queues. When dealing with nonmirrored queues, you only receive a *publisher confirm* back (or a successful transaction) after the channel has routed the message to all of the queues specified by the bindings that the message matched. When you switch to using mirrored queues,

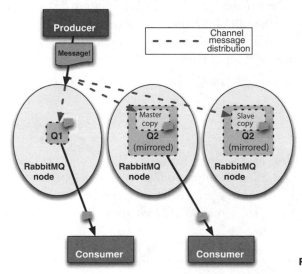

Figure 5.5   Mirrored queue behavior

Rabbit uses the same concept, but extends it to the slave copies of the queues as well. So if you need to ensure a message isn't lost, you can use a publisher confirmation on the message and Rabbit will notify you when all of the queues and their slave copies have safely accepted the message. But if a mirrored queue's master fails before the message has been routed to the slave that will be become the new master, the publisher confirmation will never arrive and you'll know that the message may have been lost. But that only covers how publishers handle the failure of a mirrored queue's master node. What happens to consumers attached to the failed master copy?

If a mirrored queue loses a slave node, any consumers attached to the mirrored queue don't notice the loss. That's because technically they're attached to the queue's master copy. But if the node hosting the master copy fails, all of the queue's consumers need to reattach to start listening to the new queue master. For consumers that were connected through the node that actually failed, this isn't hard. Since they've lost their TCP connection to the node, they'll automatically pick up the new queue master when they reattach to a new node in the cluster. But for consumers that were attached to the mirrored queue through a node that didn't fail, RabbitMQ will send those consumers a *consumer cancellation* notification telling them they're no longer attached to the queue master. If your AMQP client library understands consumer cancellation notifications, it'll raise an exception and your app will know it's no longer attached to the queue and needs to reattach. On the other hand, if your client library doesn't understand consumer cancellations, you're in a bind. The client has no way of telling your app that its consumption loops point to a master queue copy that no longer exists. So your app will sit there dumb and happy, thinking there's nothing in the queue to consume. Unfortunately, there's no clever way around this situation (such as Rabbit closing the consumer's channel to force an exception). So if your client library doesn't understand consumer cancellation notifications, you should avoid mirrored queues until it does. Otherwise, you could end up with a wake-up call in the middle of the night from your monitoring system telling you that your queues are chock full of unconsumed messages.

After cancellation notifications, the only remaining item to watch out for with mirrored queues is messages that have been consumed but not acknowledged. When the master node of a mirrored queue fails, Rabbit has to make a decision about any messages that have been delivered to consumers, but not yet acknowledged by them. Even though the messages were delivered to a consumer, Rabbit can't tell the difference between acknowledgements that were lost during the failover and messages that weren't acknowledged at all. So to be safe, consumed but unacknowledged messages are requeued to their original positions in the queue (or to the back of the queue in versions before 2.7.0).

5.7 Summary

When you started this chapter, you were completely at the mercy of a single Rabbit node to keep your apps powered and communicating. Now you no longer need to fear Rabbit failure, because your RabbitMQ cluster will keep your infrastructure powered and humming along. More important, you understand the ins and outs of how clustering is implemented internally so you can make intelligent design choices for your RabbitMQ architectures. These choices can maximize uptime and scalability while minimizing your vulnerability to message loss. But clustering RabbitMQ is only half the battle. Even with a hard charging Rabbit cluster at the heart of your infrastructure, your apps still only connect to one node. If that one cluster node dies, they're adrift about where to connect next in the cluster so they can keep operating without a hiccup. Clustering is Rabbit's end of the high-availability bargain. It's time to talk about how to write your apps so they can survive individual node failure and hold up their end of that bargain.

Writing code that survives failure

This chapter covers

- Understanding load balancing
- Installing and configuring HAProxy to load balance Rabbit
- Writing code that reconnects and intelligently survives failure

Building a RabbitMQ cluster to ensure availability and performance is only half the battle of ensuring a resilient messaging infrastructure. The other half is writing applications that expect node failure and knowing how to reconnect to the cluster when it happens. There are a number of strategies for handling reconnection to the cluster, but the one we'll focus on is using a load balancer to handle node selection. By using a load balancer you not only reduce the complexity of the failure handling code in your apps, but you also ensure even connection distribution across your cluster. But even with a load balancer, there's more to writing an app that can handle node failure than establishing a new connection to the cluster. Your apps also need to be prepared to re-create exchanges and queues that may

107

not have survived the failure of the original node. This is particularly true when using two standalone Rabbit nodes in an active/standby configuration (which we'll cover in chapter 7). Before you start writing failure-handling code in your apps, we'll look at what it takes to use a load balancer with RabbitMQ.

6.1   *Load balancing your Rabbits*

Depending on your background, you might be wondering what the heck a *load balancer* is. A load balancer presents a single IP address behind which lie multiple servers. Let's say you have three web servers powering your website named web1.acme.com, web2.acme.com, and web3.acme.com. Without a load balancer, your customers would have to manually go to web1 and if it was down try web2 or web3 instead. Not only is this a lot to ask of your customers, it also gives you no control over how much load is on each of the servers at any given time. If you have a load balancer, you could create an IP address on the load balancer that you name www.acme.com. Then when a customer connects to www, the load balancer transparently proxies the connection to web1, web2, or web3 based on whichever has the lowest connection load. If web1 were to fail, the load balancer is also smart enough to detect this and stop sending connections to web1, instead making web2 and web3 pick up the load. To your customer, it looks like you have one huge server called www and that's all they need to care about. All of the load balancing and failed server detection is handled by the load balancer transparently (see figure 6.1).

When using a load balancer with RabbitMQ, your cluster nodes are the servers behind the load balancer and your producers and consumers are the customers. Your apps only need to know the frontend IP of the load balancer; it'll transparently connect them to the cluster node with the lowest connection load. If you want to grow your cluster for more performance, you don't need to change any of your apps—you just need to join the new node to the cluster and then add the node to the load

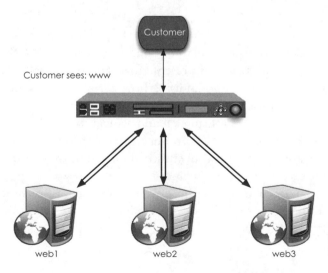

Figure 6.1   Load balancing multiple web servers to appear as one

balancer's configuration. There's no change to your applications. Without a load balancer, your apps would have to be manually configured with knowledge of every cluster node's IP. They'd also have to handle cluster node selection and failed server detection on their own. Since each app would be handling its own node selection, you'd have no way to evenly spread the load across the cluster. The load distribution would be essentially random. So by using a load balancer in front of your Rabbit cluster, you let it handle the complexities of node selection, failed server detection, and load distribution (see figure 6.2).

Many different load balancers are out there, but they fall into one of two categories: hardware appliances or software. Hardware appliances are beefy dedicated network systems that can handle millions of connections a second without blinking an eye. They also usually offer advanced clustering so that two load balancers can act as a single unit to remove the load balancer as a single point of failure. If you have a hardware load balancer already, there's no reason why you can't use it to load balance RabbitMQ clusters. Just use your appliance in layer 4 load balancing mode. But for most situations, a software load balancer is more than adequate. You're more likely to hit the upper limit of the number of nodes a cluster can support than to outstrip a software load balancer's ability to feed the cluster. Of the many software load balancers out there, we'll use HAProxy. It's freely available, is extremely reliable, and handles heavy loads across the internet for sites like StackOverflow. Also, it'll run on nearly any UNIX-based platform and is extremely easy to configure. Instead of talking about how

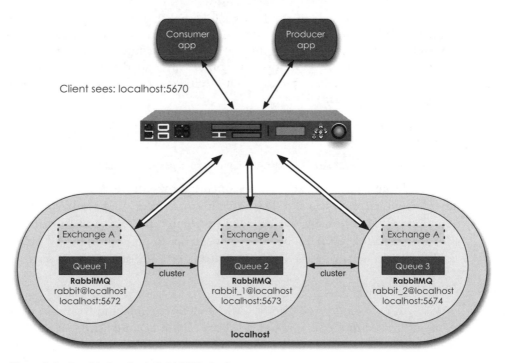

Figure 6.2 Load balancing a RabbitMQ cluster

great HAProxy is, let's show you by installing it and configuring it to load balance a RabbitMQ cluster.

6.1.1   *Installing HAProxy*

Installing HAProxy is simple. Most modern Linux distributions have HAProxy available in their packaging systems, but we'll build it from source. The first step is to download HAProxy to your development system and unpack the archive:

```
$ wget http://haproxy.1wt.eu/download/1.4/src/haproxy-1.4.14.tar.gz
Resolving haproxy.1wt.eu... 88.191.124.161
Connecting to haproxy.1wt.eu|88.191.124.161|:80... connected.
HTTP request sent, awaiting response... 200 OK
Length: 812238 (793K) [application/x-gzip]
Saving to: `haproxy-1.4.14.tar.gz'

100%[=============================>] 812,238      192K/s   in 4.1s

2011-03-29 19:16:56 (192 KB/s) - `haproxy-1.4.14.tar.gz' saved

$ sudo tar xfz haproxy-1.4.14.tar.gz
```

With the source unpacked you need to run make to build the HAProxy executable. Before you can run make, you need to select the target platform. If you're building on a Linux 2.6 system you'll want to set TARGET=linux26 to enable epoll support. For all other UNIX-based systems, TARGET=generic is usually the right choice. Without further ado, let's kick off the build.

> **NOTE** *epoll* is a feature of the Linux 2.6 kernel that enables event-based network software like HAProxy to be notified when new packets are waiting instead of the software having to poll on a regular interval. This can reduce CPU usage and improve performance on heavily loaded systems. FreeBSD has a similar feature called *kqueues* which HAProxy can take advantage of by setting TARGET=freebsd.

```
$ cd haproxy-1.4.14
$ sudo make TARGET=generic
...
gcc  -g -o haproxy src/haproxy.o src/sessionhash.o src/b...
```

You should now have an executable named haproxy in the build directory. If everything is built correctly you should be able to run haproxy --help to see its configuration options. Finally, copy the haproxy executable to /usr/local/sbin so that it's available on your UNIX path. Now all you need is a configuration file for HAProxy so it can begin load balancing the RabbitMQ cluster on your development system.

6.1.2   *Configuring HAProxy*

HAProxy uses a single configuration file to define everything from the frontend IPs being advertised to the servers behind them. The following listing shows the configuration you'll use to load balance your local Rabbit cluster.

Listing 6.1 HAProxy configuration for local RabbitMQ cluster

```
global                                                          Logging
    log 127.0.0.1    local0 info                               options
    maxconn 4096
    stats socket /tmp/haproxy.socket uid haproxy mode 770 level admin
    daemon

defaults                                                        Load
    log     global                                             balancing
    mode    tcp                                                defaults
    option   tcplog
    option   dontlognull
    retries   3
    option redispatch
    maxconn   2000
    timeout connect    5s                                    ❶ Front-end IP for
    timeout client 120s                                        consumers and
    timeout server 120s                                        producers

listen rabbitmq_local_cluster 127.0.0.1:5670
    mode tcp                                                 Load
    balance roundrobin                                       balancing
    server rabbit 127.0.0.1:5672 check inter 5000 rise 2 fall 3  ❷ options
    server rabbit_1 127.0.0.1:5673 check inter 5000 rise 2 fall 3
    server rabbit_2 127.0.0.1:5674 check inter 5000 rise 2 fall 3

listen private_monitoring :8100
    mode http                                                Statistics
    option httplog                                         ❹ page
    stats enable
    stats uri   /stats
    stats refresh 5s
```

Cluster ❸ (pointing to `listen rabbitmq_local_cluster`)
nodes
to load
balance

In ❶ you define the IP and port your clients will be connecting to. You use port 5670 so that it doesn't conflict with the RabbitMQ cluster nodes themselves. Then you tell HAProxy to use the round-robin algorithm ❷ to distribute the load among the backends (see figure 6.3).

The most interesting part is ❸ where we define the backends:

```
server rabbit 127.0.0.1:5672 check inter 5000 rise 2 fall 3
    server rabbit_1 127.0.0.1:5673 check inter 5000 rise 2 fall 3
    server rabbit_2 127.0.0.1:5674 check inter 5000 rise 2 fall 3
```

Each backend configuration directive has five parts:

- server <name> is the internal identifier given to the backend definition.
- <IP>:<port> is the IP and port number of the backend server to connect to.
- check inter <value> defines how often in milliseconds to check that the backend is available.
- rise <value> indicates how many successful health checks a backend must complete after having failed before it is considered usable again.
- fall <value> specifies how many health checks a backend must fail before HAProxy stops using it.

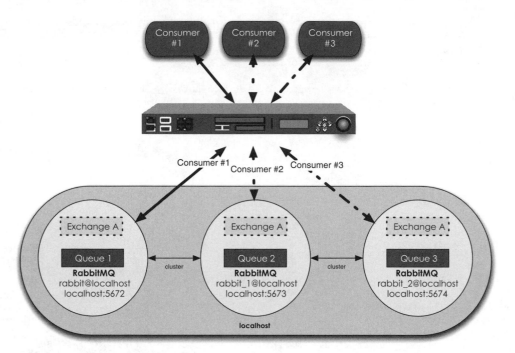

Figure 6.3   Round-robin load balancing

The final configuration section is for the statistics page ❹. It's optional but by enabling it on port 8100 you can connect to http://localhost:8100 and see HAProxy's current status, including how many connections each RabbitMQ cluster node is currently serving. This can be useful when you want to see the load across your cluster or how many nodes are currently up or down. There are many more configuration options for HAProxy that allow everything from complex load balancing rules to identifying backend nodes as backup servers that are only used if all of the main backends are down. Check out HAProxy's manual to find out more at http://haproxy.1wt.eu/download/1.4/doc/configuration.txt.

Let's start up HAProxy with your new configuration and make sure it works. Run /usr/local/sbin/haproxy -f config_file where *config_file* is the configuration file you just created. If everything went well you should be able to load a web page at http://localhost:8100/stats that looks like figure 6.4.

Now that you have a functioning load balancer on your development system, we're going dive into using it to build failover and resilience into your messaging apps.

6.2   *Lost connections and failing clients between servers*

When a cluster node fails, suddenly your app has a decision to make: where do I connect next? To be able to answer that question effectively, you must have anticipated it in your code long before it happens. Gracefully handling node failure requires a change in mentality. Clustering doesn't mean your app never experiences Rabbit

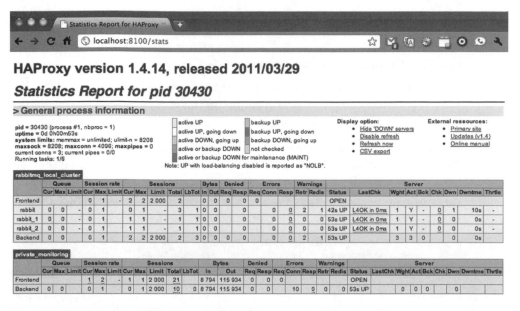

Figure 6.4 HAProxy statistics page

problems; it means when there is a problem, nodes have somewhere else to go and keep running. So the first step is to *step back* and consider what assumptions you can make before writing your code:

1 *If I reconnect to a new server, what happens to my channels and all of the consumption loops attached to them?* They're invalid now and point nowhere. You need to rebuild both.

2 *When I reconnect, can I assume that all of my exchanges, queues, and bindings are still in the cluster? Can I just reconnect and immediately start consuming from my queues again?* The answer is, no. You can't assume queues and bindings survived the node failure. You must assume that all of the queues you were consuming from were hosted on the node you were attached to—and no longer exist. The same goes for those queues' bindings, though exchanges are a different story. If you're using Rabbit's built-in clustering you can assume exchanges will survive node failure due to being replicated to every node. But if you're using an active/standby setup like we describe in the next section, you can't even assume exchanges will survive failover.

What you can take away from those questions is that you can't assume anything about the state of the cluster when you fail over to a new node. Though the Rabbit cluster has given your app a new place to connect to, you can't make any assumptions about what does and doesn't exist. In some respects, you should always treat failover as if you were connecting to a completely unrelated RabbitMQ server, rather than a cluster node with some shared state. As a result, whenever a node failure occurs, the first order of business after detecting the failure and reconnecting is to rebuild the fabric of exchanges, queues, and bindings that your app needs to operate. Before we dive into some code, let's talk about what you'll need to run it. Like the examples in chapter 3, you'll need a functional Python 2.6 installation and Pika 0.9.6 or greater installed. In addition you'll also need the following:

- A RabbitMQ cluster set up on your local development machine.
- HAProxy configured and running on the same machine, and listening on port 5670 for AMQP connections.

You'll build a sample producer and consumer that can survive cluster node failure. Building a cluster-aware consumer is the more difficult task because the consumer is what builds your messaging fabric (exchanges, queues, and bindings). As a result, it's up to the consumer to rebuild that fabric after node failure. With a standard consumer, your app's body would look something like the following listing.

Listing 6.2   Standard consumer main body

Connect to RabbitMQ ❶

```
conn_broker = pika.BlockingConnection(conn_params)          ❷ Custom
                                                               connection
channel = conn_broker.channel()                                behavior
channel.exchange_declare( exchange="cluster_test",
                          type="direct",
                          auto_delete=False)
channel.queue_declare( queue="cluster_test",                 Declare
                       auto_delete=False)                    exchanges,
channel.queue_bind( queue="cluster_test",                    queues,
                    exchange="cluster_test",               ❸ & bindings
                    routing_key="cluster_test")


print "Ready for testing!"
channel.basic_consume( msg_rcvd,                             Start
                       queue="cluster_test",                consuming
                       no_ack=False,                      ❹ messages
                       consumer_tag="cluster_test")
channel.start_consuming()
```

With the connection parameters already established, you build ❶ your connection to the server. Then you establish the channel ❷ and begin declaring ❸ exchanges, queues, and bindings (your messaging fabric). After the fabric is built, you create ❹ a consumption subscription (powered by the msg_rcvd function) and start consuming messages. At this point if you were to experience node failure, your program would crash with an unhandled exception. That's because this code doesn't know what to do when a connection error occurs. What you need to do is wrap this code in an exception handler and initiate a reconnection when the failure occurs. But where do you start wrapping? What parts of the main body need to be rerun after a failure event? All of them. If you don't assume any of the messaging fabric survives node failure, then all of your main body needs to be executed every time an error occurs. If you rewrite the main body with this in mind, it'll look something like the following listing.

Listing 6.3 Cluster-aware consumer main body

```
while True:
    try:
        conn_broker = pika.BlockingConnection(conn_params)

        channel = conn_broker.channel()
        channel.exchange_declare( exchange="cluster_test",
                                  type="direct",
                                  auto_delete=False)
        channel.queue_declare( queue="cluster_test",
                               auto_delete=False)
        channel.queue_bind( queue="cluster_test",
                            exchange="cluster_test",
                            routing_key="cluster_test")

print "Ready for testing!"
channel.basic_consume( msg_rcvd,
                       queue="cluster_test",
                       no_ack=False,
                       consumer_tag="cluster_test")
channel.start_consuming()
except Exception, e:
    traceback.print_exc()
```

On fault, reconnect to RabbitMQ ❶

❷ Establish connection to RabbitMQ

❸ Declare exchange, queues, bindings

❹ Start consuming messages

❺ Trap connection errors and print them

By wrapping the main body in a try...except block you can now detect connection failures ❺ and prevent them from crashing the consumer. In this case, you trap out any errors and print them to the screen. But this is only half of the solution. You're no longer crashing when a node fails but you still need to reconnect and rebuild the fabric. To do that you wrap the entire main body (including the new try...except block) with an infinite loop ❶. When the app first starts, it enters the loop and then builds the connection ❷ and the fabric ❸. Then it pauses the loop to start consuming ❺. As long as there are no errors, this is as far as the outer loop will ever progress. But the minute a node fails, a connection error is experienced. This causes control to pass from the consumption code ❹ to the outer exception handler ❺. The exception handler then prevents the program from crashing by trapping the error, prints it to the screen, and then passes control back to the outer loop. Now the loop starts the whole connection process over from scratch ❶ by building a new connection ❷ and fabric ❸ just like before. It's a simple change, but one that enables your program to handle node failure within a RabbitMQ cluster. It'll also handle a variant of node failure we haven't discussed yet, but that you need to know about.

So far when we've talked about a cluster node failing from your app's perspective, we've always said it's the node the app is connected to. You might've assumed that as long as the node connected to your app doesn't fail, then your app has nothing to worry about. That's not entirely true. If you remember how queues operate in a cluster, you'll note that they only exist on one node. Since your app doesn't know which node a queue is on when it starts consuming, it's possible that your app is connected to node A in the cluster but is consuming from a queue on node B. So what happens when node B fails? The app doesn't experience a connection error but the queue it's supposedly consuming from no longer exists. If you're running a version of RabbitMQ earlier than 2.4.0 you're somewhat out of luck. Your consumer will sit there dumb and happy, doing nothing forever (at least until you restart it). This limitation is more a property of AMQP than RabbitMQ itself. But with RabbitMQ 2.4.0 came a new extension to AMQP called *cancellation notification.* With cancellation notifications, your consumer receives a notification when its subscription terminates for any reason other than the consumer canceling it. In Pika this manifests as an exception raised in the consumption code. This will be trapped by your exception handler and your reconnect/rebuild code will reestablish the connection and rebuild the fabric. With all of the pieces in place, the following listing shows what the consumer looks like all together.

Listing 6.4 Cluster-aware consumer

```
import sys, json, pika, time, traceback

def msg_rcvd(channel, method, header, body):
    message = json.loads(body)

    print "Received: %(content)s/%(time)d" % message          Print and
    channel.basic_ack(delivery_tag=method.delivery_tag)       acknowledge
                                                              message

if __name__ == "__main__":        Broker settings
    AMQP_SERVER = sys.argv[1]
    AMQP_PORT = int(sys.argv[2])
                                                              Establish
    creds_broker = pika.PlainCredentials("guest", "guest")    broker
    conn_params = pika.ConnectionParameters( AMQP_SERVER,     connection
                                     port=AMQP_PORT,
                                     virtual_host="/",
                                     credentials=creds_broker)

    while True:        On fault, reconnect to RabbitMQ
        try:
            conn_broker = pika.BlockingConnection(conn_params)    Establish
                                                                 connection
                                                                 to RabbitMQ
            channel = conn_broker.channel()        Custom connection behavior
            channel.exchange_declare( exchange="cluster_test",    Declare
                                type="direct",                    exchange,
                                auto_delete=False)                queues,
            channel.queue_declare( queue="cluster_test",         bindings
                                auto_delete=False)
            channel.queue_bind( queue="cluster_test",
                                exchange="cluster_test",
                                routing_key="cluster_test")
                                                                 Start
            print "Ready for testing!"                          consuming
            channel.basic_consume( msg_rcvd,                     messages
                                queue="cluster_test",
                                no_ack=False,
                                consumer_tag="cluster_test")
            channel.start_consuming()
        except Exception, e:                   Trap connection
            traceback.print_exc()              errors and print them
```

As you can see, converting any consumer app to be cluster-aware isn't difficult. It just requires understanding what happens inside of RabbitMQ when a node fails and accommodating those behaviors in your code. Now let's fire up your consumer and see what happens:

```
$ python cluster_test_consumer.py localhost 5670
Ready for testing!
```

Hmmm ... you're connected to the cluster through the load balancer and have built your fabric (check out http://localhost:8100 to see which cluster node you're connected to). But your consumer isn't doing anything interesting yet. What you need is a cluster producer to give your consumer some content to display! The producer is short-lived and doesn't need any fancy failure-handling code. This is because every invocation of the producer establishes a new connection from scratch, which enables the load balancer to select a new functional node. The following listing shows what your producer looks like.

Listing 6.5 Cluster-aware producer

```
import sys, time, json, pika

AMQP_HOST = sys.argv[1]                                          ❶ Establish
AMQP_PORT = int(sys.argv[2])                                       connection
                                                                   to broker
creds_broker = pika.PlainCredentials("guest", "guest")
conn_params = pika.ConnectionParameters(AMQP_HOST,
                                        port=AMQP_PORT,
                                        virtual_host = "/",
                                        credentials = creds_broker)

conn_broker = pika.BlockingConnection(conn_params)

channel = conn_broker.channel()                                 ❷ Connect to
                                                                  RabbitMQ and
                                                                  send message
msg = json.dumps({"content": "Cluster Test!",
                  "time" : time.time()})
msg_props = pika.BasicProperties(content_type="application/json")

channel.basic_publish(body=msg,
                      exchange="cluster_test",
                      properties=msg_props,
                      routing_key="cluster_test")

print "Sent cluster test message."
```

The first part of the producer ❶ is setting up the connection like you've done before. It's determining the IP address and port of the RabbitMQ "server" from the first and second command-line arguments passed to the producer. You're also using the built-in guest account that comes with every Rabbit install for authentication. Then you create a JSON message ❷ to send to your consumer that contains the phrase Cluster Test! and the current timestamp. The last thing you do before publishing the message is to set the content_type header of the message so that your consumer knows your message is JSON-encoded. Finally you publish the message and send it jetting through Rabbit to your consumer. What does this look like on the command-line?

```
$ python cluster_test_producer.py localhost 5670
Sent cluster test message.
```

And if you check back on your running consumer …

```
$ python cluster_test_consumer.py localhost 5670
Ready for testing!
Received: Cluster Test!/1301531152
```

Bingo! The message was injected into one node of the cluster by your producer and received on another node by your consumer! Now let's see the real proof in the pudding and restart the node that's connected to your consumer. First, use http://localhost:8100 to figure out which cluster node name your consumer is connected to. It should be the node listed with a 1 in the Cur column under Sessions in the HAProxy stats page. Then from your RabbitMQ installation directory, run ./sbin/rabbitmqctl -n node_name stop_app, where *node_name* is the node name you identified in the HAProxy stats. Now if you check back on your consumer, you should see some connection errors followed by a successful reconnection to the cluster:

```
$ python cluster_test_consumer.py localhost 5670
Ready for testing!
Traceback (most recent call last):
  File "cluster_test_consumer.py", line 57, in <module>
    channel.start_consuming()
  File "/Library/Python/2.6/site-packages/pika-0.9.6-py2.6.egg/
  pika/adapters/blocking_connection.py", line 293, in start_consuming
    self.transport.connection.process_data_events()
  File "/Library/Python/2.6/site-packages/pika-0.9.6-py2.6.egg/
  pika/adapters/blocking_connection.py", line 87, in process_data_events
    raise AMQPConnectionError
AMQPConnectionError
Ready for testing!
```

The second Ready for Testing! line indicates your consumer has successfully recovered from the node failure and reconnected to the cluster. Now if you publish a new message into the cluster you should see it echoed from your newly reconnected consumer:

```
$ python cluster_test_consumer.py localhost 5670
Ready for testing!
Traceback (most recent call last):
 File "cluster_test_consumer.py", line 57, in <module>
   channel.start_consuming()
 File "/Library/Python/2.6/site-packages/pika-0.9.6-py2.6.egg/
 pika/adapters/blocking_connection.py", line 293, in start_consuming
   self.transport.connection.process_data_events()
 File "/Library/Python/2.6/site-packages/pika-0.9.6-py2.6.egg/
 pika/adapters/blocking_connection.py", line 87, in process_data_events
   raise AMQPConnectionError
AMQPConnectionError
```

```
Ready for testing!
Received: Cluster Test!/1301531677
```

Everything works! You now have a fully clustered RabbitMQ setup, complete with a load balancer to handle node selection and cluster-aware consumer and producers that can keep trucking when a cluster node dies. At this point you could call it a day with the satisfaction that you have RabbitMQ's built-in clustering under your belt. But the built-in clustering doesn't cover every use case. For example, what if you absolutely can't risk losing any messages in a durable queue when a node fails? Current versions of RabbitMQ will restore the durable queue and its contents when its node rejoins the cluster, but versions before 1.8.0 didn't. This necessitated an alternate approach with active and standby standalone RabbitMQ servers that could allow you to failover without losing the old queue's contents.

6.3 *Summary*

Clustering RabbitMQ is only half of what you need to make a resilient messaging infrastructure. The other half is up to your applications. Now you know how to write them to be resilient in the face of cluster node failure by reconnecting to new nodes and rebuilding the fabric your apps need to keep operating. Equally as important, you can now set up and use a load balancer to be the glue that determines which cluster nodes have failed and intelligently route your apps to new nodes when they reconnect. These techniques, when combined with a RabbitMQ cluster, give you a robust messaging infrastructure that can get hit with a failure without your applications missing a beat. But there are still a couple of unanswered questions about making Rabbit highly available. For example, how can you design a Rabbit infrastructure where the durable queues on that node aren't unavailable to your apps when a node goes down? Also, what about designing a Rabbit architecture that can survive losing a whole data center and the clusters in it? For the answers to those questions, we need to break out our shovels and dive into a couple of warrens.

Warrens and Shovels: failover and replication

This chapter covers

- Understanding active/standby pairs (warrens)
- Creating warrens with load balancers
- Building long-distance replication using Shovel

So far when we've talked about high availability, it's always been in the context of RabbitMQ's built-in clustering. But clustering isn't the only way to build resiliency into your Rabbit infrastructure, and depending on your needs it's not always the right way either. Clustering makes you trade the benefit of all the nodes acting as single unit to distribute the load for the drawback of not being able to use durable queues on downed nodes until the nodes are restored. Also, clustering won't give you what you need to build a RabbitMQ architecture that's distributed across more than one data center. So though clustering might initially sound like a Swiss army knife for our availability problems, you still need a couple of other tools in your toolbox. That's where warrens and Shovel come in.

Leveraging the knowledge you've acquired so far, you'll learn how to build active/standby pairs of standalone RabbitMQ servers that let you trade scalability for more flexibility when it comes to durable messaging. Then you'll see how you can use the Shovel plugin to replicate the contents of queues on a Rabbit server in one city over long distances to a Rabbit server (or cluster) in another. When you're done you'll have a complete toolbox for any high availability situation. Best of all, if you've designed your apps with the new techniques you learned in the last chapter, you can use them unchanged to take advantage of these new RabbitMQ topologies. Let's get started by jumping into understanding active/standby pairs, or as we call them, *warrens*.

7.1 *Warrens: another way of clustering*

In versions of RabbitMQ prior to 1.8.0 there was an "interesting" behavior when a cluster node containing a durable queue went down. If a client re-created the durable queue while the node was still down, then the contents of the old queue would be lost when the downed node came back up. The restored node would essentially say "Oops, this queue already exists; I don't need my copy." When the contents of the old queue were valuable, this was a huge problem. Since version 1.8.0, a different behavior has taken over. When a node with a durable queue goes down, that queue can't be re-created. Any client that attempts to redeclare the queue will receive a 404 NOT_FOUND AMQP error. When the downed node is restored, so is the durable queue and its contents (providing the messages were delivered with delivery_mode 2). But until that node is restored, any messages that would've been delivered to it are either black-holed or errors are sent to the clients that set mandatory publish flags.

If your application can't risk losing messages or deal with the latency of continuously republishing messages until their downed queue returns, then you need what we call *warrens*. In our parlance, a warren is a pair of active/standby standalone servers with a load balancer in front handling failover (see figure 7.1). The advantage to this setup is that it's truly shared-nothing. There's no coordination between the active and standby servers, so any problem affecting the active server won't be automatically transferred to the standby or vice versa. The separation between them is so complete that you could run different versions of RabbitMQ on both. This would allow you to roll out a new version of RabbitMQ into production while keeping the old version around as a precaution. There are many reasons and situations where it's advantageous to have two completely independent RabbitMQ servers available to handle each others load. Whatever the reason, a warren can be useful when Rabbit's built-in clustering doesn't quite fit the bill.

We'd be remiss if we didn't mention that there's another way to set up a warren for high availability. A different school of thought says, "I want my standby node to have *all* of the messages that were in the active node when it failed." Our approach with load balancers and shared-nothing architecture doesn't give you this. Instead our approach gives you an immediate place to start publishing and consuming messages again, and when you restore the active node, it allows your consumers to reattach and drain the messages that were in the queues when the active node went down. You don't lose any messages old or new, but you do have to wait for the active node to be restored for the old messages to become available again. The other school of thought

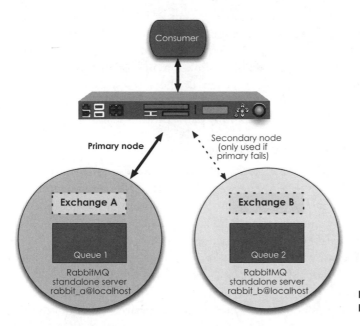

Figure 7.1 Load balancer-based warren

for building a warren says you should instead build it with shared storage between your active and standby servers with RabbitMQ not running on the standby node (see figure 7.2). Then when a failure of the active server happens you use Pacemaker[1] to transfer the RabbitMQ IP address to the standby node and then start up Rabbit on that node to pick up your current metadata, contents, and state from the shared storage. There are only a couple of problems with that setup in our opinion. First, the storage is shared, so if some kind of corruption kills your active node, that corruption will be present on the standby node too and prevent RabbitMQ from starting there. Second, you need to be sure that the standby RabbitMQ has the same node name and UID as RabbitMQ on the primary node. If either of these aren't true, the standby Rabbit won't be able to access the files on the shared storage and fire up. Lastly, using this setup for a warren means your standby Rabbit isn't actually running. So there's a possibility that something will have changed on the standby node that will prevent Rabbit from starting up when you need it. That's a lot of complexity and we prefer simple.

Due to the fact that corruption gets replicated and the lack of a fully running RabbitMQ on both nodes with the shared storage approach, we prefer the load balancer–based warren and that's the one we'll show you. But if a shared storage warren sounds appealing or fits your use case better, there's a good tutorial on the RabbitMQ website that explains how to set it up: http://www.rabbitmq.com/pacemaker.html. Lastly, if you've built your app using the principle of "assume

---

[1] Pacemaker is a set of cluster utilities for Linux that handle IP failover between active and standby nodes, as well as automatically start up the protected application on the standby node when failure occurs. Pacemaker is available from http://www.clusterlabs.org/.

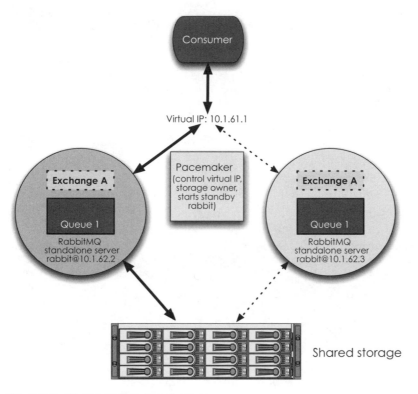

Figure 7.2   Shared storage–based warren

nothing" and you always rebuild your fabric when your app reconnects, then your app can use the load balancer–based warren without any changes.

7.2 *Setting up load balancer–based master/slave clusters*

Actually setting up a load balancer–based warren is simple and builds on all of the concepts you've acquired so far. First, you'll start two RabbitMQ nodes on your development system and name them `rabbit_a` and `rabbit_b` so they don't conflict with the local cluster nodes you already have running (run from your Rabbit installation directory):

```
$ RABBITMQ_NODE_PORT=5675 RABBITMQ_NODENAME=rabbit_a \
./sbin/rabbitmq-server -detached
Activating RabbitMQ plugins ...
$ RABBITMQ_NODE_PORT=5676 RABBITMQ_NODENAME=rabbit_b \
./sbin/rabbitmq-server -detached
Activating RabbitMQ plugins ...
```

With your active/standby nodes running, you now need to set up a new HAProxy configuration to treat `rabbit_b` as a backup server so it'll only be used when `rabbit_a` goes down. In fact the warren configuration for HAProxy (shown in the following listing) looks remarkably similar to the cluster configuration.

> **Listing 7.1   HAProxy configuration for a load balancer–based warren**

```
# HAProxy Config for Local RabbitMQ SLB Warren

global
    log 127.0.0.1     local0 info
    maxconn 4096
    stats socket /tmp/haproxy_2.socket uid haproxy mode 770 level admin
    daemon

defaults
    log     global
    mode    tcp
    option     tcplog
    option     dontlognull
    retries    3
    option redispatch
    maxconn    2000
    timeout connect    5s
    timeout client 120s
    timeout server 120s

listen rabbitmq_local_cluster 127.0.0.1:5680

    mode tcp
    balance roundrobin

    server rabbit_a 127.0.0.1:5675 check inter 5000 rise 2 fall 3

    server rabbit_b 127.0.0.1:5676 backup check inter 5000 rise 2 fall 3

listen private_monitoring :8101
    mode http
    option httplog
    stats enable
    stats uri /stats
    stats refresh 5s
```

← Logging options

Load balancing defaults

❶ Frontend IP for consumers and producers

Load balancing options

Active node

Backup node ❷

❸ Statistics page

Here the HAProxy local socket ❶ and stats page ❸ have been changed to avoid conflicts with the Rabbit cluster HAProxy instance. The more interesting change, though, is ❷ the addition of a new HAProxy configuration option: backup. When you add backup to a backend server directive you're telling HAProxy to only use that backend server when all of the nonbackup servers are unavailable. If you check the warren's HAProxy stats page (see figure 7.3) by going to http://localhost:8101/stats, you'll see rabbit_b is a light blue color instead of the normal light green for an available server (like rabbit_a). Light blue means rabbit_b is available but is a backup server (an unavailable backup server is colored red like any other backend server).

To test out your newly minted warren let's start up the consumer from the cluster section by running python cluster_test_consumer.py localhost 5680:

```
$ python cluster_test_consumer.py localhost 5680
Ready for testing!
```

You're connected and ready for action. Test it by running python cluster_test _producer localhost 5680:

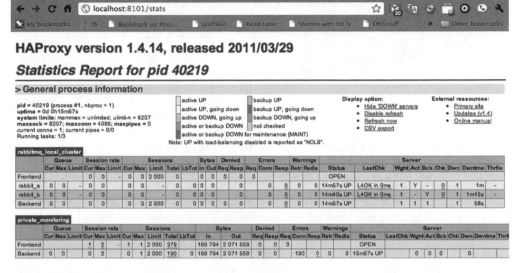

Figure 7.3 HAProxy statistics page for your warren

```
[producer output]
Sent cluster test message.
 [consumer output]
Ready for testing!
Received: Cluster Test!/1301612486
```

Looks like everything is working like clockwork. It's time to test failover. You'll fail rabbit_a by stopping its Erlang app. From your RabbitMQ installation directory run ./sbin/rabbitmqctl -n rabbit_a stop_app. Now remember you told HAProxy to only health-check backend servers every 5 seconds (inter 5000) and then to require a backend server to fail three times (fall 3) before it's considered unavailable. So you'll need to wait 15 seconds before your consumer's reconnections will succeed. Once HAProxy has failed over to the standby RabbitMQ, you should see the following:

```
$ python cluster_test_consumer.py localhost 5680
Ready for testing!
Received: Cluster Test!/1301612486
Traceback (most recent call last):
  File "cluster_test_consumer.py", line 58, in <module>
    channel.start_consuming()
  File "/Library/Python/2.6/site-packages/pika-0.9.6-py2.6.egg/
  pika/adapters/blocking_connection.py", line 293, in start_consuming
    self.transport.connection.process_data_events()
  File "/Library/Python/2.6/site-packages/pika-0.9.6-py2.6.egg/
  pika/adapters/blocking_connection.py", line 87, in process_data_events
    raise AMQPConnectionError
AMQPConnectionError
...
Ready for testing!
```

If you check the HAProxy stats page (http://localhost:8101/stats) you should see a 1 under the `Cur` heading in the `Sessions` section. That confirms that your consumer is connected to the backup server. Now if you publish again with `python cluster_test_producer localhost 5680`, does the message still reach the consumer?

```
[producer output]
Sent cluster test message.
[consumer output]
...
Ready for testing!
Received: Cluster Test!/1301612545
```

Yes it does! You have a fully functional active/standby RabbitMQ warren with a load balancer–based failover. The best part is that you can be assured that when the failover occurs, you don't have to worry about RabbitMQ failing to start on the standby node, because it's already running! Since Rabbit is running on both the active and standby nodes at all times, you can monitor both all the time and know immediately if your standby has become unavailable before it's ever called on. That's something else you can't do with a shared storage–warren.

With clustering and warrens under your belt, you're covered when it comes to handling failure and scaling within your data center. But what do you do when you need to replicate messages between Rabbits in different data centers? That's when you need a *Shovel*.

7.3   *Long-distance communication and replication*

RabbitMQ clustering is great for expanding your messaging performance inside one data center, but where it breaks down is when you need to route messages from a Rabbit server in one city to a Rabbit server in another. You might try to use clustering to bridge your geo-diverse data centers, but you'll run into a couple of show stoppers. First and foremost, you have no control over the cluster nodes on which RabbitMQ chooses to place your queues. So even if you had two cluster nodes in Chicago and a third in Los Angeles, you'd have no way of ensuring that queue A is in one city and queue C is in the other. Second, Erlang's OTP communication framework doesn't tolerate latency well. So those expensive WAN links between Chicago and LA are going to cause havoc and all sorts of strange behavior within your cluster. Then there's the fact that RabbitMQ has no strategy to cope with network partitioning if that WAN link fails. Right about now is when you might be wondering, "So how *do* you handle geo-diverse infrastructures with RabbitMQ?" The answer is to use a Shovel. But before you can use it, you need to know some background on how Shovel works.

7.3.1   *Shoveling your Rabbits: an introduction to the Shovel plugin*

Shovel is a plugin for RabbitMQ that enables you to define replication relationships between a queue on one RabbitMQ server and an exchange on another. Originally designed by LShift (one of the original parents of Rabbit Technologies), Shovel is now maintained by RabbitMQ's core development team. Like most RabbitMQ plugins,

Shovel is its own Erlang application that just happens to be loaded by Rabbit on startup. Unlike most plugins, Shovel doesn't deeply integrate with the Rabbit core—when you define a replication relationship between two servers in Shovel you specify the full URL of both servers including username and password (say, `amqp://guest:guest@localhost:5675/`). In some respects, Shovel could've been written as a standalone Erlang application instead of as a RabbitMQ plugin. But by virtue of being a RabbitMQ plugin, you can rely on RabbitMQ to automatically start Shovel and the defined replication relationships every time you boot Rabbit.

Perhaps a real-world example would demonstrate how Shovel can help. Farmer Jacques runs Avocados Supreme Limited, a large avocado farming company in Southern California. Jacques has a problem: for many years, Avocados Supreme has operated out of a single warehouse in Goleta, California, but recently the warehouse has been operating at 80% and sometimes orders experience delays when inventory runs out. To fix this, Jacques opens up a second warehouse down the road in Carpinteria (see figure 7.4). The only purpose of the Carpinteria warehouse is to carry extra inventory and ship orders when Goleta runs out.

One of the crown jewels in the Avocados Supreme operation is their order-processing system that uses RabbitMQ to link their website to fulfillment in the Goleta

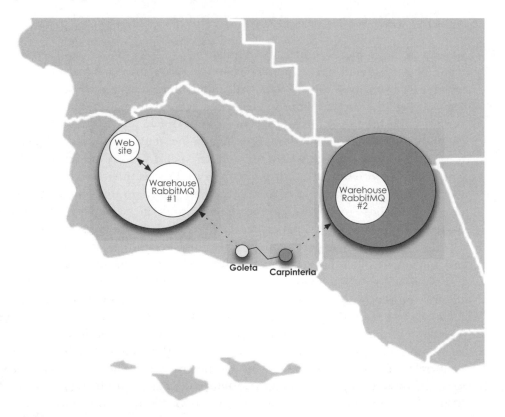

Figure 7.4 Warehouse map topology

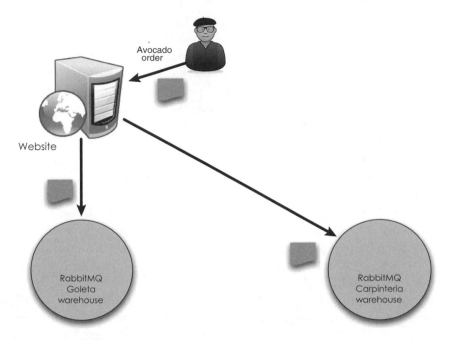

Figure 7.5   Order processing without Shovel

warehouse. With the Carpinteria warehouse now online, Pierre (Avocado Supreme's technology architect) has been in a pickle trying to figure out how to link in the new warehouse to receive orders Goleta can't fulfill. Since he can't use RabbitMQ clustering to bridge the two warehouses, Pierre had been planning on updating the website to start publishing to RabbitMQ servers in both Goleta and Carpinteria. But Pierre's concerned that this will slow down ordering on the website since the web app now has to publish to both Goleta (where the website is) and to Carpinteria (a much longer round trip) before he can confirm the order to the customer (see figure 7.5). Not to mention that Pierre now has to modify the web app to do this, when one of the reasons why he chose messaging was the ability to route messages without changing the frontend code. While Pierre is bemoaning his choices, he discovers Shovel.

After doing some experimenting, Pierre discovers he can use Shovel to create a new queue in Goleta that subscribes to the incoming_orders exchange that the website publishes to. Then he can tell Shovel to consume these messages and republish them over the WAN link to the incoming_orders exchange in the Carpinteria RabbitMQ where they'll be routed to the backup order fulfillment (see figure 7.6). The best part is the website doesn't have to slow down order confirmation at all. It can keep publishing to the Goleta RabbitMQ that's on the same LAN and give zippy order confirmations back to avocado-loving customers. Then Shovel can asynchronously replicate those orders to Carpinteria without the website ever being aware or affected by the increased latency. It's a perfect scenario for Pierre, who receives a beach vacation to Monterey for his brilliance.

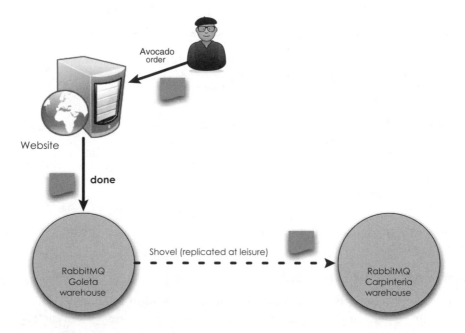

Figure 7.6 Order processing with Shovel

So whether you need to replicate messages between RabbitMQ servers across the country or across the street, Shovel is your go-to solution. So how do you install Shovel and start the message-replicating magic?

7.3.2 Installing Shovel

Installing Shovel is straightforward. As of RabbitMQ 2.7.0, the `rabbitmq-shovel` and `amqp_client` plugins are packaged with Rabbit; you just need to enable them (make sure `/etc/rabbitmq/` exists before you enable the plugins). From your RabbitMQ working directory, run the following:

```
$ ./sbin/rabbitmq-plugins enable amqp_client
The following plugins have been enabled:
  amqp_client
Plugin configuration has changed. Restart RabbitMQ for
changes to take effect.
$ ./sbin/rabbitmq-plugins enable rabbitmq_shovel
The following plugins have been enabled:
  erlando
  rabbitmq_shovel
Plugin configuration has changed. Restart RabbitMQ for
changes to take effect.
```

If you're running a version of RabbitMQ older than 2.7.0, you'll need to retrieve and install the plugins yourself. To do so, first download the `rabbitmq-shovel` and `amqp_client` plugins from http://www.rabbitmq.com/plugins.html and install them in the `./plugins/` directory of your RabbitMQ installation:

```
$ cd ./plugins/
$ wget http://www.rabbitmq.com/.../v2.6.1/amqp_client-2.6.1.ez
Resolving www.rabbitmq.com... 208.91.1.36
Connecting to www.rabbitmq.com|208.91.1.36|:80... connected.
HTTP request sent, awaiting response... 200 OK
Length: 154928 (151K) [application/andrew-inset]
Saving to: `amqp_client-2.6.1.ez'
100%[===============================>] 154,928  120K/s in 1.3s
$ wget http://www.rabbitmq.com/.../v2.6.1/rabbitmq-shovel-2.6.1.ez
Resolving www.rabbitmq.com... 208.91.1.36
Connecting to www.rabbitmq.com|208.91.1.36|:80... connected.
HTTP request sent, awaiting response... 200 OK
Length: 42131 (41K) [application/andrew-inset]
Saving to: `rabbitmq-shovel-2.6.1.ez'
100%[==================================>] 42,131  112K/s in 0.4s
```

That's all there is to it. Well, not quite. You still need to configure Shovel and start up your RabbitMQ brokers.

7.3.3 *Configuring and running Shovel*

All of Shovel's configuration information, from replication relationships to reconnection settings, goes into the `rabbitmq.config` file. Like the rest of RabbitMQ's config file, Shovel's configuration is formatted as a valid Erlang tuple called `rabbitmq_shovel` with configuration directives nested inside. Since the configuration can look fairly complicated, let's look at the following listing, which shows how your `rabbitmq.config` with a Shovel configuration looks, and then examine the individual parts.

Listing 7.2 rabbitmq.config file with Shovel configuration

```
[
    {mnesia, [{dump_log_write_threshold, 100}
            ]},
    {rabbit, [{vm_memory_high_watermark, 0.4}
            ]},
    {rabbitmq_shovel,
       [{shovels,
          [{avocado_order_shovel,
             [{sources, [{broker, "amqp://guest:guest@localhost:5675/"},
                        {declarations,
                            [{'queue.declare',
                                 [{queue, <<"backup_orders">>},
                                  durable]},
                             {'exchange.declare',
                                 [{exchange, <<"incoming_orders">>},
                                  {type, <<"direct">>},
                                  durable]},
                             {'queue.bind',
                                 [{exchange, <<"incoming_orders">>},
                                  {queue, <<"backup_orders">>},
                                  {routing_key, <<"warehouse">>}]}]
                        ]}]},
              {destinations, [{broker, "amqp://guest:guest@localhost:5676"},
```

```
                                    {declarations,
                                      [{'queue.declare',
                                        [{queue, <<"warehouse_carpinteria">>},
                                            durable]},
                                       {'exchange.declare',
                                        [{exchange, <<"incoming_orders">>},
                                         {type, <<"direct">>},
                                         durable]},
                                       {'queue.bind',
                                        [{exchange, <<"incoming_orders">>},
                                         {queue, <<"warehouse_carpinteria">>},
                                         {routing_key, <<"warehouse">>}]}
                                      ]}]},
                               {queue, <<"backup_orders">>},
                               {ack_mode, no_ack},
                               {publish_properties, [{delivery_mode, 2}]},
                               {publish_fields, [{exchange, <<"incoming_orders">>},
                                           {routing_key, <<"warehouse">>}]},
                               {reconnect_delay, 5}
                            ]}
                          ]
                        }]
                      }
                   ].
```

Right under the `rabbitmq_shovel` directive you see a subsection called `shovels`. This is a list of shovel definitions where each shovel defines a replication relationship between two RabbitMQ servers. In this case, you only have one shovel defined called `avocado_order_shovel`. Within that shovel, you define the `sources` that your messages to be replicated will come from and the `destinations` where those messages will go to. Both `sources` and `destinations` contain the same types of configuration directives:

- `broker` or `brokers`—URL defining the server, username, password, and vhost of the RabbitMQ server you'll be shoveling messages from (or to). If a RabbitMQ cluster is your source or destination, use `brokers` and follow it with more than one URL string wrapped in [] (for example, `["amqp://server1...", "amqp://server2..."]`). This will let Shovel fail over to another cluster node if the primary node fails.
- `declarations`—List of AMQP commands to declare the queues, exchanges, and bindings that need to be in place for the shovel to operate.

The `declarations` are the trickiest to understand. They're nested inside a list (array) where each member is an Erlang tuple defining the AMQP command to run along with another list of tuples that provide the arguments to that AMQP command:

```
{declarations,
   [{'queue.declare',
          [{queue, <<"backup_orders">>},
            durable]},
     {'exchange.declare',
          [{exchange, <<"incoming_orders">>},
```

```
                {type, <<"direct">>},
                durable]},
     {'queue.bind',
         [{exchange, <<"incoming_orders">>},
          {queue, <<"backup_orders">>},
          {routing_key, <<"warehouse">>}]]}
   ]}]},
```

For example, this declarations section instructs Shovel to declare a queue called backup_orders and an exchange called incoming_orders (remember our rule about not assuming any of our fabric is in place). Then you tell the shovel to bind backup_orders to incoming_orders using the routing key warehouse. You may notice a couple of funny things about those directives. First, all of the strings aren't simply quoted; they also have double angle brackets around them: <<"backup_orders">>. The angle brackets tell Erlang not to treat the information as a string but as a special data type called a *binary*. You don't have to understand what a binary is, only that Shovel will crash on startup if you forget the angle brackets. The other funny thing you may notice is that the durable argument doesn't get wrapped in curly braces like all of the other arguments. This is because durable doesn't take a value. It's either present or it's not. You only need the curly braces when it's an argument that takes a value. Otherwise, the AMQP commands and their arguments should look familiar to you, and you can specify any of the arguments you'd normally have in the language of your choice. For example, though you wouldn't normally want to, you could define the backup_orders queue as auto_delete. Like durable, since auto_delete doesn't take a value, just add it (separate by a comma) without curly braces after durable in the queue.declare arguments list.

After you've defined the sources and destinations, you also need to define some general settings for the shovel. All of these settings take values, so they're wrapped in curly braces. The settings you can define are

- queue—The name of the queue in the source server that Shovel will listen on for messages to replicate.
- ack_mode—Whether Shovel should acknowledge message receipt on the source before completing delivery to the destination.
- prefetch_count—How many messages Shovel will internally buffer at any given time. The internal buffer is a stopover point between the source and destination that's *not* protected during failure of Shovel.
- publish_properties—A list of properties to set specifically when publishing messages to the destination. For example {delivery_mode, 2} will set the delivery_mode to durable (2). By default, Shovel replicates the properties of the source message when publishing to the destination unless a property is specifically overridden in publish_properties.

- `publish_fields`—Similar to `publish_properties`, but defines the `exchange` to publish messages into on the destination server and the `routing_key` to tag on the messages. If `exchange` or `routing_key` isn't defined, Shovel replicates the omitted settings from the original message.

- `reconnect_delay`—How many seconds to wait to reconnect to a source or destination after being disconnected.

So in your case you want to tell Shovel to consume messages from the `backup_orders` queue on the source server and deliver them to the `incoming_orders` exchange on the destination server with the routing key `warehouse`. You don't want to auto acknowledge the messages (for example, `ack_mode` set to `on_confirm` or `on_publish`), but you do want the messages published as durable (delivery mode 2). Finally, you want Shovel to wait 5 seconds before reconnecting if it becomes disconnected. Putting this all together, here's what it looks like in the configuration file:

```
{queue, <<"backup_orders">>},
{ack_mode, no_ack},
{publish_properties, [{delivery_mode, 2}]},
{publish_fields, [{exchange, <<"incoming_orders">>},
                  {routing_key, <<"warehouse">>}]},
{reconnect_delay, 5}
```

Figure 7.7 shows the topology your Shovel defines. You're taking orders from the `backup_orders` queue on Rabbit server `localhost:5675` and publishing them into the `incoming_orders` exchange on Rabbit server `localhost:5676`.

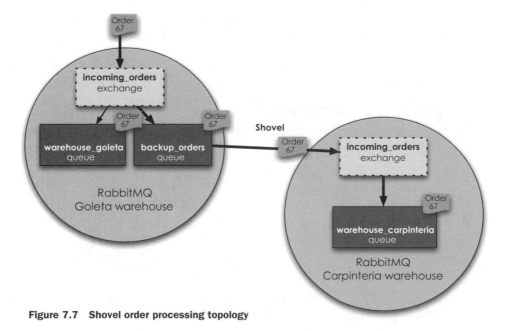

Figure 7.7 Shovel order processing topology

Now that your Shovel configuration is complete, it's time to fire up your source and destination Rabbit servers and see how it works. You'll spin up two standalone RabbitMQ nodes on your development system for the test. Since both the source and destination servers will be using the same `rabbitmq.config` file, you'll end up with two identical shovels running: one on the source and one on the destination. Normally, you'd only want one shovel, but since you're running both nodes locally, one configuration file for both is simpler for testing. If you still have `rabbit_a` and `rabbit_b` running from the warrens section, go ahead and stop them now, because you'll reuse them for this example. Once they're stopped, change to your RabbitMQ installation directory and run `RABBITMQ_NODE_PORT=5675 RABBITMQ_NODENAME=rabbit_a./sbin/rabbitmq-server` to start the source node (you're not using the `-detached` option so that you can see errors in your config file if they exist). Since your first terminal is occupied with the source node in the foreground, open a new terminal and then run `RABBITMQ_NODE_PORT=5676 RABBITMQ_NODENAME=rabbit_b./sbin/rabbitmq-server` to start the destination node. With both your source and destination running, you're going to need a consumer and producer to test the setup. Variants of your cluster consumer and producer modified to handle avocado orders should do nicely. First let's look at the consumer, shown in the following listing.

> **Listing 7.3 Shovel test consumer**

```
import sys, json, pika, time, traceback
def msg_rcvd(channel, method, header, body):
    message = json.loads(body)

    print "Received order %(ordernum)d for %(type)s." % message
    channel.basic_ack(delivery_tag=method.delivery_tag)

if __name__ == "__main__":
    AMQP_SERVER = sys.argv[1]
    AMQP_PORT = int(sys.argv[2])
    creds_broker = pika.PlainCredentials("guest", "guest")
    conn_params = pika.ConnectionParameters( AMQP_SERVER,
                                             port=AMQP_PORT,
                                             virtual_host="/",
                                             credentials=creds_broker)

    conn_broker = pika.BlockingConnection(conn_params)
    channel = conn_broker.channel()

    print "Ready for orders!"
    channel.basic_consume( msg_rcvd,
                           queue="warehouse_carpinteria",
                           no_ack=False,
                           consumer_tag="order_processor")
    channel.start_consuming()
```

Annotations:
- **Print and acknowledge order** → points to the `print "Received order..."` / `channel.basic_ack` lines
- **Broker settings** → points to the `if __name__ == "__main__":` block
- **Establish broker connection settings** → points to `creds_broker` / `conn_params`
- **Establish connection to RabbitMQ** → points to `conn_broker` / `channel`
- **Start processing orders** → points to `print "Ready for orders!"`

It's not much different than the consumers you built in chapter 4 for processing alerts. Your producer (shown in the following listing) is even simpler, with the only change being the format of the avocado order you're sending.

Listing 7.4   Shovel test producer

```
import sys, json, pika, random
AMQP_HOST = sys.argv[1]
AMQP_PORT = int(sys.argv[2])                              Establish
AVOCADO_TYPE = sys.argv[3]                                connection
                                                      ◁  to broker
creds_broker = pika.PlainCredentials("guest", "guest")
conn_params = pika.ConnectionParameters(AMQP_HOST,
                                        port=AMQP_PORT,
                                        virtual_host = "/",
                                        credentials = creds_broker)
conn_broker = pika.BlockingConnection(conn_params)
channel = conn_broker.channel()

msg = json.dumps({"ordernum": random.randrange(0, 100, 1),   ◁   Connect to
                  "type" : AVOCADO_TYPE})                         RabbitMQ
msg_props = pika.BasicProperties(content_type="application/json")  and send
channel.basic_publish(body=msg, mandatory=True,                   message
                      exchange="incoming_orders",
                      properties=msg_props,
                      routing_key="warehouse")
print "Sent avocado order message."
```

Your consumer takes two command-line arguments: the destination host name and the destination port. The producer takes the same arguments but adds a third: the avocado type (hass, fuerte, and so on—any single word will do). You're going to publish an avocado order into the source node with the producer, and then through the magic of Shovel, receive and print the order from the consumer attached on the completely independent destination server. Let's fire up your consumer and connect it to the destination node:

```
$ python shovel_consumer.py localhost 5676
Ready for orders!
```

Now let's send it an avocado order by publishing into the source node:

```
$ python shovel_producer.py localhost 5675 hass
```

Back on the consumer, you should see something like this:

```
$ python shovel_consumer.py localhost 5676
Ready for orders!
Received order 66 for hass.
```

Hot diggity, you have a working shovel that's enabling publishes on one RabbitMQ server to be consumed on a completely independent one. Though more tedious to set up than clustering, Shovel extends the reach of RabbitMQ by allowing you to create even more robust topologies that now include federation between independent RabbitMQ servers and clusters. In the future RabbitMQ will support robust federation natively, but until then Shovel will provide you the federation you need *today*.

7.4   *Summary*

It's been a long trip through all the options for making Rabbit resilient, but when we started you were at the mercy of server failure taking down your Rabbits and knocking your messaging infrastructure offline. Now you no longer have to fear the power cord. If what you really need is absolute high availability with no possibilities of message loss, you can build a warren using two standalone RabbitMQ servers, with a load balancer making them appear as one to your applications. If for some reason you then need to extend this reliability to bridge Rabbits in multiple data centers, you know how to use Shovel to provide the replication to make that a reality. Perhaps most important, you know how to make your applications resilient in the face of individual Rabbit failure. By making them assume nothing about the state of the servers they're connecting to and implementing reconnecting functionality, your consumers and producers can take advantage of any of the RabbitMQ redundancy options you've learned and survive node failure without missing a beat. Your apps and Rabbits are now robust, resilient, and ready for production! But what good is a robust and distributed RabbitMQ infrastructure if it's a pain to administer? To answer that question, we're heading next into the wonderful world of the RabbitMQ management plugin.

Administering RabbitMQ
from the Web

This chapter covers

- Advantages of the Management plugin over the `rabbitmqctl` script
- Enabling RabbitMQ Management plugin
- Management plugin features
- Management users, queue, and exchanges from the web console
- Introduction to the Management plugin REST interface

So far our way of administering RabbitMQ has been based on the command line via the `rabbitmqctl` script. After typing `rabbitmqctl` so many times, you may have dreamed about a way to administer the server from a graphical interface, since there's `phpMyAdmin` for MySQL or `Futon` for CouchDB. The need for such a graphical interface led the RabbitMQ community to produce several web admins for RabbitMQ with more or less the same features: displaying queue stats, adding users, creating vhosts, and so on. Thankfully the RabbitMQ team listened to the call from the community and developed the *RabbitMQ Management plugin*. Along the way, they improved the server's Erlang API in order to collect more stats about the broker usage, such as messages sent per second, queue usage rates, and more. In this chapter you'll learn about using this plugin, from enabling it to using its web interface to manage users, queues, and exchanges. Further on you'll learn about the new REST API, which can be easily accessed via the new `rabbitmqadmin` script.

8.1 Beyond rabbitmqctl: the RabbitMQ Management plugin

First things first—so far we haven't discussed much about plugins. They're a way to extend the behavior of the server in ways that weren't envisioned by its creators. Plugins for RabbitMQ are written in Erlang and they run together with the server in the same Erlang VM. We'll have a chapter later devoted to building your own RabbitMQ plugin; therefore, in this one we'll focus on enabling and working with one of them. Let's see why you need the Management plugin, what its features are, and how to get it enabled and running on your machines.

8.1.1 Why you need the Management plugin

Say you love your `rabbitmqctl` script (we do as well). We understand if you ask why you'd ever need to use this plugin. Here are some reasons.

The `rabbitmqctl` script is cool and it lets you do a lot of things for managing your server, but it has a couple of shortcomings. First, to run the `rabbitmqctl` script, your current Linux user needs to have access to the *Erlang cookie* that was used to start the server. Since the server will probably be running as `root` or as a `rabbit` user, you need access to their files. That's not a problem if you have a one-man team or a small number of developers, but what happens with big teams? Managing permissions for that file can get messy. Do you share passwords across the teams? And the story doesn't end there. When you have access to the content of the `.erlang.cookie` file it means you can connect directly from an Erlang console to the RabbitMQ process. This means you can perform pretty destructive operations on the server—accidentally or not—no one will stop you.

Apart from the security problems, not all the team members on a project are CLI addicts. We've worked in projects where even the product owner was interested in knowing how many background notifications were left on the queue. Besides that, sometimes you just want to click and see the information with nice colors; it's easier to understand than text output produced by the `rabbitmqctl` script.

8.1.2 Management plugin features

What does the Management plugin looks like? Figure 8.1 shows a nice web interface where you can access the following features:

- Overview server stats—messages delivered, server memory information, number of Erlang processes, and so on
- Import/Export server configuration
- Monitor connections to the server
- List open channels

Figure 8.1   The RabbitMQ Management plugin main interface

- List/Add exchanges
- List/Add queues
- Modify queue bindings
- List/Add users
- List/Add vhosts

Now let's get your fingers to work and enable the plugin.

8.1.3   Enabling the Management plugin

With the latest release of RabbitMQ (2.7.0 as of this writing), installing plugins became simple. As a matter of fact there's nothing to install anymore since the newer server packages come with the plugins bundled in the distribution. The only thing you need to do is to enable them. If you go to the folder where you installed RabbitMQ, you can see the plugins that you have available by entering the following command:

```
$ ls plugins/
README
amqp_client-2.7.0.ez
eldap-2.7.0-git.ez
erlando-2.7.0.ez
mochiweb-1.3-rmq2.7.0-git.ez
rabbitmq_auth_backend_ldap-2.7.0.ez
rabbitmq_auth_mechanism_ssl-2.7.0.ez
rabbitmq_consistent_hash_exchange-2.7.0.ez
rabbitmq_federation-2.7.0.ez
```

```
rabbitmq_jsonrpc-2.7.0.ez
rabbitmq_jsonrpc_channel-2.7.0.ez
rabbitmq_jsonrpc_channel_examples-2.7.0.ez
rabbitmq_management-2.7.0.ez
rabbitmq_management_agent-2.7.0.ez
rabbitmq_management_visualiser-2.7.0.ez
rabbitmq_mochiweb-2.7.0.ez
rabbitmq_shovel-2.7.0.ez
rabbitmq_shovel_management-2.7.0.ez
rabbitmq_stomp-2.7.0.ez
rabbitmq_tracing-2.7.0.ez
rfc4627_jsonrpc-2.7.0-git.ez
webmachine-1.7.0-rmq2.7.0-hg.ez
```

The files ending with the .ez extension are the plugins and their supporting libraries. For example, the management plugin that you want to enable depends on others like the AMQP Erlang client amqp_client-2.7.0.ez and the webmachine plugin webmachine-1.7.0-rmq2.7.0-hg.ez, among others. To enable the Management plugin, you have to run the following command from the broker sbin folder:

```
$ ./rabbitmq-plugins enable rabbitmq_management
The following plugins have been enabled:
  mochiweb
  webmachine
  rabbitmq_mochiweb
  amqp_client
  rabbitmq_management_agent
  rabbitmq_management

Plugin configuration has changed. Restart RabbitMQ
for changes to take effect.
```

As you can see, the rabbitmq_management plugin was enabled[1] along with the supporting plugins, but you still need to restart the broker for the changes to take effect:

```
./rabbitmqctl stop
$ ./rabbitmq-server -detached
Activating RabbitMQ plugins ...
6 plugins activated:
* amqp_client-2.7.0
* mochiweb-1.3-rmq2.7.0-git
* rabbitmq_management-2.7.0
* rabbitmq_management_agent-2.7.0
* rabbitmq_mochiweb-2.7.0
* webmachine-1.7.0-rmq2.7.0-hg
```

If everything went well, you can point your browser to http://localhost:55672/mgmt/ where you should be welcomed by an authentication prompt asking for a username and a password. In the meantime you can use guest as user and password. Once you

---

[1] If after running the command ./rabbitmq-plugins enable rabbitmq_management you got an error regarding file permissions, then you probably need to modify the permissions of the folder /etc/rabbitmq/. Do that by chowning that folder to the user that runs the rabbitmq process and then try again to enable the plugin.

submit the information, you should see the management interface as in figure 8.1. If you're not running the server in `localhost`, then you'll have to modify that URL to fit your environment.

By following such easy steps, you got the plugin up and running. Now it's time to learn how to use it, so let's move on to the next section to start playing with it. Let's manage RabbitMQ with the click of a mouse.

8.2   *Managing RabbitMQ from the web console*

Let's look again at figure 8.1. As you can see, you have a navigation menu on top where you can browse several items like *Connections, Exchanges,* or *Queues.* Then the interface presents a general overview of the server status. You can see how many messages are ready to be delivered from all of your queues, how many are waiting to be acknowledged, and the total number of messages. This information can be useful when debugging your applications because, for example, the number of unacked messages tells you about the work your consumers are performing. If the number starts to get too high, that could be a sign that your consumers are getting slow. The good thing is that you can see this information right on the front page, without clicking 20 times to reach it. There's more to it in the web console; in this section you'll learn how to monitor the Erlang VM to find out the number of processes running on it, and also see how to export your configuration into JSON format, as well as how to import your configuration back to the server.

8.2.1   *Monitoring the Erlang VM*

If you scroll down the page a bit you'll see some useful information about the Erlang node where RabbitMQ is running. As you saw in chapter 3, you can use the node name information to remotely connect to RabbitMQ and perform advanced administration operations on it. Another interesting value is the number of Erlang processes: if it reaches the limit, then RabbitMQ will stop working. You can increase the limit by modifying the `+P` option in the `SERVER_ERL_ARGS` from the `rabbitmq-server` init script.[2] Other important values that you can see there are the installed versions of RabbitMQ and Erlang. Whenever you send a bug report to the RabbitMQ mailing list, you should attach those values because that will make it easier for people to diagnose the problem and be able to help you.

On the next table you can see which port and host RabbitMQ is listening on. How many times have you scratched our head because you couldn't connect to the server and at the end the problem was wrong connection options? Here you can see the correct options to avoid such problems.

---

[2] The file where this option may be found will vary depending on how you installed RabbitMQ. If you followed the installation instructions in chapter 1, then the `rabbitmq-server` script will be inside the `sbin` folder.

8.2.2 Importing configuration from JSON files

When you get to the end of the *Overview* page you can see a nice feature: you can export the server configuration as a JSON file. You can then edit it and import it back. Let's see what this file looks like for the installation on your machine right now. Click on Download Broker Configuration and save the file to your hard drive. The following listing shows a formatted version of such file. Yours will be slightly different depending on your setup.

Listing 8.1   RabbitMQ JSON config

```
{
"rabbit_version":"2.3.1",

"users":
    [{"name":"guest",
      "password_hash":"6r578x5zS5/8oo1acUUiebYkRiU=",
      "administrator":true}],

"vhosts":[{"name":"/"}],
"permissions":[{"user":"guest", "vhost":"/", "configure":".*",
                "write":".*", "read":".*"}],

"queues":[
    {"name":"smart_proxy", "vhost":"/", "durable":true,
        "auto_delete":false, "arguments":{}},
    {"name":"control", "vhost":"/", "durable":true,
        "auto_delete":false, "arguments":{}}],

"exchanges":[
    {"name":"char_count_server", "vhost":"/", "type":"direct",
        "durable":true, "auto_delete":false, "internal":false,
        "arguments":{}},
    {"name":"control", "vhost":"/", "type":"topic",
        "durable":true, "auto_delete":false, "internal":false,
        "arguments":{}},
    {"name":"char_count", "vhost":"/", "type":"direct",
        "durable":true, "auto_delete":false, "internal":false,
        "arguments":{}}],

"bindings":[]}
```

For the sake of testing, try to add a new virtual host called book. Modify the vhost line as in the following snippet:

```
"vhosts":[{"name":"/"}, {"name":"book"}],
```

Save your changes and upload the new file by clicking on the Upload button and selecting your modified .json file. Once you've selected the file, click the Upload Broker Configuration button. If everything went well, you should see a confirmation message as in figure 8.2. With this simple mechanism, you can update your server configuration with ease. Also you can export and version the configuration files so you can keep track of the server configuration at different points in time. Every time you make a change in the config, you can keep the old settings *just in case.*

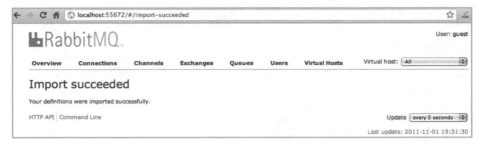

Figure 8.2   Importing JSON configuration

Let's continue exploring the features provided by the Management plugin; in this case, let's see how you can manage the users that can access your server.

8.3   *Managing users from the web console*

Your next step will be to learn how to manage users from the web interface. You've been using the default guest user in the book, which is fine for learning purposes, but if you want to run RabbitMQ in production you need to take the precaution of creating your own users and passwords. So in this section you'll learn the easy way of doing that via the web console. User management doesn't end at user creation; you also have to grant permissions to users. The second part of this section will deal with that task.

8.3.1   *Creating users*

Remember that when you opened the management page for the first time, you were prompted for user and password information, and replied using guest:guest as values? It's time to change that, because you don't want your systems to be running with the default user settings. Click on the Users link on the upper navigation menu, and you should see the dialog box shown in figure 8.3.

You'll be presented with a list of the current users on the system. Below the list is a form where you can add a new user. As in figure 8.3, create a user called rmqinaction using rmqinaction as the password too. Finally, set the user as an administrator by entering administrator in the tags field. The Management plugin supports the concepts of user roles, which will determine what the user can do in the management interface. Your users can be part of the management role, which means they can log in to this interface. If you set the user as part of the monitoring role, then they can see connections and node-related information. Your rmqinaction user was set as administrator to grant access to all the features the Management plugin offers. In figure 8.4 you can see the confirmation of your new user.

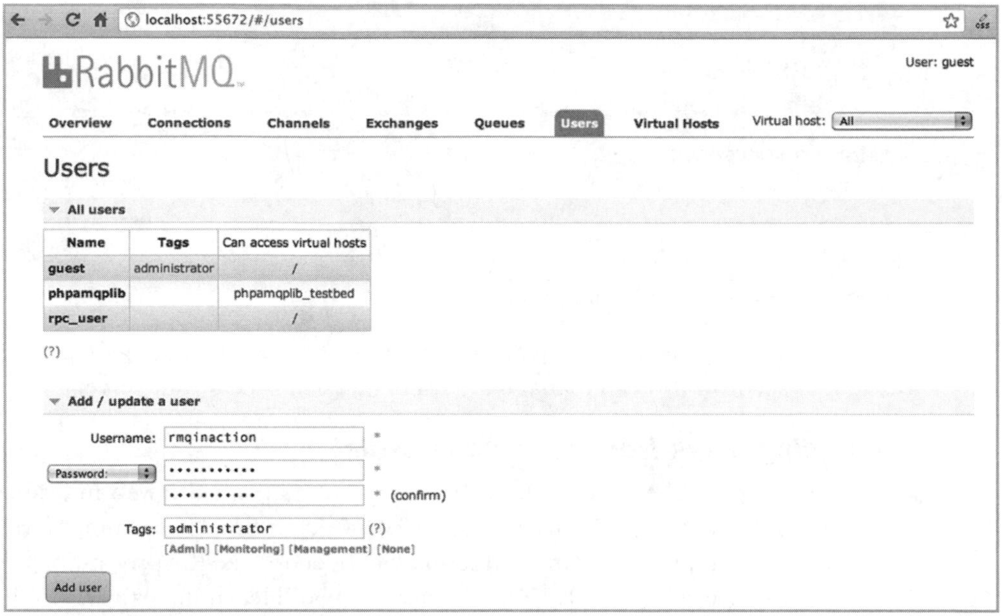

Figure 8.3   Creating new users

Figure 8.4   New user confirmation

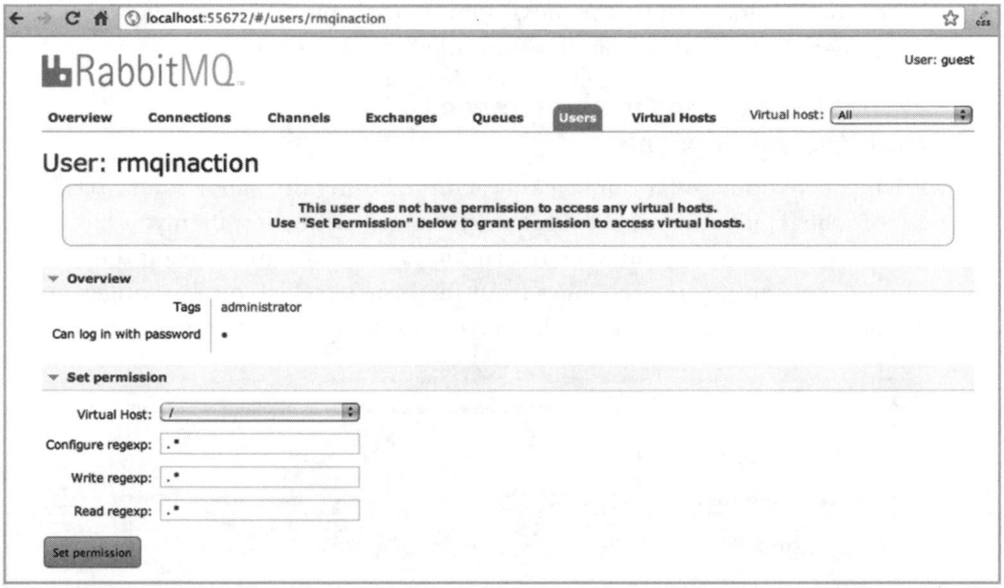

Figure 8.5 Managing users' permissions

8.3.2 *Managing users' permissions*

As you can see from figure 8.5, the user that you just created doesn't have permissions to access any virtual host so it's time to change that. Let's grant the permissions to configure the server and to write and read from queues. Click on the user name to go to the permissions settings dialog box, shown in figure 8.5.

Use the default settings that the Management plugin presents, as in the figure, so just click on the Set Permission button to save those changes.

As a last note on user management, you can also delete users from this page by clicking the Delete button as in figure 8.6.

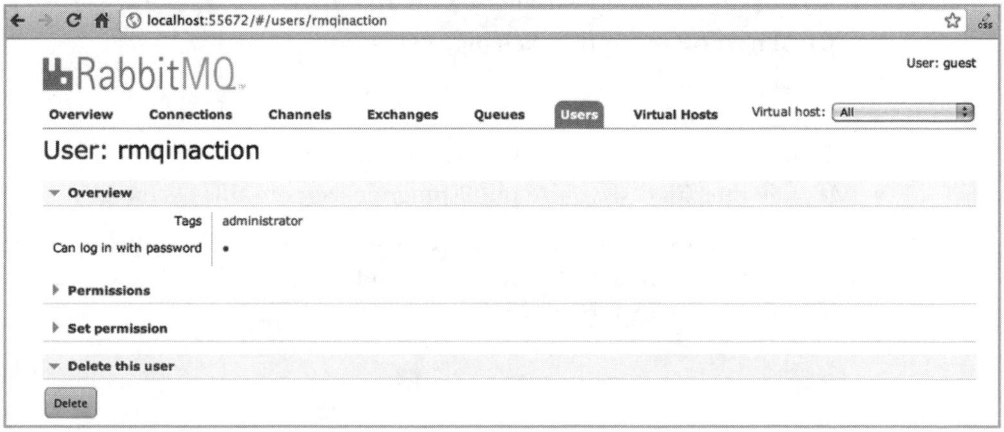

Figure 8.6 Delete users

With your users set up, the next step is to learn about managing queues and exchanges. Let's do that from the convenience of your browser.

8.4   *Managing exchanges and queues from the web console*

What you've done so far can be easily achieved using the `rabbitmqctl` script, but with `rabbitmqctl`, if you wanted to create exchanges or queues, then you had to resort to your library of choice and write a script for such a task in it. Using the Management plugin, you can create exchanges from the browser. Click on Exchanges on the navigation menu. You'll get a list of the current exchanges on the server, as in figure 8.7.

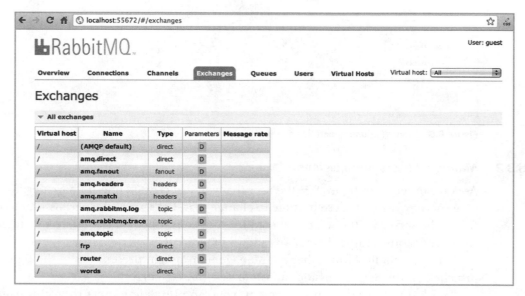

Figure 8.7   Listing exchanges

In the exchange list you get the following information:

- Virtual host on which the exchange exists
- Exchange name
- Exchange type
- Parameters list; D stands for durable for example.
- Message rate (in case you're publishing messages to this exchange)

By clicking on the exchange name, you can see more details about it, such as the exchange bindings. You can also add new bindings and even delete the exchange completely. See figure 8.8 for an example.

Figure 8.8 is an image showing the RabbitMQ web console displaying exchange details.

← → C ⌂ | 🔍 localhost:55672/#/exchanges/%2F/amq.direct   ☆ | css

⊞RabbitMQ

User: guest

Virtual host: [All   ⬦]

Overview   Connections   Channels   **Exchanges**   Queues   Users   Virtual Hosts

Exchange: amq.direct

▼ **Overview**

Type	direct
Parameters	durable: true
Virtual host	/

▼ **Message rates**

Incoming (?)   Outgoing (?)

... no publishes ...   ... no publishes ...

▼ **Bindings**

Outgoing from amq.direct

(amq.direct) → ... no bindings ...

Add binding

Figure 8.8 Viewing exchange details

Finally, if you go back to the exchange list page and scroll down, you'll see the form that allows you to create a exchange, as you can see in figure 8.9.

Let's create one using `test` as the name, `direct` as the exchange type, and leaving all the other options as they appear on the form. Click Add Exchange and ta-da! In figure 8.10 you can see your new exchange created with a couple of clicks and keystrokes.

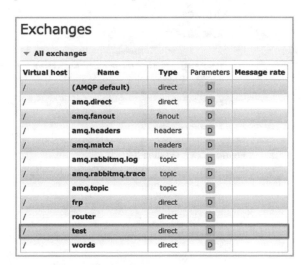

▼ **Add a new exchange**

Virtual host:	[/ ⬦]
Name:	[test] *
Type:	[direct] *
Durability:	[Durable ⬦]
Auto delete: (?)	[No ⬦]
Internal: (?)	[No ⬦]
Alternate exchange: (?)	[ ]
Arguments:	[ ] = [ ]

[Add exchange]

Figure 8.9 Adding an exchange

Exchanges

▼ **All exchanges**

Virtual host	Name	Type	Parameters	Message rate
/	(AMQP default)	direct	D	
/	amq.direct	direct	D	
/	amq.fanout	fanout	D	
/	amq.headers	headers	D	
/	amq.match	headers	D	
/	amq.rabbitmq.log	topic	D	
/	amq.rabbitmq.trace	topic	D	
/	amq.topic	topic	D	
/	frp	direct	D	
/	router	direct	D	
/	test	direct	D	
/	words	direct	D	

Figure 8.10 New exchange

8.4.1 *Listing queues*

In this chapter you've seen how the Management plugin aids comprehension of your RabbitMQ architecture by providing visual representations of the fabric you've been building. To nail down the point, let's compare listing queues using `rabbitmqctl` versus the management web console.

Move to the `sbin` folder of your RabbitMQ installation and do the following:

```
$ ./rabbitmqctl list_queues -p '/' name messages_ready \
    messages_unacknowledged messages
Listing queues ...
char_count_server-queue     0    0    0
myQueueDE    0    0    0
smart_proxy    0    0    0
myQueueEN    0    0    0
control    0    0    0
...done.
```

Then go back to your browser and click on the Queues link. Compare that with the table you see in figure 8.11.

You even got some extra goodies such as information telling you whether the queue is exclusive, the queue's status, and the queue's message rates—the latter being information that you can get only via the Management plugin. This last feature likely convinced you to use the plugin!

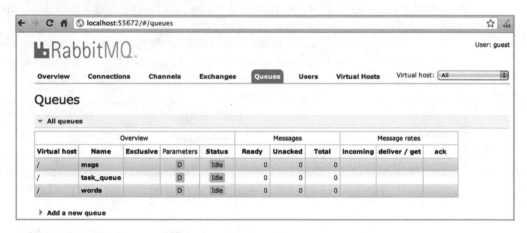

Figure 8.11   Queues list

8.4.2 Creating queues

Another thing you can't do from the `rabbitmqctl` script is create queues. You sure can from the plugin web console. As you did when creating an exchange, type `test` as the queue name and then click the Add Queue button. In figure 8.12 you can see what the form looks like once filled.

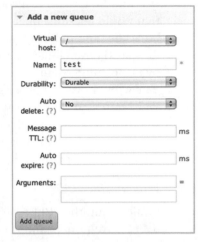

Figure 8.12   Adding a queue

Your new queue will appear on the list. If you click on it, you can inspect its properties in detail. An interesting feature here is that you can delete it or purge it directly from the browser. That means if you have some queue in your server lying around but not in use anymore, you can just click Delete and the queue is gone.

In figure 8.13 you can see details about the status of a particular queue, for example, how many messages are ready to be delivered by consumers or how many of them have pending acks. With this tool, it's easy to see how much memory is used by this queue, so you can use this information to monitor the health of the system in ways that weren't possible before by just using the `rabbitmqctl` script.

The Management plugin doesn't end at the web interface. For it to be really useful to sysadmins, it has to provide command-line tools that allow access to its features from a machine that lacks a window system, like most *nix servers. The Management plugin also comes packed with a new command-line interface that will add flexibility to the management process, liberating your sysadmins from their mice.

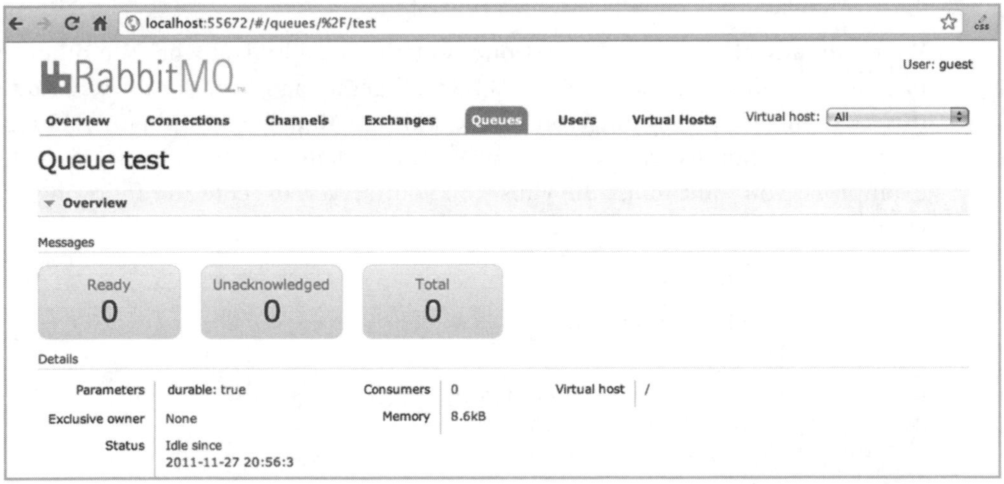

Figure 8.13   Queue details

8.5   *Back to the command line*

It would be great if you could automate all that you've seen so far—say, write a script that would get some queue details, like number of messages held in memory waiting to be acked, and publish that to a graphing tool like Ganglia or Graphite. If you want to do that via the Management plugin web interface, you'll have to get your hands dirty by performing some screen scraping. This means that if the web interface changes on a new plugin version, your script will break. There has to be a better way of doing this. Well, suffer no more, for there's a new command-line tool, the *RabbitMQ Management CLI*. In this section we'll go through the reasons for yet another command-line tool. Then you'll install the new `rabbitmqadmin` script and use it to automate tasks like purging queues, creating exchanges, and more.

8.5.1   *Why another CLI?*

"Wait … another CLI tool? But in chapter 2 you guys taught me about the `rabbitmqctl`." We understand your questions and they're perfectly valid. As we already mentioned at the beginning of this chapter, the `rabbitmqctl` script is the default way of administering RabbitMQ, but it has its own shortcomings, like dealing with Erlang cookies, for example. Apart from that, it's hard to integrate with other programming languages and tools, since you need to be parsing the output it produces in its own format. It'll be better if, for example, you could get a list of queues in JSON format and let your JSON library of choice parse the results to give you back a Python hash. Such features justify the investment in learning this CLI API. Let's see how it works.

Point your browser to http://localhost:55672/. You'll see three options there:

- Management: Web UI
- Management: HTTP API
- Management: Command Line Tool

We've already played with the first one, so let's take a look at what the other options have to offer. If you click on HTTP API, you'll get a page with the documentation for this REST interface. Anything you can do with the Management plugin (Management Web UI), you can also do by using `curl`[3] and invoking commands on this API. As an example, if you want to list the vhosts on your server, execute the following code on your terminal:

```
$ curl -i -u guest:guest http://localhost:55672/api/vhosts
```

You'll get the following output:

```
HTTP/1.1 200 OK
Server: MochiWeb/1.1 WebMachine/1.7 (participate in the frantic)
Date: Wed, 23 Mar 2011 20:07:22 GMT
Content-Type: application/json
```

---

[3] `curl` is a command-line tool for transferring data with URL syntax. It supports several formats like HTTP, RTMP, IMAP, and many more. In case you need to install it on your machine, you can get the program from its website: http://curl.haxx.se/.

```
Content-Length: 30
Cache-Control: no-cache

[{"name":"/"},{"name":"book"}]
```

You can also add new vhosts from here:

```
$ curl -i -u guest:guest -H "content-type:application/json" \
    -XPUT http://localhost:55672/api/vhosts/rmqinaction

HTTP/1.1 204 No Content
Server: MochiWeb/1.1 WebMachine/1.7 (participate in the frantic)
Date: Wed, 23 Mar 2011 20:12:28 GMT
Content-Type: application/json
Content-Length: 0
```

And list all the vhosts back to see the one you just created:

```
curl -i -u guest:guest \
http://localhost:55672/api/vhostsHTTP/1.1 200 OK
Server: MochiWeb/1.1 WebMachine/1.7 (participate in the frantic)
Date: Wed, 23 Mar 2011 20:12:57 GMT
Content-Type: application/json
Content-Length: 53
Cache-Control: no-cache
[{"name":"/"},{"name":"book"},{"name":"rmqinaction"}]
```

Of course you can delete it if you don't need it anymore:

```
$ curl -i -u guest:guest -H "content-type:application/json" \
    -XDELETE http://localhost:55672/api/vhosts/rmqinaction
HTTP/1.1 204 No Content
Server: MochiWeb/1.1 WebMachine/1.7 (participate in the frantic)
Date: Wed, 23 Mar 2011 20:14:05 GMT
Content-Type: application/json
Content-Length: 0
```

By following this REST API you can easily automate tasks that so far have been only possible via a clickable interface. For sure, sysadmins will be happier with this tool. If you want to learn about the available methods of the REST API, you can do so by pointing your browser to the excellent documentation that's distributed with the Management plugin. See it at http://localhost:55672/api. Something interesting to notice if you've been paying attention to the response headers is that the response is sent as application/json, which means parsing the results will be as hard as knowing how to use a JSON library in your language of choice (which you probably already do).

8.5.2 *CLI administration the easier way*

The preceding method is convenient and flexible, but there's still an easier way to administer the server: the *command-line tool*. The command-line tool is a Python script that you can download directly from your RabbitMQ Management plugin installation and execute on your machine. The advantages of this script over the REST-based API is that you don't need to hand-craft your requests. The rabbitmqadmin will wrap the REST API and let you use a clean interface to interact with it, so instead of running the following command to list the queues on the server,

```
$ curl -i -u guest:guest http://localhost:55672/api/queues
```

you could do this:

```
./rabbitmqadmin list queues
```

Much better, no? Let's get it installed then.

8.5.3 *Installing rabbitmqadmin script*

Setting up the `rabbitmqadmin` admin script is dead simple: the only requirement is to have Python installed. Assuming you do have Python installed, then what you have to do is to fetch the script out of the Management plugin and make it executable. You accomplish that with the following two commands:

```
$ wget http://localhost:55672/cli/rabbitmqadmin
    $ chmod +x rabbitmqadmin
```

This will place a `rabbitmqadmin` script in your current folder that can be easily invoked from the terminal. By using this you can avoid learning all the intricacies about `curl`. Let's see it in action:

```
$ ./rabbitmqadmin -V "/" list exchanges
```

```
+-------+------------------+---------+--------+---------+----------+
| vhost |       name       |  type   |  auto  | durable | internal |
|       |                  |         | delete |         |          |
+-------+------------------+---------+--------+---------+----------+
| /     |                  | direct  | False  | True    | False    |
| /     | amq.direct       | direct  | False  | True    | False    |
| /     | amq.fanout       | fanout  | False  | True    | False    |
| /     | amq.headers      | headers | False  | True    | False    |
| /     | amq.match        | headers | False  | True    | False    |
| /     | amq.rabbitmq.log | topic   | False  | True    | False    |
| /     | amq.topic        | topic   | False  | True    | False    |
| /     | test             | direct  | False  | True    | False    |
+-------+------------------+---------+--------+---------+----------+
```

As you can see, the output is formatted, returning some pretty tables with the information related to the exchanges that are part of the `"/"` vhost. Let's strip apart the command you just invoked: `rabbitmqadmin` is the name of the executable file, the Python script you just downloaded; `-V "/"` is the option used to specify the vhost you want to use; finally, `list exchanges` is the command you want to execute.

8.5.4 *Purging queues, creating exchanges, and more*

Say that for some reason you had a consumer acting awry, unable to consume and ack messages from the queue it was subscribed. By the time you notice the problem, you have a queue filled up with messages that aren't relevant anymore. You could write a simple script to purge the queue using AMQP, or you can just call the following command:

```
$ ./rabbitmqadmin purge queue name=test
queue purged
```

Let's go back to the example of creating new exchanges. Let's see how you can declare a *direct* exchange called `cli_test` authenticating with the user `guest` and password `guest`:

```
$ ./rabbitmqadmin -u guest -p guest declare exchange \
name=cli_test type=direct
exchange declared
```

Another interesting command is the ability to close connection, say because of misbehaving consumers that are unable to ack messages, thus disrupting the message flow. First you'll get a list of connections, getting only the `connection name` property:

```
$ ./rabbitmqadmin list connections name
+-----------------+
|      name       |
+-----------------+
| 127.0.0.1:64659 |
+-----------------+
```

If you want to disconnect said consumer, you can do it by calling the `close connection` command:

```
$ ./rabbitmqadmin close connection name="127.0.0.1:64659"
connection closed
```

Though we don't describe every command in detail, we've presented the basics of using the `rabbitmqadmin` script and from here it'll be easy for you to get started and perform other tasks.

8.6 Summary

When it comes to system administration, some people prefer command-line tools and others prefer GUI programs. In this chapter, you've seen that there are plenty of choices when it comes to administering a RabbitMQ server. The good thing is that the tools we presented in this chapter are all produced by the RabbitMQ developers, which means they're maintained and on par with the latest features. Depending on your taste, you'll feel inclined to use the web UI, which is convenient for everyday development, to get a visual representation of what's happening on the server. The web UI will make it easier to work in teams and even your marketing people can now see how many campaign emails were delivered to customers. If you want to automate such tasks, you can resort to the REST-based API that you can invoke via `curl`. Since you'll get the responses as JSON objects, it becomes easy to integrate with your current tools and languages. Finally, if you want to extract some information from the server but require something simpler than manually building your HTTP requests with `curl`, you can resort to the `rabbitmqadmin` script to get nicely formatted output to help you manage and monitor your RabbitMQ installations.

In the next chapter we'll dig deeper into the REST API, learning how to automate several administration tasks like user and vhost provisioning. Start warming up your fingers, because we'll get our hands dirty with some Python code.

Controlling Rabbit
with the REST API

This chapter covers

- Limitations and abilities of the Rabbit REST API
- Managing Rabbit permissions from code
- Accessing messaging statistics and counters
- Automating user and virtual host creation

Up to this point, you've been limited in your ability to configure RabbitMQ servers from apps or scripts. Sure, you could write code that runs `rabbitmqctl` and then tries to "scrape" the output for results but that's a brittle solution and is likely to break anytime the guys at Rabbit decide to change `rabbitmqctl`'s output. In reality, both `rabbitmqctl` and the management web UI are designed for interaction with something that has a heartbeat. So where does that leave you when you want to automate the deployment of your RabbitMQ servers with tools like Chef, Puppet, or even CFEngine? Also, what about the more basic need to monitor RabbitMQ? How are you supposed to write health check scripts to keep an eye on your Rabbits without a programmatic window into RabbitMQ's inner workings?

If you've been working through the book linearly, you're already familiar with the RabbitMQ Management plugin (check out chapter 8 for installation instructions). It provides web-based access that allows you to manage and control a RabbitMQ server from your browser. Via the included web UI, an administrator can do everything from creating users and vhosts to viewing queue statistics and overall configuration. The best part is that when you install the Management plugin, you not only get the web UI, you also get a RESTful web API for free. The API provides to your apps and scripts the same full functionality as the web UI or `rabbitmqctl`.

When Rabbit HQ released the Management plugin, they not only gave developers a human-friendly web UI, they also included a RESTful web management API. The API is a simple, language-neutral, and Erlang-free way to configure and keep tabs on your Rabbit nodes running the Management plugin. The Erlang-free part is particularly important, because though Erlang provides the foundation for RabbitMQ to be distributed, scalable, and stable, you may want to control Rabbit from systems that do not have Erlang installed. Fortunately, the RabbitMQ management API uses HTTP to communicate, so you can talk to it from any programming or scripting language that has an HTTP client library.

NOTE For those not familiar with the term, *REST* stands for *Representational State Transfer*. It describes a convention for HTTP-based APIs that encodes the item you're changing and the state of the action on the item in the URL. For example, you could have a non-RESTful API that has a single URL like `http://my-api.com/calls`, and then put the particulars about the item and action in the body of the request. But if you want to do any sort of data mining on the API server's logs, all you'll see is a list of requests for `/calls`. Not very helpful. When you use a RESTful convention for your API, you end up with a URL like `http://my-api.com/item` (where *item* is the name of the item you're acting on) and then use standard HTTP verbs like POST, PUT, and DELETE to create, modify, or delete the item. Now your logs are full of useful information showing exactly the item being manipulated, and the action (verb) performed on it. For more information on REST, check out http://en.wikipedia.org/wiki/Representational_State_Transfer.

Before we dive into writing programs that interact with the management API, we need to cover some ground about what the API does (and doesn't) allow you to do. Once that's under your belt, you'll be ready to start looking at how to create access credentials for your API clients, and then begin using that access to view internal RabbitMQ statistics and perform changes to the Rabbit server like adding users and virtual hosts. Let's get started and see what the management API has to offer!

9.1 *What can you do with the RabbitMQ REST API?*

The first thing to understand about the API is that it is fully RESTful, so the name of the item you're manipulating is always included in the URL. For example, if you wanted to see the statistics for the queue named `branches` in the `oak` virtual host, you'd construct the following URL and send it as an HTTP GET request to the server:

http://localhost:55672/api/queues/oak/branches.[1] If you were to run this request using cURL, you'd see something like this:

```
$ curl -i -u guest:guest
http://localhost:55672/api/queues/oak/branches
HTTP/1.1 200 OK
Server: MochiWeb/1.1 WebMachine/1.7 (participate in the frantic)
Date: Tue, 05 Jul 2011 22:55:25 GMT
Content-Type: application/json
Content-Length: 739
Cache-Control: no-cache

{"memory":9136,"messages":0,"consumer_details":[],
 "idle_since":"2011-7-516:55:1","exclusive_consumer_pid":"",
 "exclusive_consumer_tag":"","messages_ready":0,
 "messages_unacknowledged":0,"messages":0,"consumers":0,
 "backing_queue_status":{"q1":0,"q2":0,
 ...
```

> **NOTE** *cURL* is a free program that lets you manually send and receive HTTP requests from the command line. It's available in most Linux/UNIX distributions and can also be downloaded directly from http://curl.haxx.se/download.html.

Wow, besides the fairly readable HTTP headers, what does that load of jumble mean? The headers give you a clue. If you look at the Content-Type header, you see that the response is encoded as application/json. For those not familiar with it, *JSON* stands for *JavaScript Object Notation* and is an alternative to XML for encoding data (check out http://en.wikipedia.org/wiki/JSON for a deep dive on JSON). JSON allows you to encode data using familiar structures like hash tables, arrays, strings, and integers that programming languages already understand (and, more importantly, that you already understand). If you understand JavaScript, you've probably figured out that the API is returning all the data about the queue as a hash table. For example, the memory element of the hash table tells you how much RAM (in bytes) the queue is currently consuming. When working with the management API, every call will return either an empty body (for actions that create or delete items) or a JSON hash table containing the data you requested (for actions that list or show items).

Just as important as the data an API request can return is the HTTP verb you use to make the request; you used a GET request. The RabbitMQ API interprets GET as meaning "show me all the details/settings about the item located at/api/queues/oak/branches." Besides GET, you can also use POST, PUT, or DELETE when talking to the API. POST and PUT create items, whereas DELETE does what it says—it deletes things. POST and PUT aren't interchangeable, and some API calls require POST to create the item referenced in the URL whereas others use PUT (see the reference link at the end of the section for a detailed list of where to use PUT or POST). Let's assume for a minute that

---

[1] For the examples in this chapter we assume that RabbitMQ is running on localhost and that you haven't modified the Management plugin's default listening port of 55672.

the `branches` queue doesn't exist yet, and you want to create it using the API. By using the same URL as before but changing the verb to PUT, you can convert the request to create the queue instead of returning its details:

```
$ curl -i -u guest:guest -X PUT -H
"Content-Type: application/json" \
 -d '{"auto_delete": false, "durable": false}' \
http://localhost:55672/api/queues/oak/branches

HTTP/1.1 204 No Content
Server: MochiWeb/1.1 WebMachine/1.7 (participate in the frantic)
Date: Tue, 05 Jul 2011 23:24:46 GMT
Content-Type: application/json
Content-Length: 0
```

All right, so you didn't *just* change the verb to PUT. You also added the JSON hash table `'{"auto_delete": false, "durable": false}'` into the body and added a Content-Type header so that the API would know the data in the body is JSON-encoded. The body of your request told the API to turn off the `auto_delete` and `durable` flags when creating the `branches` queue. The flags have the same effect here as the `auto_delete` and `durable` flags did when creating queues in the Python examples earlier in the book. In fact, just like in the Python AMQP examples, the API requires the flags to be specified when creating queues. If you had left the body empty, you would've received an API error. Whether you're creating a queue with the API or setting permissions, any time you use a PUT or POST verb, encode the parameters for the function you're calling as a JSON hash table in the body.

So you can create queues and view their statistics, but what else can you do? Here are a few other things the API will enable your scripts to do:

- View a list of the current connections and their details—`/api/connections`
- Download or upload the complete configuration of your RabbitMQ broker, including queues, exchanges, and bindings— `/api/all-configuration`
- List all of the nodes in a cluster (and their statistics)—`/api/nodes`
- Create or view a RabbitMQ user— `/api/users/<user>`
- View or create a virtual host— `/api/vhosts/<vhost>`
- Set the permissions for a user— `/api/permissions/<vhost>/<user>`

Since the management API (and plugin) is always being enhanced, that's just a small list of the functions the API provides. You can always see the most current (and complete) list of API calls and the HTTP verbs they support by loading http://localhost:55672/api in your web browser. Enough explanation though! Let's create some credentials so you can start writing scripts that use the API!

9.2 *Granting your clients access*

You may have noticed that both of the API requests you made using cURL had `-u guest:guest` as an argument. Just like any app accessing RabbitMQ through AMQP, scripts accessing the management API use normal RabbitMQ usernames and passwords to authenticate and gain access (supplied using HTTP Basic authentication). For example, if you have a monitoring script that should only be able to check on queue statistics, you could create a new Rabbit user whose permissions for the virtual host were

- Read: .*
- Write: (empty)
- Config: (empty)

This would allow the script (and anyone who knew the script's Rabbit username and password) to only monitor the queues but not publish to them or change their configuration.

So how do you create a username for API access? Simple: create a user via `rabbitmqctl` and set the `admin` property to true. Let's create a user called `monitor` that your scripts can use to monitor statistics in the default (/) virtual host (but not write or change anything). From your RabbitMQ directory run

```
$ sbin/rabbitmqctl add_user monitor monitorMe
Creating user "monitor" ...
...done.

$ sbin/rabbitmqctl set_admin monitor
Setting administrative status for user "monitor" ...
...done.

$ sbin/rabbitmqctl set_permissions -p / monitor "" "" ".*"
Setting permissions for user "monitor" in vhost "/" ...
...done.
```

That's all there is to it! The important part is the `set_admin` command. Without setting the `admin` flag on the username, it won't be allowed to access the API regardless of the permissions that are set. The last command (`set_permissions`) grants the `monitor` user no configure or write permissions, and full read permissions within the default (/) virtual host. With your `monitor` user in hand, you're ready to write your first API script and start viewing queue statistics.

9.3   Accessing statistics

There are many times on a daily basis when you need to see how many messages are sitting in a particular queue. Sometimes it's to debug a new app you're writing; other times it's to monitor in production the ratio between messages waiting to be consumed and those that have been delivered to a consumer and are still unacknowledged (the latter can be a useful metric for discovering messages that are crashing your consumers). You could use `rabbitmqctl` to list the total message count in your queues, but this has two major disadvantages:

1 You can only run `rabbitmqctl` from computers that have Erlang installed and the same Erlang cookie as the RabbitMQ server.
2 `rabbitmqctl` will only show you the *total* number of messages in the queue. It won't differentiate between delivered messages waiting for acknowledgement and messages waiting to be consumed in the first place.

Sounds like a perfect job for the Rabbit management API! You'll use Python's built-in `httplib` and `json` libraries to communicate with Rabbit and encode/decode the requests and responses. Since you want to be able to run your query statistics script from the command line, you need to start by parsing the command line arguments, as in the following listing.

Listing 9.1   queue_stats.py—acquire initial settings

```
import sys, json, httplib, urllib, base64          ❶ Validate
                                                       argument
if len(sys.argv) < 6:                                  count
    print "USAGE: queue_stats.py server_name:port auth_user " + \
        "auth_pass VHOST QUEUE_NAME"
    sys.exit(1)

server, port = sys.argv[1].split(":")              Assign
username = sys.argv[2]                             arguments
password = sys.argv[3]                             to memorable
vhost = sys.argv[4]                              ❷ variables
queue_name = sys.argv[5]
```

The utility takes five arguments besides the program name: server name/port (in `host:port` notation), username for API authentication, password for API authentication, name of the virtual host containing the queue, and the queue name whose statistics you want to view. After you've validated ❶ that the minimum number of required arguments is present, you assign them ❷ to more memorable variables based on the argument's position in the argument list. The only unusual bit is `server, port = sys.argv[1].split(":")`. Since you're passing the hostname and port of the Rabbit server as a single argument delimited by `:` (`localhost:55672`), you split that argument into its individual hostname and port parts. The `split` command splits the argument at `:` and returns an array containing the separated parts (for example, `"localhost:55672"` becomes `["localhost", "55672"]`). The separated parts are then assigned into the `server` and `port` variables.

With the arguments parsed, you're ready to build the request. All API queue operations are located under the `/api/queues` path. So, if you want to access a particular queue, you just extend the path to indicate the virtual host containing the queue you want and that queue's name: `/api/queues/<vhost>/<queue_name>`. The following listing shows an example.

Listing 9.2   queue_stats.py—build the request

```
vhost = urllib.quote(vhost, safe='')              ◄─❶ Build API path
queue_name = urllib.quote(queue_name, safe='')
path = "/api/queues/%s/%s" % (vhost, queue_name)
 method = "GET"                                    ◄── Set request method
```

You may notice that you escaped ❶ both the virtual host name and queue name before putting them into the request's path. If you don't quote the virtual host, then specifying the default virtual host (`/`) will raise an API error since the server considers `/` a path

separator. By first escaping the virtual host name, the request path /api/queues///
test_queue becomes /api/queues/%2F/test_queue and can be understood by the
API server. Finally, you set the HTTP method to GET so that the server will know you
want to retrieve details about the queue rather than create it. With the request path
and method set, you're ready to fire off the request to the server, as the in the following
listing.

Listing 9.3   queue_stats.py—issue API request

```
conn = httplib.HTTPConnection(server, port)
credentials = base64.b64encode("%s:%s" % (username, password))
headers = {"Content-Type" : "application/json",
           "Authorization" : "Basic " + credentials}
conn.request(method, path, "", headers)
response = conn.getresponse()
if response.status > 299:
    print "Error executing API call (%d): %s" % (response.status,
                                                  response.read())
    sys.exit(2)
```

Connect to API server ❶

❷ Base64 credentials

❸ Set headers

❹ Send request

Receive response ❺

The script first establishes an HTTP connection ❶ with the API server. At this point,
the server is waiting for the API request and authorization credentials. Since the
Rabbit API uses HTTP Basic authentication, you need to package ❷ the username and
password into a single string in the format username:password and then Base64-
encode the string.[2] Then you need to create a dictionary (hash table) containing the
HTTP headers ❸ for the request. One of those headers is the Authorization header
that contains your Base64-encoded credentials appended to the ASCII string "Basic".
The other header is Content-Type and is equally important because it lets the API
server know your request body (if there is one) will be encoded as JSON. Since your
utility is only issuing GET requests, the request bodies will always be empty, but it's
good form to set the Content-Type so you don't forget when it does matter (PUT or
POST requests). Finally, you send ❹ the prepared request to the API server and receive
the response ❺ back. If there are any issues fulfilling the request, the API server will
set the HTTP response code to a 4xx or 5xx value. Since anything higher than 299 is
an unacceptable response code, you check that the code is lower than 299 ❺ and if it
isn't, exit with an error to the user. If there isn't an error, you're ready to parse the
response and display the queue details to the user, as in the following listing.

Listing 9.4   queue_stats.py—parse and display queue statistics

```
payload = json.loads(response.read())

print "\tMemory Used (bytes): " + str(payload["memory"])
print "\tConsumer Count: " + str(payload["consumers"])
print "\tMessages:"
```

❶ Decode response

❷ Display queue statistics

---

[2]   Base64 is a way of encoding text and binary data so that it can be represented by only ASCII characters. The
HTTP Basic authentication specification requires the username:password string to be Base64-encoded
before it's sent. For more information on Base64 check http://en.wikipedia.org/wiki/Base64.

```
print "\t\tUnack'd: " + str(payload["messages_unacknowledged"])
print "\t\tReady: " + str(payload["messages_ready"])
print "\t\tTotal: " + str(payload["messages"])
sys.exit(0)
```

Since the API server always returns information as a JSON hash table, you have to first JSON-decode ❶ the response. This converts the JSON-encoded hash table into the actual hash table type supported by your programming language. For Python, this means the response is converted into a Python dictionary. The beauty of the response being JSON-encoded is that once the decoding is done, you can access the fields in resp_payload just like any other dictionary (hash table). For example, extracting the amount of memory used by the queue is as easy as accessing ❷ the memory element of the resp_payload dictionary.[3]

So what does it look like if you run the utility?

```
$ python queue_stats.py localhost:55672 guest
guest / test
'test' Queue Stats
------------------
    Memory Used (bytes): 9104
    Consumer Count: 3
    Messages:
        Unack'd: 3
        Ready: 4
        Total: 7
```

You can see from the output that the test queue in the default (/) virtual host is consuming 9104 bytes of memory, has three consumers attached to it, and contains a total of seven messages. Not only can you tell that the queue contains seven messages, you can see that three of them have been delivered to consumers and are waiting for those consumers to acknowledge them, and the other four are waiting to be delivered to the next available consumer. All of this information at your fingertips in less than 60 lines of code—and you can access it from anywhere in your infrastructure! That's the power of the Rabbit management API. It empowers you to introspect and control your Rabbits from anywhere that has network access. But for all this talk about *controlling* RabbitMQ, so far all we've done is read statistics. Let's actually change the configuration of your RabbitMQ server.

9.4   *Automating vhost and user provisioning*

Before the management API came along, one of the biggest hassles in deploying RabbitMQ was automating the creation of the virtual hosts and users that apps need. Frequently, when deploying your apps with automated deployment tools like Chef or Puppet, the recipe to deploy your app is run on a server that's different from the

---

[3] There are many more statistics in the resp_payload dictionary than just the ones we display. Inside there's also information on how many of the messages are persistent, how many messages are pending acknowledgement, the average ingress and egress rates of messages in the queue, and much more. Simply add print repr(resp_payload) before sys.exit(0) in the code from the listing to see all of the different fields.

RabbitMQ server the app needs to communicate with. When all you have is `rabbit-mqctl` to create users and virtual hosts, that's a problem, because it means Erlang and `rabbitmqctl` must be installed on every app server for the sole purpose of creating users and vhosts on the central RabbitMQ server. Wouldn't it be nice if there was a way to create users and vhosts from the servers running your apps without having to put Erlang on every one (and synchronize them all to the same Erlang cookie)? Since we live in the age of the Rabbit management API, fret no more intrepid Rabbit developer! You can write a command-line script that will let you create, delete, show, and list users by using the management API (extending the script to provision vhosts will be simple). No Erlang or cookies required!

Since we've already covered how to connect, authenticate, and send a basic API request, we'll focus on what makes a request that creates or deletes users (or vhosts) different. Let's start by looking at the `user_manager.py` script in its entirety, as shown in the following listing.

Listing 9.5   user_manager.py—RabbitMQ user manager

```
import sys, json, httplib, base64                          ❶ Assign
                                                              arguments
if len(sys.argv) < 5:
    print "USAGE: user_manager.py server_name:port " + \
          "auth_user auth_pass",
    print "ACTION [PARAMS...]"
    sys.exit(1)

server, port = sys.argv[1].split(":")
username = sys.argv[2]
password = sys.argv[3]
action = sys.argv[4]

if len(sys.argv) > 5:
    res_params = sys.argv[5:]
else:
    res_params = []

base_path = "/api/users"                                   ❷ Build API path

if action == "list":
    path = base_path
    method = "GET"
if action == "create":
    path = base_path + "/" + res_params[0]
    method = "PUT"
if action == "delete":
    path = base_path + "/" + res_params[0]
    method = "DELETE"
if action == "show":
    path = base_path
    method = "GET"

json_args = ""                                             ❸ Build JSON arguments
if action == "create":
    json_args = {"password" : res_params[1],
                 "administrator" : json.loads(res_params[2])}
```

Issue API ❹ request ⌐▷

```
                   json_args = json.dumps(json_args)

conn = httplib.HTTPConnection(server, port)
credentials = base64.b64encode("%s:%s" % (username, password))
conn.request(method, path, json_args,
               {"Content-Type" : "application/json",
                "Authorization" : "Basic " + credentials})
response = conn.getresponse()
if response.status > 299:
    print "Error executing API call (%d): %s" % (response.status,
                                                  response.read())
    sys.exit(2)
resp_payload = response.read()
if action in ["list", "show"]:
    resp_payload = json.loads(resp_payload)

    if action == "list":
        print "Count: %d" % len(resp_payload)
        for user in resp_payload:
            print "User: %(name)s" % user
            print "\tPassword: %(password_hash)s" % user
            print "\tAdministrator: %(administrator)s\n" % user
    if action == "show":
        print "User: %(name)s" % resp_payload
        print "\tPassword: %(password_hash)s" % resp_payload
        print "\tAdministrator: %(administrator)s\n" % resp_payload
else:
    print "Completed request!"

sys.exit(0)
```

◁⌐ **Parse and display ❺ response**

Process list results ❻ ⌐▷

❼ Process show results ◁

◁⌐ **Create and delete requests ❽ have no result**

As with the queue statistics script, you validate ❶ the command-line arguments and assign them into more memorable variables. The only difference so far is that the number of arguments has grown. Instead of the final arguments indicating a vhost and queue name, they now represent the action to take (create, delete, list, show) and parameters for that action. For example:

```
$ python user_manager.py localhost:55672 guest guest \
 create myuser password true
```

This will connect to the localhost API server using the username and password guest, and will create a new user called myuser whose password is password and who is an administrator (true). If you change the true to false, the user won't be created as an administrator.

Next you start building ❷ the request's path. The base path for all use API calls is/ api/users. To this path you then append the username (located in 0 index of the res_params array) you want to perform the action on:

```
base_path = "/api/users"

if action == "list":
    path = base_path
    method = "GET"
if action == "create":
```

```
        path = base_path + "/" + res_params[0]
        method = "PUT"
if action == "delete":
        path = base_path + "/" + res_params[0]
        method = "DELETE"
if action == "show":
        path = base_path + "/" + res_params[0]
        method = "GET"
```

Here is where you can see clearly how the API interprets different HTTP verbs on the same request path. If you set the method to PUT, then the API server will create the user specified by/api/users/<username>. But setting the method to DELETE for the same request path will cause the user to be deleted. Similarly, GET will be interpreted by the API server as an instruction to return details about the user in a JSON hash table. The only oddball is what you do to *list* all users. Rather than issue GET on /api/users/<username> (which would specify a specific user), you issue the GET request on/api/users. Since that request path specifies no user in particular, the API server returns a list of all the users in the RabbitMQ server (the server returns a list of hash tables, where each hash table has the full details for a user).

After the path is built, you need to determine ❸ whether the request being crafted is supposed to create a user. If it is, you need to build a JSON-encoded hash table that contains the password and administrator status for the new user:

```
json_args = ""
if action == "create":
    json_args = {"password" : res_params[1],
                 "administrator" : json.loads(res_params[2])}
    json_args = json.dumps(json_args)
```

The hash table for creating a user needs two fields: password and administrator. password contains a plaintext version of the desired password, and administrator is a Boolean set to either true or false. With the request now built, you connect and send ❹ the request just as you did with the queue statistics script. The only difference is that you now specify a request for the body when the action is to create a user.

Once the request has been sent and you've verified that the server didn't return an error, you read ❺ the response and get to work. If the action was to create or delete a user ❽, there's no result so you just print a confirmation that the request succeeded to the user. If the requested action was to list or show users, then you JSON-decode the response. After the response has been decoded, you have a native Python data structure you can work with. If the user requested a list of users, then the response is an array of hash tables. So you need to iterate ❻ through the list of users and print the name, password_hash, and administrator status for each user:[4]

---

[4] You may notice that we're using Python's string formatting capabilities. For example, "User: %(name)s" % user tells Python to create a new string, substituting the value of user["name"] at the position of %(name)s in the string. You could use the syntax "User: " + user["name"] and have the same result.

```
if action == "list":
    print "Count: %d" % len(resp_payload)
    for user in resp_payload:
        print "User: %(name)s" % user
        print "\tPassword: %(password_hash)s" % user
        print "\tAdministrator: %(administrator)s\n" % user
```

If the action was to show a *specific* user, then the response won't be an array of hash tables. Instead, the response will itself be a single hash table, similar to what you saw with the queue statistics script, except that this time the hash table ❼ contains the name, password_hash, and administrator status for the user:

```
if action == "show":
    print "User: %(name)s" % resp_payload
    print "\tPassword: %(password_hash)s" % resp_payload
    print "\tAdministrator: %(administrator)s\n" % resp_payload
```

You now have a fully featured utility that can create, delete, show, and list users on any RabbitMQ server that has the Management plugin installed. Let's see what creating and then showing a user looks like with the utility:

```
$ python user_manager.py localhost:55672 guest guest \
  create newuser newpass true
Completed request!

$ python user_manager.py localhost:55672 guest guest \
  show newuser
User: newuser
    Password: o/ZEH9Z86FNUtzu2MzNlmDSTDFE=
    Administrator: True
```

Though you'd probably want to add more stringent argument validation to the script for production use, the fact is you *could* use it as-is to manage the creation of users from any system. In fact, the authors use a similar script for automating RabbitMQ user creation when deploying apps. By building this script you've learned how to not only show a single item via the management API, but how to show lists of items and how to create and delete those items. You can apply these concepts to working with any of the different item/resource types available via the API (users, queues, exchanges, connections, permissions, and so on). In the source code companion for this chapter we've included a script called user_vhost_manager.py. It extends this user manager script to manage the creation of vhosts, and also enables the manipulation of user/vhost permissions.

9.5 Summary

Before we began, you were limited to managing your Rabbit servers by hand either through rabbitmqctl or the management web UI. You were completely unable to write automated scripts or utilities that could integrate with Rabbit to help you manage its configuration or monitor its internal state. But by learning how the Rabbit management API works, you're now able to build tools that let you monitor queue state and manage your users according to your own needs. You're no longer at the mercy of managing your RabbitMQ servers by hand—now you can write utilities that use the management API to automate Rabbit provisioning to custom suit the processes of your organizations. With the management API at your disposal, the only limit to the Rabbit management tools you can build is your own imagination. One of the areas that the API opens up is automated monitoring of RabbitMQ's health. Now that you understand how to build tools with the API, you're ready to look at using those skills in more depth to enhance the monitoring of your Rabbit infrastructures and make sure they're running in tip-top shape.

Monitoring: Houston, we have a problem

10

This chapter covers

- Basics of writing Nagios health checks
- Using both AMQP and the REST API to monitor Rabbit internals
- Verifying that Rabbit is available and responding
- Watching queue levels for early detection of consumer problems
- Checking for undesirable configuration changes in the messaging fabric

Your RabbitMQ server is up and running and your snazzy dog walking app is bringing in thousands of orders nationwide. Everything seems to be going great when you suddenly get the call: customers are getting errors from your web app and the flow of orders has stopped completely. The RabbitMQ server has died, and to make matters worse it appears that it's been down for hours. If only you'd been proactively notified the instant RabbitMQ went offline instead of having to wait for your customers to tell you and losing thousands of dollars in orders in the process. Setting up Rabbit to be highly available and writing your apps to use it are only two legs of the stool. Things can still go bump in the night. If you're going to run a truly

167

reliable operation, you need to monitor Rabbit to make sure it's running and that the messages you publish into it are getting consumed as expected. Properly monitored, you can find out not only when things have gone horribly wrong (like the Rabbit server dying), but also when your messaging infrastructure is suffering—well before it takes down your customers and your bottom line. For example, wouldn't it be great to know that your dog walking order queue suddenly has 10 million messages waiting to be consumed when it normally averages 1,000 messages? Or perhaps it would be a good idea to know when that order queue suddenly has had its `durable` setting changed from durable to transient before a power outage hits and causes all those orders to disappear? In this chapter you're going to learn how to write programs that can monitor Rabbit and all of these aspects of our messaging infrastructure. You'll then be able to take these monitoring programs and plug them into the monitoring and alerting framework of your choice so you can be alerted when things have gone off course with your messaging. Let's get started by learning how to monitor RabbitMQ internals both over AMQP and with the REST API.

10.1   RabbitMQ monitoring: keeping an eye on your warren

Monitoring RabbitMQ isn't just about making sure that port `5672` is open and accepting TCP connections. With a complicated system like Rabbit it's better if you can simulate an AMQP client to make sure that you can actually acquire a channel after you connect. It would also be great if you could use the REST API to find out if all of the different Erlang components that make up Rabbit are running and talking correctly to each other. To do any of this, you first have to understand how write a health check that your monitoring system can understand. In this case, that system is going to be Nagios, so let's look at what Nagios is and what a health check has to do to talk to it.

10.1.1   Writing health checks for Nagios

Many different commercial and open source monitoring frameworks are available today. Of these, one of the most popular is Nagios. It's freely available from http://nagios.org and has a flexible API that makes it easy to write your own health check programs in any language you choose. In addition, many of the other open source monitoring frameworks (like Zenoss and Zabbix) also support the Nagios health check API, making it possible for your Rabbit health checks to be used with many other monitoring systems besides Nagios. So what's a Nagios health check and how does it work?

A Nagios health check is a standalone program that monitors a service when it's run and indicates the healthiness of the service (or lack thereof) by its exit code when the program terminates. You technically don't even need Nagios to run a health check—you can execute it anytime from the command line and manually observe the output. A Nagios health check can be written as anything from a Python program to a BASH script as long as it prints the human-readable status of the thing it's monitoring to `STDOUT` and returns one of the following four integer exit codes:

- *0—OK*—The service being checked is functioning normally and is completely within any thresholds given to the health check via command-line arguments.

- *1—WARNING*—The service is running in a degraded state (or has encountered a problem) but the issue isn't urgent. For example, say you're monitoring RAM usage. If you had configured the health check with a *warning* threshold of 2 GB and a *critical* threshold of 4 GB, a WARNING exit code would be returned for any RAM usage between 2 GB and 4 GB.
- *2—CRITICAL*—The service is down, unresponsive, and/or has crossed the critical threshold for the metric being monitored. Using the RAM usage example, the health check would return a CRITICAL exit code when RAM usage is over 4 GB.
- *3—UNKNOWN*—Technically this means that the status of the service or metric being monitored couldn't be determined. For example, if the health check were monitoring the number of messages in a queue and it couldn't connect to the server, instead of returning a critical status it could return *unknown* as the status. Returning the status as unknown only makes sense when you're unable to sample the current state of the metric. If the metric you're monitoring *is* connectivity and you can't connect, then definitely return critical instead of unknown.

Now that you understand what Nagios expects from a health check program, let's build one in the following listing. Though you can use any language to write your health checks, for these examples you'll use Python again and the Pika AMQP library you installed in chapter 4. Your first health check is going to be simple—it's not going to check anything. It's going to take warning, critical, unknown, or ok as an argument and exit with that Nagios status code.

> **Listing 10.1 nagios_check.py: health check that returns Nagios status codes**

```
import sys, json, httplib, base64

status = sys.argv[1]                          Return requested
                                              Nagios status code
if status.lower() == "warning":
    print "Status is WARN"
    exit(1)
elif status.lower() == "critical":
    print "Status is CRITICAL"
    exit(2)
elif status.lower() == "unknown":
    print "Status is UNKNOWN"
    exit(3)
else:
    print "Status is OK"
    exit(0)
```

If you run `python nagios_check.py critical` you should get a human-readable message on `STDOUT` and 2 as the exit code:

```
> python nagios_check.py critical
Status is CRITICAL
> echo $?
2
```

Excellent! Your health check returned the correct status message, and `echo $?` tells you the exit code is correct for critical status (2). If Nagios were running this health check itself, you'd get an alert that read Status is CRITICAL. Though Nagios doesn't understand what that message means, it does understand that 2 as your exit code indicates that the health check is in critical status. All of our health checks will build on this example to add logic that actually checks a live service, and also to take command-line arguments so that you can tell the health check what service to monitor and what constitutes a critical or warning threshold.

Before we jump into making a health check that can see whether RabbitMQ is alive and capable of building channels, we need to talk about Nagios itself. Though you'll be building health checks that can be used by Nagios, we won't cover configuring Nagios to use them. This will let us focus on how to monitor different aspects of Rabbit. If you want to learn more about Nagios and how to install it, a great place to start is the documentation site: http://www.nagios.org/documentation.

Enough housekeeping! Let's see whether your RabbitMQ server is alive and healthy!

10.1.2 Checking that RabbitMQ is alive with AMQP simulation checks

Without writing a line of code, you could use the TCP health check that comes with most monitoring systems to do a simple TCP connect to check whether Rabbit is responding on port 5762. This would tell you that the RabbitMQ daemon is running, but it wouldn't tell you whether the daemon is functioning. For example, what if RabbitMQ is running out of memory? It's possible that the daemon could be functional enough to complete the TCP handshake but has insufficient memory to actually respond to AMQP commands. What you need to truly determine whether Rabbit is capable of servicing requests is to actually issue AMQP commands. So let's build an AMQP ping health check. It'll return a critical status if any of the following conditions are true:

- The RabbitMQ server doesn't respond to TCP connections.
- When issuing an AMQP command, the Pika library times out before receiving a response.
- You experience a protocol error while building an AMQP channel.

Only if none of those conditions are true will the program return an OK status from the health check. The health check code itself looks like a simplified version of your initial Hello World consumer.

> **Listing 10.2   amqp_ping_check.py**

```
import sys, pika

EXIT_OK = 0                                    ①  Nagios status codes
EXIT_WARNING = 1
EXIT_CRITICAL = 2
EXIT_UNKNOWN = 3
                                               ②  Parse command-line
server, port = sys.argv[1].split(":")             arguments
vhost = sys.argv[2]
```

```
username = sys.argv[3]
password = sys.argv[4]

creds_broker = pika.PlainCredentials(username, password)
conn_params = pika.ConnectionParameters(server,
                                    virtual_host = vhost,
                                    credentials = creds_broker)
try:
    conn_broker = pika.BlockingConnection(conn_params)
    channel = conn_broker.channel()
except Exception:

    print "CRITICAL: Could not connect to %s:%s!" % \
    (server, port)
    exit(EXIT_CRITICAL)

print "OK: Connect to %s:%s successful." % (server, port)
exit(EXIT_OK)
```

③ Establish connection to broker

④ Connection failed, return CRITICAL status

⑤ Connection OK, return OK status

After creating a few constants to refer to the status codes ❶ that Nagios will expect the health check to return, you get right to parsing the command-line arguments passed to the check ❷. Since this health check is simply verifying that the RabbitMQ server is able to respond to AMQP commands, it only needs to be passed four arguments when it's invoked: the server name and port for the RabbitMQ server, the virtual host (vhost) on which to build the channel, and the username and password that permit access to the vhost. Wait a minute—that's five arguments, not four. To simplify the number of arguments you have to pass to the check, combine the hostname and port into a single argument delimited by a colon. For example, if the Rabbit server you want to check the health of is running at localhost on port 5672, you'd pass the argument as localhost:5672.

Once you've parsed the connection parameters from the command-line arguments, you attempt to connect to the server ❸ using those credentials and then build a channel: channel = conn_broker.channel(). What's different from the earlier examples is that if an exception is thrown for any reason when you try to connect, you exit immediately with a critical exit code ❹ (and print that you couldn't connect). In previous examples, when an error occurred, you'd catch the error and immediately try to reconnect to keep your consumer running. In this case, since a bad connection is exactly what you're trying to tell Nagios about, you don't want to cleanly hide the error. Rather, by catching the generic Exception error class, all exceptions will match your error handling code and return a critical status (exit code 2) to Nagios for any issue related to connecting to the Rabbit server (including timeout errors). Finally, if building the connection and channel didn't trigger any errors, you return ❺ with an exit code of 0 (the value of EXIT_OK) to let Nagios know that your health check was successful.

What's important to notice in this simple health check is that Nagios has no intimate knowledge of RabbitMQ at any point in the process. In fact, Nagios never even knows what RabbitMQ is. All that Nagios knows is that the exit code is either 2 if there's a critical error determined by the health check, or 0 if everything is running smoothly. That's what makes writing health check programs for Nagios so simple, and why so many other monitoring frameworks support the Nagios model of health checks written as standalone programs that return exit codes 0 through 3. With your shiny new health check in hand, let's give it a test drive and see what happens with a healthy RabbitMQ server:

```
$ python amqp_ping_check.py localhost:5672 / guest guest
OK: Connect to localhost:5672 successful.
$ echo $?
0
```

Terrific, the RabbitMQ server running on your local development machine is running and able to process AMQP commands. Also, as required, the exit code when the check is successful is 0 (echo $? will always show you the exit code from the previously run command). But how can you test to make sure the health check detects an unhealthy RabbitMQ server? To simulate an internal Rabbit failure, you'll use the rabbitmqctl stop_app command you learned about when dealing with clustering:

```
$ rabbitmqctl stop_app
Stopping node rabbit@Phantome ...
...done.
$ python amqp_ping_check.py localhost:5672 / guest guest
CRITICAL: Could not connect to localhost:5672!
$ echo $?
2
```

As desired, your new AMQP-based health check for Rabbit successfully detects a failed Rabbit and returns an error code of 2 to indicate a critical failure to the monitoring framework. With your new health check in hand, you can easily configure your monitoring framework of choice to start monitoring your Rabbit server and notify you when it's unable to service connections. But what if you want your health check not to stop at simply building a channel, but rather want to fully test that you can publish a message and consume it? You could extend your AMQP health check with this additional functionality, but if you have the Rabbit management API installed, you have an even better option at your disposal. Let's look at how you can build a health check that uses the REST API to do a full produce/consume test for you and lets your health check know the result.

10.1.3 Checking aliveness with the REST API

Testing that RabbitMQ is accepting new connections and able to build an AMQP channel is a good way to test that a Rabbit server is healthy. But as we've all learned the hard way, if you don't test every part of a process you rely on, you can get bitten when the part you don't test fails. With that in mind, let's take the monitoring a step further and test the process of publishing a message into RabbitMQ and then consuming that message to verify it was routed correctly.

You could simply extend your AMQP health check to fully test the routing process, but your check would have the added complexity of creating queues and making sure messages don't build up if the health check doesn't complete. Fortunately, you have another option. One of the features of the REST API that ships with the Rabbit management plugin is an API call that tests the health of the Rabbit server internally. The aliveness-test, as it's called, performs three steps to verify the health of a Rabbit server:

1 Create a new queue to receive the test message.
2 Publish a test message with the name of the queue as the routing key into the default exchange.
3 Consume the message when it arrives in the queue, and error out if it doesn't arrive.

Since this check runs internally inside the Erlang virtual machine (alongside RabbitMQ) it's not affected by network issues that might prevent you from connecting to Rabbit's port (5672) externally. Though this means that using the API to health check Rabbit lets you focus on internal message routing issues that may be occurring, it also means that the check won't tell you whether a firewall rule is preventing outside consumers (like your dog walking app) from connecting to Rabbit at all. So in reality, it's advisable to use the AMQP health check you built in the previous section in conjunction with an API-based health check to ensure you have complete monitoring coverage of your Rabbit server. It's also important to note that the aliveness-test API call uses an intelligent implementation of its check process, which doesn't delete the queue it creates. This means you won't fill the Mnesia database with thousands of queue metadata transactions if your health check runs repeatedly in short intervals. So how do you write a health check around the aliveness-test API call? Use HTTP to make an API request in the form /api/aliveness-test/<vhost> where <vhost> is the name of the virtual host where the API should create the test queue. The following listing shows the code.

Listing 10.3 api_ping_check.py: REST API–based health check for RabbitMQ

```
import sys, json, httplib, urllib, base64, socket

EXIT_OK = 0                                                    ← 1 Nagios status codes
EXIT_WARNING = 1
EXIT_CRITICAL = 2
EXIT_UNKNOWN = 3

server, port = sys.argv[1].split(":")                          ← 2 Parse arguments
vhost = sys.argv[2]
username = sys.argv[3]
password = sys.argv[4]
                                                               3 Connect to server
conn = httplib.HTTPConnection(server, port)                    ←

path = "/api/aliveness-test/%s" % urllib.quote(vhost, safe="")
method = "GET"
                                                               5 Issue API
credentials = base64.b64encode("%s:%s" % (username, password))    request  ←

try:
```

Build API path 4

```
conn.request(method, path, "",
             {"Content-Type" : "application/json",
              "Authorization" : "Basic " + credentials})
```

Could not
connect,
return
critical
status ⓺

```
except socket.error:
    print "CRITICAL: Could not connect to %s:%s" % (server, port)
    exit(EXIT_CRITICAL)

response = conn.getresponse()

if response.status > 299:
    print "CRITICAL: Broker not alive: %s" % response.read()
    exit(EXIT_CRITICAL)

print "OK: Broker alive: %s" % response.read()
exit(EXIT_OK)
```

⓻ **RabbitMQ not**
responding/
alive, return
critical status

⓼ **RabbitMQ alive,**
return OK status

As with the AMQP health check, the first things you do are set up constants ❶ for the exit codes and parse ❷ the command-line arguments. This health check takes exactly the same arguments as the AMQP health check, with the change that the *server* and *port* are for the API server (instead of the RabbitMQ server itself). Where you start to diverge from the AMQP health check is that you're building an HTTP connection ❸ to the API server rather than an AMQP connection. Once you've built the HTTP connection to the API server, you then create the request path for the aliveness-test call ❹. At the end of the path, you append the vhost to be used for creating the test queue. Since it's possible to have a vhost named / (the HTTP path separator), you also need to escape any special characters in the vhost name using urllib.quote before appending it to the path. The safe="" argument tells urllib.quote that it should escape all special characters without exception (by default urllib.quote won't escape / characters). Also, you set the request method to GET since you're retrieving information via the API rather than modifying or creating it.

Once you've created the HTTP connection and request path, you're ready to encode your credentials ❺ and transmit the request to the API server.[1] If you're unable to connect to the API server ❻, you return EXIT_CRITICAL as your status exit code. You could return a warning or unknown status instead, since technically you only know that the API server is down as opposed to the RabbitMQ server itself. But since the API runs as a plugin to RabbitMQ, it's unlikely that the API server would be down if the RabbitMQ server wasn't down as well.

Providing you're able to connect to the API server and transmit your request, you'll receive a response object back. The response object stores the HTTP status code in response.status, and the body text of the response as a file descriptor you can access using response.read(). All that you care about is the HTTP status code. If the aliveness-test call is successful, it'll return a 200-level HTTP status code. Any other code above 299 is either an error or additional instructions to the client. As a result, if you receive an HTTP status code above 299 ❼, you can return a critical status (EXIT _CRITICAL) to Nagios to indicate that the health check failed. Otherwise, the call was

---

[1] Chapter 9 on the REST API has more information on how to craft the HTTP Basic authentication header.

successful and the broker is alive ❽. Since the body of a successful call is simply the JSON string {'status' : 'ok'} (a status you already know from the HTTP status code), you can either ignore the body entirely or in this case append it to the human-readable response from your health check.

So what happens if you run your API ping health check against your local development machine?

```
> python api_ping_check.py localhost:55672 / guest guest
OK: Broker alive: {"status":"ok"}
> echo $?
0
```

The health check correctly determines that the RabbitMQ server is alive and able to produce and consume messages. But what happens if you simulate a node failure and rerun the health check?

```
> rabbitmqctl -n rabbit@Phantome stop_app
Stopping node rabbit@Phantome ...
...done.
> python api_ping_check.py localhost:55672 / guest guest
CRITICAL: Broker not alive: <html><head><title>500 Internal
Server Error</title></head><body><h1>Internal Server Error</h1>The
server encountered an error while processing this request:<br><pre>
{exit,{aborted,{no_exists,[rabbit_user,<<"guest">>]}},
      [{mnesia,abort,1},
       {rabbit_misc,dirty_read,1},
       {rabbit_auth_backend_internal,internal_check_user_login,2},
       {rabbit_access_control,'-check_user_login/2-fun-0-',4},
       {lists,foldl,3},
       {rabbit_mgmt_util,is_authorized,3},
       {webmachine_resource,resource_call,3},
       {webmachine_resource,do,3}]]}</pre><P><HR>
       <ADDRESS>mochiweb+webmachine
       web server</ADDRESS></body></html>
> echo $?
2
```

Wow, that's a lot of output. Nagios is only looking for the exit code (2) to determine that the health check failed, but it'll send you everything from CRITICAL:... to ...</html> in the alert that it generates. What the aliveness-test call is returning to you in the body, and which your health check is outputting verbatim, is the internal Erlang crash report that was generated because the API couldn't talk to RabbitMQ. So if someone were to stop the RabbitMQ node, not only would your monitoring system be able to alert you thanks to your new health check, but it would also give you the detailed Erlang crash report that you can use to track down why Rabbit is having issues.

You now have the ability to monitor not only that RabbitMQ is able to accept connections, but also that it's able to successfully route messages. But what happens if someone were to change one of your durable queues to nondurable and thereby make it vulnerable to message loss? How can you protect against dangerous changes to your Rabbit configuration that wouldn't normally be noticed by checking the

RabbitMQ server's health? Easy: just write a health check that can monitor a queue (or exchange) configuration.

10.1.4 *Creating a watchdog for configuration changes*

Verifying that RabbitMQ is running and healthy is only part of ensuring the reliability of your messaging infrastructure. You also need to make sure that your messaging fabric isn't accidentally changed into a configuration that would cause message loss for your apps. For example, imagine that your hard-working fellow developer Rolf is deploying the latest version of your dog walking app. Since you wisely wrote the app to configure the queues, exchange, and bindings it will need, you don't have to worry that the app will crash if the RabbitMQ server is missing parts of that fabric when the app starts (the app will just create what's missing). But this autoconfiguration of the fabric by the app is going to cause problems this morning because Rolf had a late night of quashing the final bugs in Dog Walker 10.0 and made a typo. Accidentally, Rolf erased the code that creates the `walking_orders` queue upon app startup. Realizing his problem, he retyped the queue declaration back into the app's code before he committed the code to the production repository. The issue is that when Rolf retyped

the queue declaration, he forgot to make the queue durable. This is a big problem, because if a power failure hits the RabbitMQ server in production, all the dog walking orders in the queue will vaporize when the power is cut. But since the queue exists and is named correctly, you wouldn't notice any problems until a power outage occurs, at which point it's too late. Since we're all Rolf from time to time, you need to create a health check that can monitor the configuration of a queue so that you're notified proactively if it changes. Consult figure 10.1.

Before the creation of the Rabbit Management plugin and API, it was difficult to monitor queue (or exchange) configuration. About the only way you could verify a queue's configuration was to attempt to redeclare the queue with the desired parameters, and trust that RabbitMQ would reject the redeclaration if the configuration was different from the queue that already existed. The biggest issue with this approach is that it can actively change

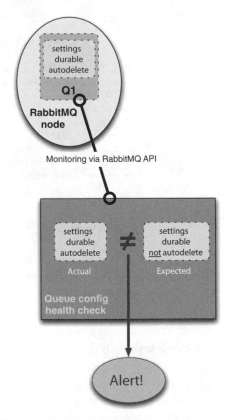

Figure 10.1 Queue configuration health check

the messaging fabric since you're declaring a queue to see if a failure occurs. In other words, if the health check has a bug it could trigger the very condition (a queue adversely changing configuration) it's trying to detect. Fortunately, with the existence of the RabbitMQ API, you now have a better way.

One of the calls provided by the Rabbit management API allows you to view the configuration of any queue in any vhost: /api/queues/<vhost>/<queue>. Not only can you view the configuration, you can also view statistics about the queue like how much memory it's consuming or the queue's average messaging throughput. In the following listing, let's use curl to take a quick look at the configuration and status of a sample queue called my_queue in the / vhost (note that / is encoded in the URL as %2F).

Listing 10.4   /api/queues/<vhost>/<queue> curl output

```
$ curl -i -u guest:guest http://localhost:55672/api/queues/%2F/my_queue
HTTP/1.1 200 OK
Server: MochiWeb/1.1 WebMachine/1.7 (participate in the frantic)
Date: Tue, 16 Aug 2011 23:25:14 GMT
Content-Type: application/json
Content-Length: 670
Cache-Control: no-cache

{
    "memory":8400,                                    ❶ Queue memory usage
    "idle_since":"2011-8-16 17:24:46",
    "exclusive_consumer_pid":"",
    "exclusive_consumer_tag":"",
    "messages_ready":0,                               ❷ Message counts
    "messages_unacknowledged":0,
    "messages":0,
    "consumers":0,
    "backing_queue_status":
    {
        "q1":0,
        ...
    },
    ...
    "name":"my_queue",
    "vhost":"/",
    "durable":true,                                   ❸ Queue configuration
    "auto_delete":false,
    "arguments":
    {
    },
    "node":"rabbit@Phantome"
}
```

Even though you've trimmed out some of the statistics for brevity (the ... portions), you can still tell a lot about the queue. For example, you can see that my_queue is consuming 8400 bytes of memory ❶, and that no messages are waiting in the queue ❷. For your current needs, you're interested in the queue configuration elements at the bottom of the JSON output ❸. Here you can see that my_queue was created with durable set to true and auto_delete set to false (the arguments array contains a list of the queue's optional configuration parameters). Armed with this kind of information, your new health check could easily monitor the durable and auto_delete parameters from the API call's output to alert you when either changes.

Like the previous health checks you've written, you'll use command-line arguments to let the check know which API server to check. But this time you need a few extra arguments. In addition to the usual server, port, vhost, username, and password details, you also need to know

- The name of the queue whose configuration is going to be monitored
- Whether the queue is supposed to have durable and/or autodelete turned on

Since the API call is going to return the value of durable and auto_delete as JSON-encoded Booleans, you're going to expect true or false on the command line in JSON format:

```
server, port = sys.argv[1].split(":")
vhost = sys.argv[2]
username = sys.argv[3]
password = sys.argv[4]
queue_name = sys.argv[5]
auto_delete = json.loads(sys.argv[6].lower())
durable = json.loads(sys.argv[7].lower())
```

This will let you JSON-decode the arguments and compare them to the values of their respective parameters from the call output. Your code to generate the HTTP request for the API call is also remarkably similar to the API ping health check. The only change is to the request path itself to point to the queue inspection call:

```
conn = httplib.HTTPConnection(server, port)

path = "/api/queues/%s/%s" % (urllib.quote(vhost, safe=""),
                              urllib.quote(queue_name))
method = "GET"

credentials = base64.b64encode("%s:%s" % (username, password))
try:
    conn.request(method, path, "",
                 {"Content-Type" : "application/json",
                  "Authorization" : "Basic " + credentials})
except socket.error:
    print "UNKNOWN: Could not connect to %s:%s" % (server, port)
    exit(EXIT_UNKNOWN)

response = conn.getresponse()
```

Issue API request

You may have noticed one other change from the HTTP connection code in the API ping health check you built: your new health check returns EXIT_UNKNOWN if it can't connect to the API server. With the API ping health check you were verifying the availability of the RabbitMQ server itself, so the API server not being available meant the health check had failed and should return EXIT_CRITICAL. But the mission of this new health check is not to monitor the availability of the Rabbit server but to keep an eye on the configuration of a queue. As a result, if you can't connect to the API server, you should return EXIT_UNKNOWN since your health check can't determine the configuration of the queue one way or the other. Whether you receive an alert from your monitoring system when this new check enters into the state unknown is up to how you configured the monitoring system (Nagios) to treat UNKNOWN. By returning UNKNOWN instead of CRITICAL, you're providing a more accurate response and giving the administrator of the monitoring system the flexibility to configure the system to handle UNKNOWN the way they think is best.

Where this check truly diverges from the checks you've written so far is in the way it handles the HTTP response from the API call, as shown in the following listing.

Listing 10.5 queue_config_check.py: API response handling

```
if response.status == 404:                          Queue doesn't exist,
    print "CRITICAL: Queue %s does not exist." % \  ❶ return critical
            queue_name
    exit(EXIT_CRITICAL)

elif response.status > 299:                         Unexpected API error,
    print "UNKNOWN: Unexpected API error: %s" % \   ❷ return unknown
            response.read()
    exit(EXIT_UNKNOWN)
                                                    ❹ Queue
response = json.loads(response.read())                auto_delete flag
                                                      incorrect, return
                                                      warning
if response["auto_delete"] != auto_delete:
    print "WARN: Queue '%s' - auto_delete flag is NOT %s." % \
            (queue_name, auto_delete)
    exit(EXIT_WARNING)                              ❺ Queue durable
                                                      flag incorrect,
if response["durable"] != durable:                    return warning
    print "WARN: Queue '%s' - durable flag is NOT %s." % \
            (queue_name, durable)
    exit(EXIT_WARNING)                              ❻ Queue exists and
                                                      flags correct,
print "OK: Queue %s configured correctly." % queue_name  return OK
exit(EXIT_OK)
```

Parse API ❸ response
(pointing to `response = json.loads(response.read())`)

The API ping health check either succeeded or failed and there was no differentiation between the failure codes. But the queue inspection API call gives you more information through the HTTP status code when it fails. If the HTTP status code is 404, you know that the queue this check is trying to validate doesn't exist ❶. Since the queue not existing is a violation of how you want the queue configured, when you see a 404, you set the exit code to EXIT_CRITICAL and output a human-readable message indicating that the check failed because the queue is missing. For any other HTTP status code greater than 299, you set the exit code to EXIT_UNKNOWN ❷ and output a human-readable message indicating that an API error that you weren't expecting occurred and include the body from the call's HTTP response. EXIT_UNKNOWN as the health check exit code is appropriate because as with the last use of the unknown status, an error you're not expecting prevents the check from determining the queue configuration one way or the other.

In the remainder of the new health check, you JSON-decode ❸ the HTTP response and compare the `auto_delete` ❹ and `durable` ❺ parameters against the values provided to the health check via its command-line arguments. If either `auto_delete` or `durable` don't match what the command-line arguments say they should be, you set the exit status code to `EXIT_WARNING` and provide a descriptive human-readable message. Now you may wonder why you're setting the health check's status to warning instead of critical if the configuration parameters you're verifying aren't correct. Honestly, it's up to you and your environment. If you care more about the queue existing and less about its actual configuration, a warning status for `durable` or `auto_delete` not matching is fine. But if it would be fatal for the queue not to be durable when a power failure occurs (as with the dog walking order queue) you definitely want to use the exit code `EXIT_CRITICAL` instead.

If everything about the queue's configuration is correct, you exit normally ❻. With this health check you can easily set up multiple instances in the monitoring system to monitor the configuration of all the queues that are vital to your apps. Similarly, if you need to make sure certain exchanges are always configured in a particular way, you can rewrite this check to use the `/api/exchanges/<vhost>/<exchange>` API call instead and monitor the exchange's configuration parameters in the response. As with most of your adventures in the book so far, you've been focusing on monitoring the aspects of a Rabbit server that apply equally whether you're running a standalone server or a cluster. But if you're running a cluster it's equally important to know when individual nodes have disappeared or their internal statistics are above desirable levels. So let's look at what it takes to make a check that can monitor the health of a RabbitMQ cluster as a whole.

10.1.5 *Monitoring your cluster status*

You might be wondering what's the point of creating yet another health check just for monitoring a RabbitMQ cluster? After all, can't you use the AMQP or API-based ping health checks you've already written to monitor all of the nodes in the cluster? Yes you could, and you'd know right away when any of those nodes went down—no special cluster health check required. But imagine for a moment that you're loading a replacement server for a node that went down due to a hard drive crash. This new server is an identical replacement all the way down to the IP address and Erlang node name of the dead system. Once you're done loading RabbitMQ onto the fresh server, you then get an alert from your monitoring system. It tells you that the AMQP ping health check for that node is now reporting RabbitMQ to be up and running again. Excellent! Your cluster is running at full strength again and your work is done! Or is it? Within an hour you start receiving customer reports that their dog walking orders aren't showing up in the queue even though the web app is confirming their orders. Suddenly you realize your mistake—you reloaded the server as an identical replacement for the dead RabbitMQ node, but you forgot to join it to the cluster! It's acting as a standalone Rabbit server, so any orders that get sent to the replacement node aren't visible to apps connected to the rest of cluster. All the while, the AMQP ping health check is reporting everything is A-OK on the replacement node. When you're depending on a RabbitMQ cluster to power your apps, it's not enough to make sure all the nodes are simply running and accepting AMQP commands. You need to ensure they're acting *together* as a single unit, and that each one is joined to the cluster. There's also another reason for creating a special health check for monitoring your RabbitMQ clusters: you need to be alerted proactively when a cluster node is running up against its maximum memory limit.

There are a number of reasons why RabbitMQ can use too much memory and run into the maximum memory cap set in the Rabbit configuration file. Here are few of the most common reasons:

- Your app has a bug that consumes a message but forgets to send an acknowledgement back to RabbitMQ. This can result in thousands or millions of messages building up and exhausting Rabbit's RAM in a high-volume environment.
- You've written an app that's using RabbitMQ to route large data (like images) to processing nodes. It doesn't take many 100 MB images to exhaust a server with only 8 GB of RAM.
- There's a shiny new feature you're using in the latest version of RabbitMQ, but it has a bug that causes a slow memory leak.

No matter what the reason, once RabbitMQ has run out of RAM, bad things often start to happen—like RabbitMQ becoming completely unresponsive or crashing. Yes, RabbitMQ will try to use disk for storing messages when it experiences memory exhaustion, but if you're running in an environment with any significant message volume your disks won't be able to keep up. When memory exhaustion happens to a node that's part of a cluster, you can start to see strange and intermittent behavior that may not make sense. For example, your AMQP channel may appear to hang when a message is published to a fanout exchange on node A, but node A appears to be fine. In reality, the channel is locking up not because of anything wrong with node A, but because node A has a binding that delivers the message to a queue on node B, which is out of RAM. Since node A can't get node B to deliver the message, the channel to node A appears to hang while you wait for the publish to timeout. It would be much better to have a health check that could monitor the cluster and let you know that one of the nodes is almost out of RAM so you can correct the problem before the node becomes unresponsive.

Fortunately, you don't need separate health checks to monitor cluster membership and the RAM usage of the members. That's because the smart guys at Rabbit HQ gave you a single API call that tells you everything you could want to know about a cluster and its members: /api/nodes. If you use curl to query /api/nodes manually, you'll get a JSON array with a dictionary for each node in the cluster:

```
$ curl -i -u guest:guest http://localhost:55672/api/nodes
HTTP/1.1 200 OK
Server: MochiWeb/1.1 WebMachine/1.7 (participate in the frantic)
Date: Thu, 18 Aug 2011 02:15:10 GMT
```

```
Content-Type: application/json
Content-Length: 4254
Cache-Control: no-cache
[
    {
        "name":"rabbit@Phantome",
        "type":"disc",
        "running":true,
        ...
        "mem_used":31537360,
        "mem_limit":1675968512,
        "mem_alarm":false,
...
```

The dictionary for each node contains statistics and configuration elements for that node. For example, you can see that the node `rabbit@Phantome` is a `disc` node and is using `31537360` bytes (30 MB) of RAM (mem_used). If you were using a standalone Rabbit server you could also query `/api/nodes` for information about that server, with the only difference being you'd get a single node dictionary instead of multiple dictionaries for the nodes in a cluster. With this basic knowledge of what to expect in the `/api/nodes` response, you're ready to start building your cluster health check. Since the health check you're basing on `/api/nodes` is going to monitor both node membership and memory usage, your check first needs to know which cluster members it should expect and what memory levels you consider warranting a warning or critical status. To acquire these settings you'll add three new arguments (node list, RAM usage warning threshold, RAM usage critical threshold) to the server, port, and credentials arguments you normally expect:

```
server, port = sys.argv[1].split(":")
username = sys.argv[2]
password = sys.argv[3]
node_list = sys.argv[4].split(",")
mem_critical = int(sys.argv[5])
mem_warning = int(sys.argv[6])
```

The node list argument is special in that the check will expect it to be a comma-delimited list of nodes (such as `rabbit@node1,rabbit@node2`). This will let users pass the node list as a single argument rather than multiple arguments that are more difficult to parse. With the check's configuration settings acquired, you're ready to make the connection to the API server in the following listing and post your request to `/api/nodes`.

Listing 10.6   cluster_health_check.py: posting the request to `/api/nodes`

```
conn = httplib.HTTPConnection(server, port)          ◁——❶ Connect to server

path = "/api/nodes"                                   ◁——❷ Build API path
method = "GET"

credentials = base64.b64encode("%s:%s" % (username, password))    ◁—— Issue API
try:                                                                  ❸ request
```

```
conn.request(method, path, "",
             {"Content-Type" : "application/json",
              "Authorization" : "Basic " + credentials})
except socket.error:
    print "UNKNOWN: Could not connect to %s:%s" % (server, port)
    exit(EXIT_UNKNOWN)

response = conn.getresponse()

if response.status > 299:
    print "UNKNOWN: Unexpected API error: %s" % response.read()
    exit(EXIT_UNKNOWN)
```

As with the previous API-based health checks, you connect to the API server over HTTP ❶ and send credentials via a Base64-encoded header ❸. The only difference is that for this health check you're posting to the /api/nodes endpoint ❷. With the request sent, you're ready to start processing the API server's response in the next listing. Since you need to check both the node membership for missing members as well as the RAM usage of each of the nodes, you'll make two passes over the array of node dictionaries containing the statistics and configurations.

Listing 10.7   cluster_health_check.py: processing the node listing

```
response = json.loads(response.read())                          ⮜── ❶ Parse API response

for node in response:                                           ⮜──┐  Cluster missing
    if node["name"] in node_list and node["running"] != False:     │  nodes, return
        node_list.remove(node["name"])                          ❷ ─┘  warning

if len(node_list):
    print "WARNING: Cluster missing nodes: %s" % str(node_list)     ❸ Node used
    exit(EXIT_WARNING)                                                 memory
                                                                       over limit
for node in response:                                           ⮜──
    if node["mem_used"] > mem_critical:
        print "CRITICAL: Node %s memory usage is %d." % \
        (node["name"], node["mem_used"])
        exit(EXIT_CRITICAL)
    elif node["mem_used"] > mem_warning:                            All nodes ❹
        print "WARNING: Node %s memory usage is %d." % \        present, used
                (node["name"], node["mem_used"])                     memory
        exit(EXIT_WARNING)                                       below limit
print "OK: %d nodes. All memory usage below %d." % (len(response),   ⮜──
                                            mem_warning)
exit(EXIT_OK)
```

After decoding the JSON array of node dictionaries to their native Python equivalents ❶, you try to match the node name element in each dictionary ❷ to the list of expected member nodes that were passed on the command line. As you iterate through the node dictionaries, if the name element in that dictionary matches an expected node name (and that node is notated as running), you remove that name from the list of expected nodes. The result is that if all of the expected member nodes are present, your list of expected nodes will be empty when you're done iterating through the node dictionaries. On the other hand, if your list of expected node names has any entries still in it, you know that those nodes weren't present or weren't running according to /api/nodes. If your check determines that nodes are missing from the cluster, then you set the exit code to EXIT_WARNING and exit without any further analysis. The reason you set the status to warning is because a missing cluster node degrades the performance of the cluster but doesn't necessarily prevent the cluster from doing its work. If you feel a missing cluster node is more serious, set the exit code to EXIT_CRITICAL instead.

Once you've verified that all of the expected nodes are present in the cluster, you then iterate through each node dictionary again to evaluate how much RAM each node is using ❸. If the mem_used element in any node dictionary is greater than the critical RAM usage threshold set via the command line, you exit with the status code EXIT_CRITICAL and output a human-readable message indicating the affected node's current RAM usage in bytes. If the node's mem_used element doesn't exceed the critical threshold, but does exceed the warning threshold for RAM usage, you instead exit with the EXIT_WARNING status code but still output the affected node's current RAM usage. Finally, if all of the expected cluster members are present and none of them exceed the warning or critical RAM usage thresholds, you exit with the EXIT_OK status code ❹ and output that all of the nodes' RAM usage is below the warning threshold number. Let's give your health check a quick run and see what happens:

```
$ python cluster_health_check.py localhost:55672 guest guest \
  rabbit@Phantome,rabbit2@Phantome 34000000 33000000
OK: 2 nodes. All memory usage below 33000000.
$ echo $?
0
```

Great, so your health check has confirmed that both rabbit@Phantome and rabbit2@Phantome nodes are members of the cluster, and that the RAM usage of both is below the critical (34 MB) and warning (33 MB) thresholds. But let's see how your check handles one of the cluster nodes disappearing:

```
$ rabbitmqctl -n rabbit2@Phantome stop_app
Stopping node rabbit2@Phantome ...
...done.
$ python cluster_health_check.py localhost:55672 guest guest \
  rabbit@Phantome,rabbit2@Phantome 34000000 33000000
WARNING: Cluster missing nodes: ['rabbit2@Phantome']
$ echo $?
1
```

So far, so good; your health check not only detects that an expected cluster mode is missing from the cluster, it correctly tells you which node is missing. Finally, you need to make sure your check correctly detects nodes crossing both the warning and critical RAM thresholds that you set:

```
$ python cluster_health_check.py localhost:55672 guest guest \
  rabbit@Phantome,rabbit2@Phantome 32000000 31000000
WARNING: Node rabbit2@Phantome memory usage is 31785552.
```

```
$ echo $?
1
$ python cluster_health_check.py localhost:55672 guest guest \
  rabbit@Phantome,rabbit2@Phantome 31000000 30000000
CRITICAL: Node rabbit2@Phantome memory usage is 31834792.
$ echo $?
2
```

By switching critical/warning RAM thresholds between 32 MB/31 MB and 31 MB/30 MB, you can see that your new check correctly detects and reports when RabbitMQ is using more RAM than it should. You now have a complete set of Rabbit-facing health checks that can let you know not only if your RabbitMQ servers individually become unavailable, but can also warn you if your Rabbit clusters are missing members or if any of those members are nearing RAM exhaustion. But what if the issue isn't the health of Rabbit, but whether your apps are properly consuming the messages they're supposed to? Your cluster health check can let you know about RAM exhaustion, but if the problem is that your dog walking app isn't properly consuming orders out of an order queue, wouldn't it be nice to know that before RAM exhaustion becomes an issue? If your message volume (or size) is low, monitoring how many messages are in a particular queue can be even more important because the message build-up may go completely unnoticed until a customer complains that their order hasn't been processed. With that in mind it's time to look at how to build health checks that can let you know when your consumers stop consuming.

10.2 *Making sure consumers are consuming*

Up to this point, we've primarily been concerned with making sure your RabbitMQ servers are running, able to route messages, and clustered properly. But we haven't talked about one of the few downsides to using messaging: it becomes harder to monitor your consumers. Let's take the dog walking site as an example. A key part of the site is the daemon that runs continuously behind the scenes to process orders recorded by the user-facing web app. If you didn't have messaging, it's likely you'd design the order processing daemon as a server app that communicates over HTTP. After collecting order information from a customer, your web app would connect to the server port the order processing app is listening on and, once connected, would transmit the order. As we've discussed before, the major disadvantage to this approach is that the web app can't get back to taking another order until the order processing app confirms custody of the order, usually after processing it. The decoupling of front-end web app from backend order processor is a huge benefit of using messaging, but the question becomes how you monitor that the order processor is functioning. When it comes to monitoring them, server-type apps that accept TCP connections are straightforward to monitor. Once you convert that app to use messaging, you can no longer just connect to the server app's listener port to make sure it's up and able to process traffic. There's no port to connect to!

Fear not! You can still monitor your order processing app that uses messaging; you just have to think differently about what to monitor. The natural side effect of any consumer not being able to consume messages and process them is that messages build up in the queues supplying the consumers. You may remember earlier in the book we encouraged writing consumers so that they don't acknowledge messages they've received until they've successfully finished processing them. One of the reasons we encouraged this approach (besides ensuring your messages don't get black-holed), is that if your consumer is continually crashing when processing messages, those messages will build up in the queues and a health check can then trigger an alert. So as you may have guessed by now, the way you'll monitor whether your consumers are functioning properly is by monitoring the message count in a queue and triggering an alert when that count crosses the warning or critical threshold you set.

As with the ping health checks you wrote earlier, there are two ways you can monitor queue message counts:

1 Use the AMQP `queue_declare()` command with the `passive=True` argument to redeclare an existing queue. When you declare a queue in AMQP, the result from the command contains the queue message count if the `passive` argument is set to `True`.

2 Leverage our old friend the Rabbit management API to pull the statistics on the queue, among which is the current queue message count.

After you've learned how to build each version of the queue count check (and the benefits of each approach), we'll look at how you can analyze your messaging traffic to figure out what the warning and critical thresholds should be for each of the queues your apps use. Without further ado, let's dive into using AMQP to monitor the message counts in your queues.

10.2.1 Monitoring queue levels through AMQP

One question you might be asking yourself is, "Why are we using AMQP for this? Wouldn't the API provide more detail?" In short, yes, the API provides a lot more detail into the number of messages that are waiting to be consumed versus the number of messages that have been delivered to a consumer but have yet to be acknowledged. Using AMQP to monitor message counts will only show you the aggregate number of messages in the queue with no differentiation between unconsumed and unacknowledged messages. But if you're using an older version of RabbitMQ that doesn't work with the Management plugin, or if for technical/security reasons you can't install the Management plugin, then using AMQP to monitor message counts is your only option. Given the choice between not monitoring your queues or using an AMQP-based check to do so, it's not much of a choice if the reliability of your applications matters.

In common with the AMQP-based ping health check you've already written, your AMQP queue count check will expect server, port, vhost, and credential arguments on the command line. It will also need additional arguments so that it will know which queue to monitor and at what thresholds a warning or critical status should be returned:

```
server, port = sys.argv[1].split(":")
vhost = sys.argv[2]
username = sys.argv[3]
password = sys.argv[4]
queue_name = sys.argv[5]
max_critical = int(sys.argv[6])
max_warn = int(sys.argv[7])
```

Your new health check will also build its connection to Rabbit identically to the AMQP ping check. But once connected, it will issue `channel.queue_declare` for the specified queue to get the current message count:

```
creds_broker = pika.PlainCredentials(username, password)
conn_params = pika.ConnectionParameters(server,
                                        virtual_host = vhost,
                                        credentials = creds_broker)
try:
    conn_broker = pika.BlockingConnection(conn_params)
    channel = conn_broker.channel()
except socket.timeout:
    print "Unknown: Could not connect to %s:%s!" % (server, port)
    exit(EXIT_UNKNOWN)

try:
    response = channel.queue_declare(queue=queue_name,
                                     passive=True)
except pika.exceptions.AMQPChannelError:
    print "CRITICAL: Queue %s does not exist." % queue_name
    exit(EXIT_CRITICAL)
```

Contained within the `response` object is the current message count for the monitored queue. But before we look at how to access that message count, it's important to note the `passive=True` argument passed to `queue_declare`. The `passive` argument tells RabbitMQ you don't want to actually declare the queue; you want to know whether it exists. With `passive` set to `True`, `queue_declare` will raise an exception if the queue doesn't exist, and will return the current message count in the queue if it does. It's crucial to make sure the `passive` argument is included not only because it's the only way to return the queue message count, but also because without it the check will *actually* try to declare the queue. Once the passive `queue_declare` operation completes, you're left with the `response` object, inside of which the message count is buried. To access that message count, you reference the `.method.message_count` attribute as in the following listing.

> **Listing 10.8   amqp_queue_count_check.py: validating the queue message count**

```
if response.method.message_count >= max_critical:
    print "CRITICAL: Queue %s message count: %d" % \
          (queue_name, response.method.message_count)
    exit(EXIT_CRITICAL)

if response.method.message_count >= max_warn:
    print "WARN: Queue %s message count: %d" % \
```

❶ Message count above critical limit

❷ Message count above warning

```
             (queue_name, response.method.message_count)
     exit(EXIT_WARNING)

print "OK: Queue %s message count: %d" % \
     (queue_name, response.method.message_count)
exit(EXIT_OK)
```

❸ Connection OK, return OK

The `message_count` attribute is an integer so it's simple to compare against the check's message count thresholds. If `message_count` is greater than the critical threshold ❶, exit with an `EXIT_CRITICAL` status code, and if it's not over the critical threshold but *is* over the warning threshold, exit ❷ with an `EXIT_WARNING` status code. On the other hand, if `message_count` exceeds neither the critical nor warning thresholds, you set the status code to `EXIT_OK` ❸ and quit. Other than the code to set up the AMQP connection to Rabbit, this health check is simple.

To test out this check, first you'll use the Rabbit management web UI covered in chapter 8 to create a queue called `my_queue`, as illustrated in figure 10.2.

With the queue created, next you'll click on the Exchanges tab in the management web UI and then click on (`AMQP default`) in the resulting listing. You use the (`AMQP default`) exchange because publishing your test message into this exchange with `my_queue` as the routing key will automatically route the message to `my_queue` without

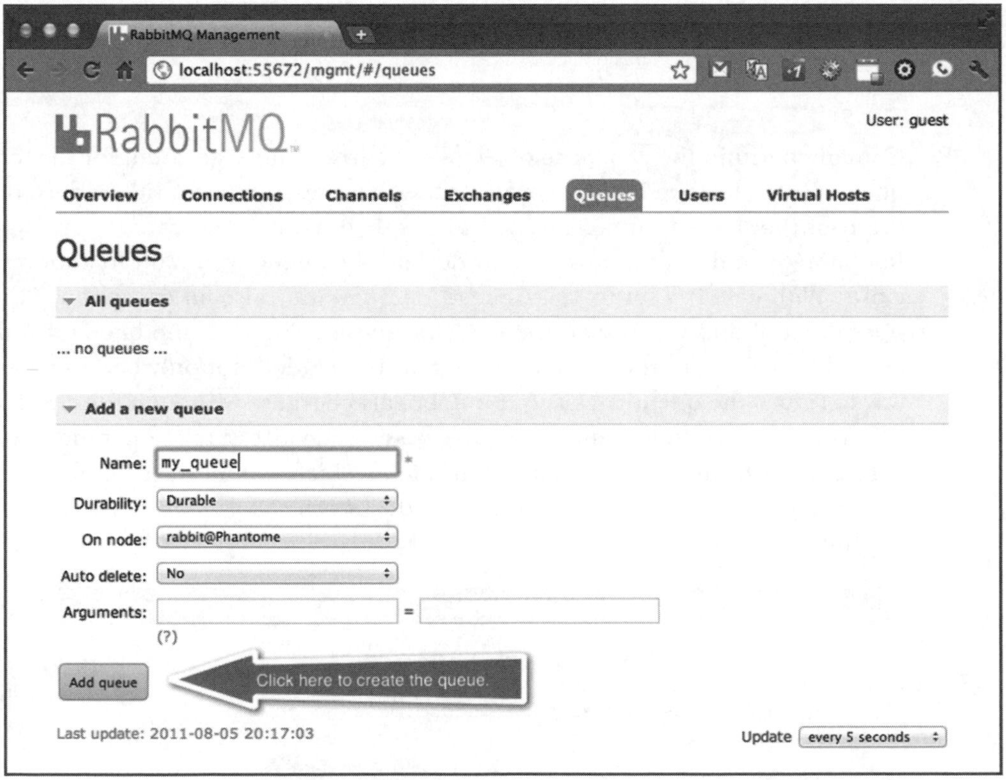

Figure 10.2   Create `my_queue`

setting up explicit bindings. Using the Publish Message controls on the (AMQP default) page in the management web UI, publish a message with the payload Any payload will do. and the routing key my_queue. After you receive the notice Message published, click Publish Message one more time to put a second copy of the message into my_queue, as in figure 10.3.

You should now have two messages waiting in my_queue, so let's run your health check to find out if it sees them:

```
$ python amqp_queue_count_check.py localhost:5672 / guest \
  guest my_queue 4 3
OK: Queue my_queue message count: 2
$ echo $?
0
```

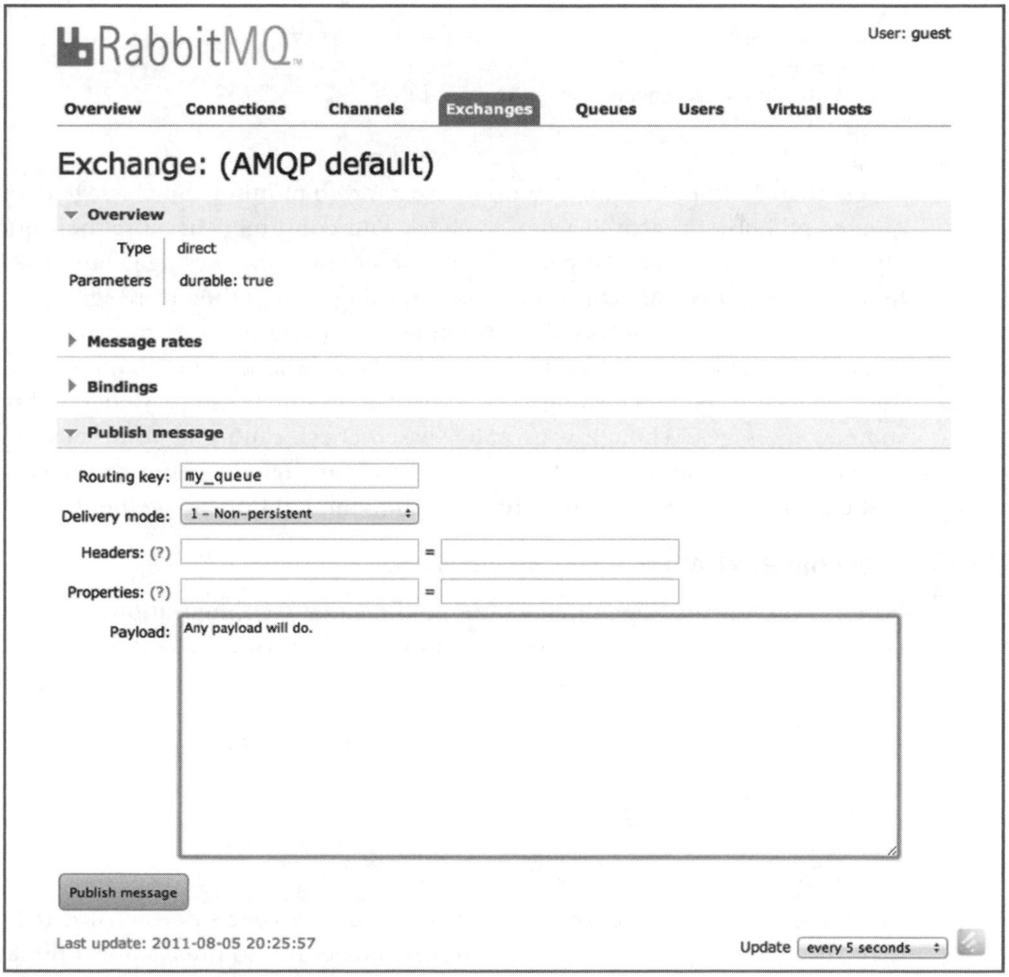

Figure 10.3   Publish test message into my_queue.

You told the health check to consider four or more messages a critical status and three or more a warning. As a result, the check returned an OK status and told you correctly that there are two messages in my_queue. Let's change the critical and warning thresholds to three and two messages respectively, and run the check again:

```
$ python amqp_queue_count_check.py localhost:5672 / guest \
  guest my_queue 3 2
WARN: Queue my_queue message count: 2
$ echo $?
1
```

As it should, your health check now returns a warning because two messages is the new warning threshold for the queue message count, but you haven't exceeded the three-message critical threshold. If you reduce the critical and warning thresholds again, but to two and one messages this time, the check should now return a critical status:

```
$ python amqp_queue_count_check.py localhost:5672 / guest \
  guest my_queue 2 1
CRITICAL: Queue my_queue message count: 2
$ echo $?
2
```

In less than 50 lines of code, you now have a way to monitor the message count in any queue and know proactively when to check your consumers because their queue message count has grown to dangerous levels. Sometimes, the message count has built too high not because your consumers are crashing, but rather the high queue count might be due to a bug where the consumers don't acknowledge messages they've successfully processed. Wouldn't it be helpful to know whether the high message count is due to unconsumed (crashing consumers) or simply unacknowledged (buggy consumers) messages? Though your AMQP-based check can't give you that information, the Rabbit API definitely can. Let's see how you can create a better queue count check that can answer those questions through using the Rabbit Management API.

10.2.2 Using the REST API to watch queue levels

When you built your health check to monitor queue configurations via the API, you may remember that there were statistics sprinkled in with the configuration information returned by /api/queues/<vhost>/<queue_name>. Among those was the number of messages currently in the queue:

```
...
"messages_ready":0,
"messages_unacknowledged":0,
"messages":0,
...
```

But the output from /api/queues/<vhost>/<queue_name> doesn't just tell you how many total messages (messages) are in the queue. It also breaks down the aggregate message count into unconsumed messages (messages_ready) and unacknowledged messages (messages_unacknowledged). This can be useful information to have. For example, let's say your dog walking order app gets temporary spikes of orders every day after your ad comes on during *The Dog Whisperer*. During the period of time after the ad, your order queues show a 10x increase in message counts. With the AMQP health check this would definitely exceed your critical threshold and would trigger a false positive alert every day. On the other hand, if you check the message counts using the API, you can see that the 10x increase is restricted to messages_ready (unconsumed messages). By creating a new message count health check using the API, you could set a much higher critical threshold for unconsumed messages while still maintaining a low threshold for unacknowledged messages. This would let you eliminate false alarms on unconsumed message counts, while still being notified quickly of bugs in your consumers that manifest as elevated unacknowledged message counts.

As with every health check so far, first you need to acquire the RabbitMQ connection and authentication information from the command line. But in addition you also need to acquire the name of the queue to monitor as well as the critical and warning thresholds for both unconsumed (ready) and unacknowledged message counts:

```
server, port = sys.argv[1].split(":")
vhost = sys.argv[2]
username = sys.argv[3]
password = sys.argv[4]
queue_name = sys.argv[5]
max_unack_critical = int(sys.argv[6])
max_unack_warn = int(sys.argv[7])
max_ready_critical = int(sys.argv[8])
max_ready_warn = int(sys.argv[9])
```

With the settings for the health check in hand, you're ready to connect to the API server. You'll use the same connection code as your previous API-based health checks, with the exception that this time you'll connect to the /api/queues/<vhost>/ <queue_name> endpoint:

```
conn = httplib.HTTPConnection(server, port)
path = "/api/queues/%s/%s" % (urllib.quote(vhost, safe=""),
                              queue_name)
method = "GET"
credentials = base64.b64encode("%s:%s" % (username, password))
try:
    conn.request(method, path, "",
                 {"Content-Type" : "application/json",
                  "Authorization" : "Basic " + credentials})
except socket.error:
    print "UNKNOWN: Could not connect to %s:%s" % (server, port)
    exit(EXIT_UNKNOWN)
response = conn.getresponse()
if response.status > 299:
    print "UNKNOWN: Unexpected API error: %s" % response.read()
    exit(EXIT_UNKNOWN)
```

Assuming that the API connection was successful, and your request didn't generate an HTTP error, you can now analyze the response to determine the current message count levels for the queue. After JSON-decoding the response, you'll extract the messages_unacknowledged and messages_ready elements from the response dictionary:

```
resp_payload = json.loads(response.read())
msg_cnt_unack = resp_payload["messages_unacknowledged"]
msg_cnt_ready = resp_payload["messages_ready"]
msg_cnt_total = resp_payload["messages"]
```

At last, with the unconsumed (ready) and unacknowledged message counts extracted, you're able to compare them against the supplied thresholds in the following listing.

Listing 10.9   api_queue_count_check.py: examine message counts

```
if msg_cnt_unack >= max_unack_critical:
    print "CRITICAL: %s - %d unack'd messages." % (queue_name,
                                            msg_cnt_unack)
    exit(EXIT_CRITICAL)
elif msg_cnt_unack >= max_unack_warn:
    print "WARN: %s - %d unack'd messages." % (queue_name,
                                        msg_cnt_unack)
    exit(EXIT_WARNING)

if msg_cnt_ready >= max_ready_critical:
    print "CRITICAL: %s - %d unconsumed messages." % (queue_name,
                                            msg_cnt_ready)
    exit(EXIT_CRITICAL)
elif msg_cnt_ready >= max_ready_warn:
    print "WARN: %s - %d unconsumed messages." % (queue_name,
                                        msg_cnt_ready)
    exit(EXIT_WARNING)

print "OK: %s - %d in-flight messages. %dB used memory." % \
    (queue_name, msg_cnt_total, resp_payload["memory"])
exit(EXIT_OK)
```

❶ Consumed but unacknowledged message count above thresholds

❷ Ready-to-be-consumed message count above thresholds

❸ Message counts below thresholds, return OK

The first thing to check is whether the unacknowledged message count has exceeded critical or warning levels ❶. If it has, you set the status exit code to EXIT_CRITICAL or EXIT_WARNING (depending on which threshold it exceeded), and output the number of unacknowledged messages currently in the queue. Providing that none of the unacknowledged message count thresholds have been exceeded, you next analyze the unconsumed (ready) message counts ❷. Similarly, if either the critical or warning thresholds for unconsumed messages have been exceeded, you again set the status exit code to EXIT_CRITICAL or EXIT_WARNING and then output the number of *unconsumed* messages. Finally, if neither the unconsumed nor unacknowledged message counts are above their critical or warning thresholds, you set the status exit code to EXIT_OK to let Nagios know everything is healthy ❸ and then output the total (unconsumed + unacknowledged) number of messages in the queue along with the amount of RAM the queue is currently consuming.

Though it's complicated to test the unacknowledged message thresholds, you should be able to use the messages still sitting in my_queue from testing the AMQP-based message count check to verify your new API-based version of the check. If you set the unconsumed critical/warning thresholds to two and one messages respectively, your API message count check should correctly detect an excessive number of unconsumed (ready) messages:

```
$ python api_queue_count_check.py localhost:55672 / guest \
  guest my_queue 2 1 2 1
CRITICAL: my_queue - 2 unconsumed messages.
$ echo $?
2
```

If you raise the critical/warning unconsumed thresholds to four and three messages respectively, your check should now consider the unconsumed message count in the queue healthy again:

```
$ python api_queue_count_check.py localhost:55672 / guest \
  guest my_queue 4 3 4 3
OK: my_queue - 2 in-flight messages. 9800B used memory.
$ echo $?
0
```

As it should, the check reports that you have a total of two messages in the queue, and that the queue is consuming 9800 bytes of memory (the exact memory usage will vary). You now have a health check that can differentiate between an excessive number of unacknowledged versus unconsumed messages in your queues. That will help you more quickly determine whether your queue counts are indicating an increased load or simply defects in your apps. The question remains: how do you determine baseline message counts for your queues so that you can set the critical and warning thresholds on your health checks?

10.2.3 *Rules of thumb for establishing a queue count baseline*

There are a number of approaches for determining what should be considered critical and warning thresholds for queue message counts. If you're converting an existing application to use messaging, the logs for that application can provide a reasonably accurate source of information. For example, if your application processes credit card orders, it's highly likely you already log each order with a timestamp to a database. It's generally a good rule of thumb to use those logs to see how many orders you process in a 10-second interval. This number should generally be your warning threshold because the health check is taking a snapshot of the queue message counts when it runs, and that snapshot generally represents a 1-second or shorter period of time. It should be unusual for the number of messages in the queue at any given time to exceed the number of messages/orders processed over 10 seconds. Similarly, set the critical threshold at the number of orders/messages processed in 20 seconds. Keep in mind that this approach is approximate and you need to monitor the actual queue levels to make sure these thresholds are correct for your environment.

The best way to determine the warning and critical message count thresholds for your environment is to monitor the queues with a graphing monitoring system like Cacti or Graphite. By modifying the message count checks to work with these systems, they can graph the actual message counts in your queues by sampling the counts at regular intervals. The resulting graphs will tell you almost exactly what your actual average unconsumed and unacknowledged message counts are. With those numbers in hand, add 20% to get your warning threshold and 100% to get your critical threshold. Generally speaking, anything between 20% and 99% above normal could be regular fluctuations. But 100% or more above normal definitely is worth looking into as a sign that something has gone awry.

10.3 *Summary*

When we started you may have had a robust RabbitMQ architecture built, but you had no way to monitor it to ensure it was truly reliable. Now you've built health check programs that can not only query a RabbitMQ server to make sure it's able to process AMQP commands, but which can also monitor actual message count levels to determine the health of the programs that are consuming from your queues. In addition, you can also keep an eye on the configuration of your queues to make sure human error doesn't change your queues from durable to nondurable and set you up for disaster during the next server failure. Monitoring RabbitMQ is a vital part of ensuring it's running properly and is efficiently powering your applications. But once you start monitoring RabbitMQ, those health checks can open your eyes to inefficiencies and issues that can be corrected by tuning Rabbit. With that in mind it's time you took a look at ways to analyze RabbitMQ's performance and behavior so you can maximize both in your applications.

11

Supercharging and securing your Rabbit

This chapter covers

- Exchange, queue, and bindings memory footprint
- Message durability and disk I/O
- SSL connections with RabbitMQ
- Setting up a private key infrastructure

In previous chapters you've seen how to design your architectures around messaging. You've seen many ways for implementing several messaging patterns using the various AMQP building blocks like exchanges, queues, and bindings. Depending on the problem at hand, you chose a particular combination of those items to bring about a solution. If you needed to distribute logs across many machines, you followed a *pub-sub* pattern using *topic* or *fanout* exchanges; if you needed point-to-point communication, then you use direct exchanges, and so on. In this chapter we'll review the performance characteristics of these design decisions. You'll see the advantages and disadvantages of using direct exchanges over topic exchanges; the minimum memory footprint an exchange, queue, or binding has; what happens when you have hundreds of bindings to a topic exchange in contrast with a fanout exchange, and more. Also you may have questions like, when is a message written to disk? How does the server cope with many *in-memory* queues? Our goal is to provide the information necessary to make decisions when it comes to capacity planning. We'll do so by analyzing the path that a message takes while traveling from the producer to the consumer, depending on the several AMQP options.

After we've talked about performance, you'll see how to secure your RabbitMQ installation and more specifically how to use SSL to establish trusted communications with the broker. We'll cover the configuration aspects to enable SSL listeners in RabbitMQ, how to generate the SSL certificates, and how to connect to the broker using SSL.

Let's move to the first section where you'll see what affects the speed of messaging delivery from an AMQP point of view.

11.1   *The need for speed*

Several factors can modify the speed at which RabbitMQ delivers messages, depending on the hardware and software configuration. On the hardware side, you have factors like network configuration, disk arrangement, number of cores, and so on. On the software level, you can configure several AMQP parameters like message durability, routing algorithm, number of bindings, and message acknowledgment strategy. Since the first totally depend on your setup, we won't cover them in this chapter. We'll focus on the AMQP specifics and on what RabbitMQ does about them.

Let's start by reviewing how message *durability* and message *acknowledgment* affect the speed of message delivery.

11.1.1   *Message durability*

When discussing software performance, everything has to be taken with a grain of salt or even two. Why? Because whatever decision you make has to take into account the context in which it's applied. For every decision you make there are pros and cons. For example, you can speed up message delivery for system logs which you might not even need to persist to disk, but when it comes to order processing for shopping carts you'd better make sure nothing is lost in the process. So although you could send logs as nonpersistent messages and consume them without acknowledgment, you can't afford such luxury when customer money is in play. So whenever you deal with these kinds of performance tweaks, you have to think of the trade-offs you're making.

When you publish messages, you have to decide whether it's okay to lose any of them. If it's okay that a couple of messages out of thousands can be lost (for whatever reason), then you may publish them with the property delivery-mode set to 1, which means *nonpersistent*. Usually you'd deliver messages as *persistent* by setting the delivery-mode to 2, but at the cost of forcing the broker to write them to disk. For example, on a Mac, RabbitMQ can easily deliver up to 12,000 messages per second. If you turn on message persistence, then that number drops to around 4,000 message deliveries per second. The number of messages is still high but has dropped considerably.

How do you manage this setting? You have to specify it as part of the message properties for every message that you publish to the server. The following code snippet is an example of how to create a nonpersistent message with the PHP library:

```
$msg = new AMQPMessage("Test Message", array('delivery_mode' => 1));
```

Another setting that will affect messaging speed is message acknowledgment. Let's take a look at it.

11.1.2 Message acknowledgment

In the previous section we looked at the settings that involve message publication; now it's time to see how you can configure during message consumption. One setting that will speed up message delivery is the `no-ack` flag that you can specify during queue subscription time. If set to true, the server will automatically dequeue the message after it's sent to the client. If for some reason the connection is lost or your client application dies, the message will be lost forever.

The speed advantage of subscribing to a queue with `no-ack` set to true comes from the fact that you don't need to send an acknowledgment back to the server after you process the message, which will speed up your consumers. On the server side, things will be simplified since RabbitMQ can forget about your message after it's delivered. Here's a Python snippet showing how to consume from a queue with `no-ack` set to true:

```
channel.basic_consume( critical_notify,
                       queue="critical",
                       no_ack=True,
                       consumer_tag="critical")
```

You'll consume from the `critical` queue using `critical` as the consumer tag as well. For every message that you receive, the callback `critical_notify` will be called. Now it's time to see what happens during message routing. In the next section we'll look at each of the main routing algorithms used by RabbitMQ.

11.1.3 Routing algorithm and bindings

In this book we've discussed three kinds of exchanges: direct, fanout, and topic. You know that each exchange type implies a particular routing algorithm that's implemented by the server. When the exchange is required to route a message, it'll select the queues where the message should go based on the message routing key and the bindings it holds to queues. The selection process will vary according to the exchange type, since each exchange type will treat the message routing key differently.

On the server side, exchanges and bindings are record entries in Mnesia, which means that when RabbitMQ is matching the message routing key, what it's doing is trying to find a binding that corresponds to that routing key. Mnesia is a highly performant database whose storage is based on Erlang's ETS and DETS tables.[1] ETS stands for *Erlang term storage* and is an in-memory storage for data, whereas DETS is the disk-based counterpart. The advantage of using Mnesia over plain ETS function calls is that Mnesia can coordinate access to the tables in a cluster. So, for example, when you create an exchange on a clustered node, Mnesia will take care of replicating the information to all the other nodes in the cluster; the same can be done while adding

---

[1] More information about ETS can be found at http://erlang.org/doc/man/ets.html.

bindings, declaring queues, and so forth. Although Mnesia works great for maintaining consistency, the extra layer on top of ETS can slow things down when you need to perform certain kind of queries like performing a routing key match. That part of the process has been optimized for the *direct* and *fanout* exchanges so you don't have to suffer Mnesia coordination penalties. For those exchange types, bindings are stored in the `rabbit_route` table, which is of the `ordered_set` type. According to the documentation for ETS tables, access time for such tables is logarithmic in relation to the number of entries in the database. Also due to the nature of the `ordered_set` table type, the RabbitMQ developers were able to perform some interesting optimizations when selecting data from the table that allowed them to bypass Mnesia for these kinds of queries. This means that RabbitMQ routing tables have the consistency guarantees offered by Mnesia while keeping the data retrieval speed offered by plain ETS tables.

DIRECT AND FANOUT EXCHANGES

The difference between the direct exchange versus the fanout exchange is that the latter ignores the routing key when it comes to querying to the `rabbit_route` table. So although you can provide a routing key during queue binding to a fanout exchange, keep in mind that the routing key will be ignored when routing messages. The same thing happens when publishing messages with routing keys to fanout exchanges: the routing key is ignored.

TOPIC EXCHANGE

The case of the topic exchange is completely different because the stored routing information is more complex. Matching a message routing key goes beyond simple string comparison, since the routing key can contain several words separated by dots (`.`). For that reason, RabbitMQ implements a `trie` data structure where the binding keys patterns are stored in a format that allows for fast querying. This series of two blog posts explain in detail the implementation of the `topic` exchange and its performance characteristics: http://www.rabbitmq.com/blog/2010/09/14/very-fast-and-scalable-topic-routing-part-1/ and http://www.rabbitmq.com/blog/2011/03/28/very-fast-and-scalable-topic-routing-part-2/. In the second of those posts, you can see that the topic exchange implementation of RabbitMQ can match 1,000,000 topics against 2,000 patterns in about 11 seconds on a 2.3 GHz machine, which leaves the topic exchange *more* than usable for your everyday messaging scenarios. Keep in mind that, usually, bindings on topic exchanges use more memory than in direct or fanout exchanges.

Finding the message destination is one thing; delivering the messages is another. Let's see what happens after the exchange processes the message routing information.

11.1.4   *Delivering messages*

After the exchange has found where the message should be routed, it'll return a list of destinations to the `rabbit_router` and later proceed to deliver copies of the messages to each of the destinations (queues or exchanges). If you published your message with the `mandatory` and `immediate` flags set to false then this process can be done asynchronously, and the server will be faster from the client point of view.

Here is where things start to get tricky, so we represented this process in figure 11.1. If the queue where the message is being delivered is empty *and* a consumer is ready to receive a message, then the message goes straight to the consumer without even touching the queue. As you can guess, this greatly improves message delivery speeds. The next question to ask is whether the consumer is in `auto-ack` mode. If the consumer is subscribed using the `no-ack` flag set to true, then the message is forgotten by the server. If that's not the case then the message will be added to a `pending-acknowledgment` list to keep track of the message. The next question is whether the message is being routed to a durable queue and whether the message was published as persistent. If so, the message is written to disk but marked as *already delivered* so while the message is sitting in the queue, it won't be sent to another consumer.

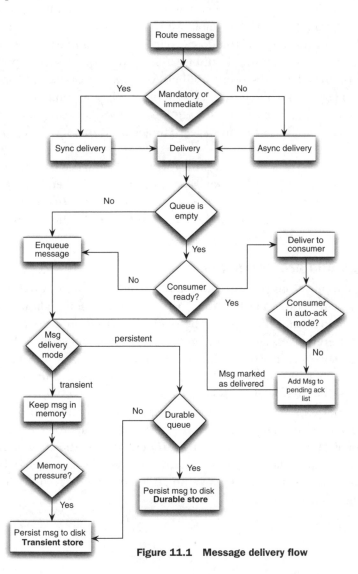

Figure 11.1   Message delivery flow

Now let's go back in time to the point when RabbitMQ checks whether the queue is empty. If the queue isn't empty, then the message is queued. If the message isn't persistent, then it's kept in memory only if there's enough memory to hold the message. If there's not enough memory, then the message will be written to disk to the transient store. In the case of persistent messages, they'll be written to disk and at the same time be kept in memory to speed up message delivery. If memory pressure occurs, then messages will get flushed to disk. By doing that, the server ensures message properties such as persistence while still delivering the messages as quickly as it can.

As you can see in figure 11.1, if the message is routed to a durable queue, then if it's written to disk, it'll go to the *durable store*; otherwise it'll go to the *transient store*. If RabbitMQ has to restart and recover durable queues, it only needs to go through the contents of the durable store, and can wipe out the transient store without worrying.

Something to keep in mind is that RabbitMQ is optimized to deliver messages as quickly as possible to consumers. If you do capacity planning and calculate your messages' ingress/egress rates, then you should try to keep your queues as empty as possible; though this isn't the latest discovery, it'll help you have a fast-paced broker. But if consumers start to lag behind and queues start to fill up, then at some point the memory alarm will fire on the server and it'll start to flush messages to disk no matter what properties were used to publish the messages. The lesson is to always keep an eye on your queue sizes.

In this section you saw how the different algorithms and message publish and subscribe settings can affect the overall system speed, and how a different flag setting like auto-ack mode can immensely affect the system performance. In the next section we'll look at the hard limits imposed on the RabbitMQ server by the hardware (RAM) and by the Erlang virtual machine itself.

11.2 Memory usage and process limits

When you design applications you usually have two basic constraints: what the chosen technology allows you to do, and what your current hardware setup allows you to do. In the previous section—and throughout the book—we've covered the first point by seeing how the different message routing and delivery algorithms affect design decisions. In this section we'll review some of the hard limits imposed by your hardware or by the Erlang virtual machine on RabbitMQ so you can plan ahead and see how much you should be able to scale up RabbitMQ in a single box. For example, one interesting metric to know about RabbitMQ is the memory required to create each of the AMQP components like queues, exchanges, and bindings. Another value to take into account is the number of Erlang processes that RabbitMQ creates for those elements, since there's a hard limit in the Erlang VM to how many processes you can create. Let's look at each of those elements in detail so you can start from solid ground when doing capacity planning calculations.

11.2.1 Memory usage

The first question to ask is what happens when you declare a queue. When you declare a queue, RabbitMQ will add several entries into various Mnesia tables, depending on the kind of queue. If the queue is declared with `durable` set to true, then there will be an entry for your queue in the tables `rabbit_queue` and `rabbit_durable_queue`. In the case of a nondurable queue, there will be an entry for it only in the `rabbit_queue` table. An entry in any of those tables will take approximately 29 words of memory. So what does that mean? In

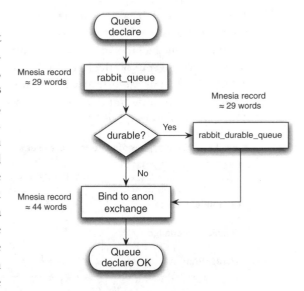

Figure 11.2   Queue declare process

Erlang the size of a `word` will depend on your system. For a 32-bit computer, the `wordsize` will be 4 bytes and in a 64-bit architecture a word will take 8 bytes. We said *approximately 29 words* because the size of the record will depend also on the name of the queue you declared. This process is shown in figure 11.2.

According to the AMQP specification, every queue is bound to the *anonymous exchange*, which means that after a queue declare there will also be an entry in the `rabbit_route` table that keeps tracks of the bindings between queues and exchanges. There might be entries in another Mnesia tables, which we'll come back to later when we take a look at bindings. An entry on the `rabbit_route` table will take approximately 44 words of memory.

All this means that when you declare a queue, you'll use 29 words of memory for the entry on the `rabbit_queue` table plus 44 words of memory for the entry on the `rabbit_route` table. If the queue is `durable`, then you'll have a 29-word entry on the `rabbit_durable_queue` table as well. Apart from that you'll also have more entries on the routing tables, as you'll soon see. Table 11.1 explains this in detail.

Table 11.1   Queue metadata memory usage

	rabbit_queue	rabbit_durable_queue
Durable queue	X	X
Transient queue	X	
Words/item	29	29

The *x* shows which tables will have new entries for a queue declare; you can also see the word size of each item stored in those tables.

When you declare an exchange, something similar happens, but in this case it's simpler. Whenever you declare a new exchange, RabbitMQ will create an entry on the `rabbit_exchange` table that will occupy approximately 29 words of memory. If the exchange is durable, an entry on the `rabbit_durable_exchange` will also be created. This can be seen in table 11.2.

Table 11.2   Exchange metadata memory usage

	rabbit_exchange	rabbit_durable_exchange
Durable exchange	X	X
Transient exchange	X	
Words/item	29	29

Now it's time to see what happens when you bind a queue to an exchange. In this case there are two situations: binding a queue to a direct or fanout exchange, or binding a queue to a topic exchange. The latter case is more complex to explain, so we'll analyze it last.

When a queue is bound to a direct or fanout exchange, RabbitMQ will create an entry in at least two Mnesia tables to keep track of the binding. Those tables are `rabbit_route` and `rabbit_reverse_route`. The size of those records are 44 words of memory. There are several combinations that will make RabbitMQ create entries on other tables. Those combinations depend on the durability properties of the queue and the exchange that participate in the binding. A durable queue bound to a transient exchange will also get a record entry on the `rabbit_semi_durable_route` table. Finally, when you bind a durable queue to a durable exchange, RabbitMQ will create an entry on the `rabbit_durable_route` table. Both those entries are 44 words of memory each. In table 11.3 you can see this in more detail.

The case of binding to a topic exchange has all the ingredients you've seen for bindings to direct and fanout exchanges, and also involves a couple more Mnesia tables: `rabbit_topic_trie_binding` and `rabbit_topic_trie_edge`. As the name of the table suggests, the binding itself will be stored in `rabbit_topic_trie_binding`. A record in that table will occupy approximately 45 words of memory. The number of parts in your topic pattern will determine the number of records inserted in the `rabbit_topic_trie_binding`. So a pattern like `a.b.c.d` will create four entries in that table with a size of 38 words of memory each.

With those numbers, you can do capacity planning for your messaging applications and determine the upper bound on RabbitMQ when it comes to RAM usage. As you can see, the footprint for queues, exchanges, and bindings is small when it comes to memory usage. As an example, you can see that on a 64-bit system, a durable queue

Table 11.3 Bindings metadata memory usage

	rabbit_route	rabbit _durable_route	rabbit _semi_durable_route	rabbit _reverse_route
Durable queue to durable exchange	X	X	X	X
Durable queue to transient exchange	X		X	X
Transient queue to transient exchange	X			X
Transient queue to durable exchange	X			X
Words/item	44	44	44	44

bound to a durable exchange will take 58 words of memory for the queue entries on the `rabbit_queue` and `rabbit_durable_queue` and 176 words for the respective entries on the `*_route` tables. That will make a total of 234 words of memory or, expressed in bytes, *234 words* times *8 bytes per word = 1872 bytes*.

Another factor that imposes a hard limit on RabbitMQ is the maximum number of Erlang processes per Erlang node. Let's look into that.

11.2.2 Erlang process count

The maximum number of Erlang processes that can be run in an Erlang node is specified when you start the node, which in this case happens when you launch RabbitMQ, for example by calling `./sbin/rabbitmq-server -detached`. The defaults set for RabbitMQ are 1048576 or 2^{20} processes per Erlang node, which should be more than enough.

Erlang applications create and destroy processes many times during their lifetime. For example, when RabbitMQ accepts a TCP connection to your AMQP client, an Erlang process will be spawned to manage that connection. At the same time, there are Erlang processes that handle the logic of the RabbitMQ message store. Other processes are there to monitor child processes to ensure they're kept alive, and so on. If you just start a RabbitMQ server, you'll have around 126 processes laying around, which is fairly low for a server like RabbitMQ. But what happens if you surpass the default limit of 2^{20}? Sadly, Erlang will crash and therefore RabbitMQ will crash too, which means you want to make sure that you set that number properly. Now 2^{20} processes is a lot and good enough for most users, but your mileage may vary. Let's see what events make that number increase so you know what to add to your capacity planning calculations.

The events you may produce as users of RabbitMQ that will increase the number of processes are new connections to the broker, new channel creations, and queue declares. A new connection will create four new processes and opening a new channel on that connection will create four new processes as well. The overhead per queue is minimal: just one process per queue. Table 11.4 shows it in a clear format.

As we said already, a limit of 2^{20} processes is more than enough in most cases; still, doing some math while planning your messaging

Table 11.4 Erlang process used by connections, channels, and queues

	Processes
New connection	4
New channel	4
Queue declare	1

architecture won't hurt anyone. Now that you have an idea of what's happening inside RabbitMQ for the different AMQP operations that you might perform, it's time to see how you can secure your RabbitMQ setup by enabling SSL.

11.3 SSL connections

When you work on a closed network inside a corporation where you deploy your applications, you can be almost 100% sure you can trust the parties involved. If *app_a* requests a connection to your RabbitMQ broker, you can easily assume that it is in fact *app_a* making the request. Most of the time there's no reason to suspect the request, but when you start to work with sensitive data like credit card information, you might need to restrict access to certain areas of your applications. Since you don't want to compromise such information, you need a way to establish encrypted connections with RabbitMQ in order to transmit data in a secure way. You can use SSL[2] as a protocol to transmit the data between messaging endpoints like consumers and producers. RabbitMQ comes with SSL support out of the box, so from your side you have to set up all the SSL machinery to use such infrastructure.

In this section we'll address how to establish secure connections to your RabbitMQ installations by using SSL. We'll use the OpenSSL library, which has support for most *nix-style operating systems as well as Windows. You can obtain more information about OpenSSL on its website at www.openssl.org/. OpenSSL and security itself are broad topics that we can't cover in detail in this chapter. If you want to get detailed information on how to secure your network with OpenSSL, we recommend that you consult the book *Network Security with OpenSSL* (Viega et al., 2002, O'Reilly Media).

In the following sections you'll see how to create an SSL Certificate Authority and from there create certificates for your clients and servers. Such a setup is often referred to as *public key infrastructure* or *PKI*. Finally, you'll use those certificates to establish an SSL connection with RabbitMQ.

11.3.1 SSL certificates

One way to exchange information in a secure way is to encrypt it using *public key cryptography*.[3] In this technique, the parties exchanging information have a private key and a public key that are mathematically related so they can be used to encrypt and decrypt

---

[2] *SSL* stands for *Secure Sockets Layer*. It's a cryptographic protocol that allows for secure network communications.

the information exchanged. Though the public key can be widely distributed, the private key must be kept, well, *private*. This technique uses asymmetric algorithms, so the key used to encrypt the message can't be used to decrypt it. If the user Bob wants to exchange data with Alice, then they exchange their respective public keys. When Alice sends data to Bob, she will encode the information using her private key and then Bob will decode the data using Alice's public key. Another use of public keys is to sign messages. The digital signature of the messages are computed based on the private key; in this way the receiver can assume that the message comes from the expected party by checking the signature against the sender's public key. Figure 11.3 depicts this process.

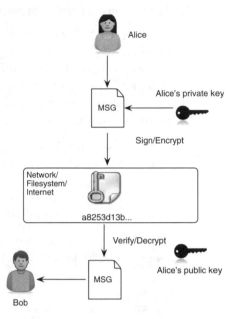

Figure 11.3 Public key encryption

Having the other party's public key is one thing. Knowing that the key actually belongs to this party is a different matter. To ensure that a key does belong to the assumed owner, the keys are exchanged together with *certificates* that prove the authenticity of the key. The certificates are emitted by trusted third parties that work as *certificate authorities* who take care of proving that the key belongs to its advertised owner. Though this may sound too complex, there's a nice analogy in the book *Network Security with OpenSSL* that compares the certificate with a passport. A passport not only has your picture but also includes some personal information about you that allows someone to certify that the picture actually belongs to whom it says it does. Of course you could have forged a passport in your basement trying to trick the authorities. To prevent that, your passport includes information about the issuing authorities from your government acting as the certificate authority for your passport. When you travel abroad, the immigration officers can identify you based on your passport and can prove its authenticity based on the watermark and other means added by your government.

To get a valid SSL certificate, you'll have to pay a trusted third-party company to issue one for you. You may want to do so if you plan to exchange data with the public, but if you just want to share data inside your organization, then you can set up your private certification authority which you implicitly trust. You'll use it to emit certificates that will be used by both RabbitMQ and its messaging clients to exchange data. In the following sections you'll learn how to set up your own certificate authority and from there you'll issue certificates for your clients and servers to be able to establish SSL connections between them.

---

[3] See the Wikipedia entry for more information on this topic: http://en.wikipedia.org/wiki/Public-key _cryptography.

11.3.2 Setting up a certificate authority

To set up your *certificate authority* you'll use the `openssl` command-line utility. This utility accepts plenty of options that are hard to remember. To make things easier, `openssl` can work with configuration files where you specify the options you want using key/value pairs. You can also track which parameters were used to generate your certificates by checking this configuration file. Let's start by creating the basic environment for your certificate authority (CA).

> **NOTE** As you already know, RabbitMQ runs on top of Erlang, so even before trying to use OpenSSL in your applications, you need to have support for it in Erlang. If you had OpenSSL installed before you built Erlang then you probably are all set to use it. If you don't have OpenSSL in your system then you'll have to install it and then reinstall Erlang with OpenSSL enabled.

You need to create a folder to hold your certificates plus the CA configuration files. Open a terminal window and then type the following commands:

```
$ mkdir rmqca
$ cd rmqca
$ mkdir certs private
$ chmod 700 private
```

First you created an `rmqca` folder to hold your files. We used the name *rmqca*, which stands for *RabbitMQ certificate authority*, but feel free to give a name that fits your organization. Once that folder is created, you then create a couple of folders: `certs` and `private`; the first will hold the certificates generated by your CA, whereas the second will hold the CA private key. Keep in mind that the CA private key *must not be disclosed to third parties*; therefore you `chmod` the private folder to be accessible only for your current user.

To be able to generate certificates, OpenSSL requires a couple more files. Since certificates created by one CA can't share the same serial number, you need to create a file where you can keep track of the last certificate's serial number. Every time you issue a new certificate, OpenSSL will take care of incrementing this number. OpenSSL expects the number to be in hexadecimal and to contain at least two digits, so when you first create such a file you have to pad the number by adding a zero to the left like this:

```
$ echo 01 > serial
```

The last file you need to create works like a database where OpenSSL will keep track of the certificates issued by your CA. We'll call this file `index.txt`; because you haven't created any certificates yet, this file will be empty. You can create it with the following command:

```
$ touch index.txt
```

Now that you have the basic environment to work with OpenSSL, you need to create your configuration file. This file will be used to provide default values to the various openssl commands that you need to run in order to create your certificate authority and to later emit certificates with it. As you'll see, the configuration is split into several sections for each of these commands, which makes it easier to follow. One of those commands is called ca and is used to set up a CA and a *certificate revocation list (CRL)*.[4] Let's create a file called openssl.conf inside the rmqca folder and then add the following content for the ca command section.

Listing 11.1 openssl.conf CA command configuration

```
[ ca ]                                          ←—❶ Section name
default_ca = rmqca

[ rmqca ]                                       ←—❷ CA configuration
dir = .
certificate = $dir/cacert.pem
database = $dir/index.txt
new_certs_dir = $dir/certs
private_key = $dir/private/cakey.pem
serial = $dir/serial

default_crl_days = 7                            ←—❸ Expiration configuration
default_days = 365
default_md = sha1

policy = rmqca_policy                           ←—❹ Policy configuration
x509_extensions = certificate_extensions

[ rmqca_policy ]
commonName = supplied
stateOrProvinceName = optional
countryName = optional
emailAddress = optional
organizationName = optional
organizationalUnitName = optional

[ certificate_extensions ]                      ←—❺ Extensions section
basicConstraints = CA:false
```

In this file you're providing default options for the ca command that you can still override on the command line when you invoke openssl. As you can see, the sections of the .conf file are marked by headers between a pair of square brackets ([]). The configuration file is a set of key/value pairs holding your configuration options. You start by declaring the ca section ❶ where you tell openssl that your default CA will be called rmqca. OpenSSL then will look for a section with that name from where it will load the remainder of the configuration options.

In the rmqca section ❷, you set up a variable called dir that points to the same directory where the .conf file is. That variable is referenced in the next few lines so you don't need to type the full path to your current folder every time. There you tell openssl that the certificate will be stored in the file cacert.pem in the same directory as the configuration file. Then you set the database to reside in index.txt. The

---

[4] Certificate revocation lists are used to inform clients when the certificates emitted by your CA have expired. Clients can download the list from the CA and then reject certificates that are revoked in your CRL.

certificates issued by your CA will be kept in the certs folder; your private key has to be taken from the private/cakey.pem file and the serial used to generate certificates will be the one stored in the file serial that you created before.

Then you need to configure the expiration time for your certificates ❸. There you say that your certificates will expire after a year, that you'll provide a CRL file every seven days, and that your certificates will be generated by using sha1[5] as the hash function.

The next part of the file configures your CA policy ❹ where you tell openssl which fields are mandatory in your certificates. For this CA, the commonName has to be provided, whereas the other fields like countryName or emailAddress are optional. (For more details, see http://www.openssl.org/docs/apps/ca.html#POLICY_FORMAT.) In that section, you specify which of the x509[6] extensions are supported by your CA, which in this case are specified under the certificate_extensions section of your config file ❺. There you set basicConstraints to CA:false. That basically means the certificates issued by your CA can't be used as certificate authorities themselves—they can't be used to sign and issue new certificates.

Now you need to configure the req command that's used to generate certificates. You'll add new sections to openssl.conf, where you'll provide new key/value pairs. Let's add the following content to the openssl.conf file.

Listing 11.2   openssl.conf req command configuration

```
[ req ]                                            ←❶ req configuration section
default_bits = 2048
default_keyfile = ./private/cakey.pem
default_md = sha1
prompt = yes
distinguished_name = root_ca_distinguished_name
x509_extensions = root_ca_extensions

[ root_ca_distinguished_name ]
commonName = hostname

[ root_ca_extensions ]                             ←❷ root extensions
basicConstraints = CA:true
keyUsage = keyCertSign, cRLSign

[ client_ca_extensions ]                           ←❸ client extensions
basicConstraints = CA:false
keyUsage = digitalSignature
extendedKeyUsage = 1.3.6.1.5.5.7.3.2

[ server_ca_extensions ]                           ←❹ server extensions
basicConstraints = CA:false
keyUsage = keyEncipherment
extendedKeyUsage = 1.3.6.1.5.5.7.3.1
```

In this section ❶ you start configuring the req command by specifying that you want to generate 2048-bit keys for your certificates. That's the minimum advised number to

---

[5] More information on SHA1 can be found at http://en.wikipedia.org/wiki/SHA-1.

[6] More information about the x509 extensions can be found at the OpenSSL website: http://www.openssl.org/docs/apps/x509.html.

consider your keys to be secure; your key will be written to the ./private/cakey.pem file and will use sha1 as the default hashing function. By setting prompt to yes, you tell the req command that it should prompt you whenever it needs to fill up the values specified under by distinguished_name. As you can see there, the distinguished _name will be taken from the next section called root_ca_distinguished_name where you set the hostname as the commonName.

Then you have the section where you provide some extensions for your root certificate ❷. In this case you set that the root certificate can be used to sign other certificates (that's the point of this whole setup). When you set up the client extensions ❸ you say that the client certificates can't be used as certificate authority themselves but can be used to sign the data they send back and forth. The extendedKeyUsage field has some particular set of numbers[7] that in this case indicates that the certificate can be used for client authentication. Finally comes the server extensions section ❹ where in this case you want certificates that are used for encrypting data and for authenticating the server. As you can see, you specify that information with a different set of values for the extendedKeyUsage key.

With those settings, you finished setting up your OpenSSL environment and are now ready to start creating certificates. Though this process was complex, you had to do it once, with the advantage that by keeping the configuration options in this file, you don't need to remember all the settings by heart. Let's move on to the next section to see how to create your own certificates.

11.3.3 *Generating the root certificate*

The first thing you need to do is to generate a CA certificate. This will be the one that you implicitly trust. All your other certificates will descend from it, and it will be used to establish the *chain of trust* between the different applications. Let's run the following commands:

```
$ openssl req -x509 -config openssl.conf -newkey rsa:2048 -days 365 \
  -out cacert.pem -outform PEM -subj /CN=RMQCA/ -nodes
```

You should see output similar to this:

```
Generating a 2048 bit RSA private key
...............................................+++
...............................................
.........................+++
writing new private key to './private/cakey.pem'
-----
```

With that command, you created your certificate which is stored in the file cacert.pem. The format will be PEM using the x509 extensions. The key will be encrypted using an rsa:2048 algorithm and will be valid for 365 days. For specific details on the req command and its options, you can consult http://www.openssl.org/docs/apps/req.html.

---

[7] For more details we refer you again to the book *Network Security with OpenSSL* by Viega et al. OpenSSL is a broad topic so if you want to learn it in detail you'll be best served by reading that book.

The next thing you'll do is to create the same certificate but using the DER format which is preferred by Microsoft products. Run the following command:

```
$ openssl x509 -in cacert.pem -out cacert.cer -outform DER
```

Now that you have your root certificate, it's time to create the client and server certificates.

11.3.4 *Generating the server certificates*

To issue your server certificate, you need to create a folder to store it in. Then you'll proceed to generate the server key and finally to certify it using your root certificate:

```
$ cd ..
$ mkdir server
$ cd server
$ openssl genrsa -out key.pem 2048
Generating RSA private key, 2048 bit long modulus
..............................................+++
................................................
.......................+++
e is 65537 (0x10001)
```

First you moved into the folder that contains the rmqca, and there you created your server folder and then moved into it. There you invoked the openssl command to generate the RSA key. What you need to do next is create a certificate request for that key:

```
$ openssl req -new -key key.pem -out req.pem -outform PEM \
  -subj /CN=$(hostname)/O=server/ -nodes
```

The certificate request now can be used by your certificate authority to provide a certificate for your RabbitMQ server. Let's create that server certificate:

```
$ cd ../rmqca/
$ openssl ca -config openssl.conf -in ../server/req.pem -out \
  ../server/cert.pem -notext -batch -extensions server_ca_extensions
Using configuration from openssl.conf
Check that the request matches the signature
Signature ok
The Subject's Distinguished Name is as follows
commonName            :ASN.1 12:'mrhyde'
organizationName      :ASN.1 12:'server'
Certificate is to be certified until Oct  5 23:10:35 2012 GMT (365 days)

Write out database with 1 new entries
Data Base Updated
```

What you did there is first change directories to the rmqca folder and, from there, you ran the openssl ca command using your openssl.conf file. The input file is the req.pem that you created before, and the output file is the cert.pem certificate that will reside inside your server folder. Now you need to repeat the same process to create the client certificate.

11.3.5 *Generating the client certificates*

Considering that the process is much the same, we won't explain it in detail this time. As in the previous case, first you create a key for your client, then you have to generate a certificate request based on that key, and finally you hand that certificate request to your certificate authority to issue the client certificate that will reside in the file called cert.pem inside the client folder. The following shows the commands that need to be run and the output they produce, which might be different on your computer:

```
$ cd ..
$ mkdir client
$ cd client
$ openssl genrsa -out key.pem 2048
Generating RSA private key, 2048 bit long modulus
....................................................
...................................................+++
.....................+++
e is 65537 (0x10001)

$ openssl req -new -key key.pem -out req.pem -outform PEM \
  -subj /CN=$(hostname)/O=client/ -nodes

$ cd ../rmqca/
$ openssl ca -config openssl.conf -in ../client/req.pem -out  \
  ../client/cert.pem -notext -batch -extensions client_ca_extensions
Using configuration from openssl.conf
Check that the request matches the signature
Signature ok
The Subject's Distinguished Name is as follows
commonName            :ASN.1 12:'mrhyde'
organizationName      :ASN.1 12:'client'
Certificate is to be certified until Oct  5 23:14:50 2012 GMT (365 days)

Write out database with 1 new entries
Data Base Updated
```

Now that you have the certificates sorted out, it's time to configure RabbitMQ to be able to use SSL when accepting incoming connections. It's worth noting that if you check the contents of the files serial and index.txt inside the rmqca folder, you'll see that the serial file now has the number 03 in it because you've generated three certificates so far and that the index.txt file lists the certificates you issued.

11.3.6 *Enabling SSL listeners in RabbitMQ*

To enable SSL with RabbitMQ, you need to add a couple of configuration values to the rabbitmq.config file. If you haven't created that file yet, now is the time to do it. The location of that file will vary depending on your operating system and the RabbitMQ distribution that you're using. For example, in a generic Unix installation, that file will go inside the /etc/rabbitmq folder. For more information on where to locate that file according to your current setup, you can consult the RabbitMQ online documentation at http://www.rabbitmq.com/configure.html#config-location.

After you've created that file, you need to add two entries to it: `ssl_listeners` and `ssl_options`. The first will enable the TCP listener for incoming connections, and the second will tell RabbitMQ where to find the server certificates and what authentication requirements it will impose on clients connecting via SSL. If you already have this file on your system, then add the configuration entries just after the ones you already have. Your configuration should then look like the following listing.

Listing 11.3   Enabling SSL with RabbitMQ

```
[
  {rabbit, [                                              ← ❶ Enable SSL listeners
    {ssl_listeners, [5671]},

    {ssl_options, [{cacertfile,"/path/to/rmqca/cacert.pem"},      ← Configure SSL
                   {certfile,"/path/to/server/cert.pem"},
                   {keyfile,"/path/to/server/key.pem"},   ← ❷ Peer validation
                   {verify,verify_peer},
                   {fail_if_no_peer_cert,false}]}
  ]}
].
```

As you know, the `rabbitmq.config` file uses Erlang syntax to specify configuration options. First you set up the `ssl_listeners` ❶ where you say that RabbitMQ will listen for SSL connections on port `5671`. Then you provide the values for the `ssl_options` key, which RabbitMQ uses internally to configure Erlang's `new_ssl` app.[8]

The options `cacertfile`, `certfile`, and `keyfile` are self-explanatory: `cacertfile` is your CA's private certificate, `certfile` is the server's own certificate, and `keyfile` is the server's key. They will be used to authenticate the server with the client and also to verify the client authenticity. The final parameters are `verify` and `fail_if_no_peer_cert` ❷, which tell the server that if the client sends a certificate, the server needs to verify its authenticity (`verify_peer`) but that if the client doesn't send a certificate, then the server won't reject the client (`fail_if_no_peer_cert`, `false`). Keep in mind that you're using SSL to establish encrypted connections—therefore the server presents its certificate to the client—but you may also want the server to be able to establish a chain of trust with the client by requesting its certificate. That's similar to how browsers work, where the server sends the certificate but the browser isn't required to send your certificate back (most people don't have their own SSL certificates when browsing the web).

Now it's time to apply this configuration to your RabbitMQ installation. Restart RabbitMQ (or start it if it wasn't running) and you should see the following entries in `rabbit.log` telling you that the new SSL listener has been started:

---

[8] For more details on the `new_ssl` application, consult its online manual at http://www.erlang.org/documentation/doc-5.7.5/lib/ssl-3.10.8/doc/html/new_ssl.html. There you can find a description of all the options it accepts.

```
$ tail -f /var/log/rabbitmq/rabbit@host.log
=INFO REPORT==== 9-Oct-2011::17:52:08 ===
started TCP Listener on 0.0.0.0:5672

=INFO REPORT==== 9-Oct-2011::17:52:08 ===
started SSL Listener on 0.0.0.0:5671
```

The next thing to do is to test your new configuration by connecting to RabbitMQ using the PHP client library.

11.3.7 *Testing your RabbitMQ SSL setup*

To test and try out your SSL setup, you'll connect to RabbitMQ using the `php-amqplib` library. PHP SSL implementation expects that your client keys, certificate, and CA certificate are all in the same file, so you'll create such a file for PHP. Go to the command line and type the following commands:

```
$ cat client/key.pem > phpcert.pem
$ cat client/cert.pem >> phpcert.pem
$ cat rmqca/cacert.pem >> phpcert.pem
```

Your PHP client will use the `phpcert.pem` file when dealing with SSL connections with RabbitMQ. Let's create your client code. Add the following content to a file called `ssl_connection.php`.

Listing 11.4 PHP OpenSSL connection

```php
<?php
require_once(__DIR__ . '/path/to/php-amqplib/amqp.inc');

define('HOST', 'localhost');                          ◁─❶ Connection options
define('PORT', 5671);
define('USER', 'guest');
define('PASS', 'guest');
define('VHOST', '/');
define('AMQP_DEBUG', true);

define('CERTS_PATH',
  '/path/to/ca/folder/');

$ssl_options = array(                                 ◁─❷ SSL options
    'cafile' => CERTS_PATH . '/rmqca/cacert.pem',
    'local_cert' => CERTS_PATH . '/phpcert.pem',
    'verify_peer' => true
);

$conn = new AMQPSSLConnection(HOST, PORT, USER, PASS, ◁─❸ Create connection
                      VHOST, $ssl_options);

function shutdown($conn){                             ◁─❹ Connection cleanup
    $conn->close();
}

register_shutdown_function('shutdown', $conn);

while(1){}
?>
```

If you run this script you'll start seeing debug information from the AMQP library showing you how it negotiates a connection with RabbitMQ. After the connection is established successfully, if you `tail` the RabbitMQ logs you should see messages similar to the following, showing you that RabbitMQ established a connection with your PHP script and then that connection was upgraded to the SSL protocol:

```
$ tail -f /var/log/rabbitmq/rabbit@host.log
=INFO REPORT==== 9-Oct-2011::21:01:03 ===
accepted TCP connection on 0.0.0.0:5671 from 127.0.0.1:64940

=INFO REPORT==== 9-Oct-2011::21:01:03 ===
starting TCP connection <0.16304.0> from 127.0.0.1:64940

=INFO REPORT==== 9-Oct-2011::21:01:03 ===
upgraded TCP connection <0.16304.0> to SSL
```

Let's see what the script is doing. First you include the AMQP library as usual and then declare ❶ some constants that you'll use as the connection configuration. What's important to note here is that you used the port 5671 for your SSL connection instead of using the default RabbitMQ port (5672). Then you created an array with the SSL options for PHP ❷ so it knows where to find your key and certificates information. You opened a connection by using the AMQPSSLConnection class ❸, passing a sixth argument with your SSL options. Finally, you prepared the connection cleanup ❹ by setting up a `shutdown` function that will take care of closing the connection when your script terminates, for example, when you press `ctrl-c` to kill the script.

With this, we finish our coverage of SSL with RabbitMQ. Now you can establish connections between the broker and its messaging clients, knowing that both ends can certify the authenticity of their peers. By checking the server certificate when you open a connection to the broker, you can be sure that the messages are coming from a trusted source. At the same time, the broker can verify the client's certificates so it won't accept connections from untrusted parties.

As we've said already many times, this is a large topic that goes well beyond what we can cover in a book about RabbitMQ. Note that depending on the language you're using, you'll have to see how to open SSL connections specifically for your platform, since the implementation details vary across vendors. Keep in mind that the PKI setup that we prepared in this section can be used in many places in your organization well beyond RabbitMQ usage. Your certificate authority isn't limited to only certify RabbitMQ brokers and their respective clients; you can also use it to certify the communication among other applications. For example, you can issue certificates for your intranet to enable secure web browsing (using HTTPS) for the company's internal websites.

11.4 *Summary*

In this chapter we covered some interesting topics like performance, capacity planning, and security. One thing that's clear is that there's no secret sauce when it comes to scaling your RabbitMQ installation. All will depend on your use case; you'll always have to consider the trade-offs. If you want to get more performance out of RabbitMQ, then you'll need to judiciously analyze the pros and cons of each of the routing algorithms provided by the different exchange types. Moreover, you saw how the combination of properties like message persistence, queue durability, and consumer acknowledgment mode will affect the path of a message through the broker, which will modify the performance characteristics of your applications. Regarding capacity planning, you saw that to calculate memory usage for your messaging fabric, you have to consider factors like the kinds of queues or exchanges you're using and which of the AMQP elements will spawn Erlang processes on the broker. Though the process limit in Erlang is high, it's not infinite, so by performing some simple math you can calculate a number that matches your needs. Finally, we covered the essentials of a broad topic like OpenSSL. You configured your broker to be able to accept SSL connections and to authenticate clients. To give your setup a test ride, you have a PHP client connecting to the server via SSL, but not without a small hassle to get PHP to accept your certificates. Such quirks happen with almost every platform that uses OpenSSL.

In the next chapter we'll enter the world of RabbitMQ plugins. You'll see which plugins you can obtain to augment your broker capabilities, but we won't stop there... you'll also build your own. Fasten your seat belt because in the next chapter you'll be programming in Erlang. You read that right: Erlang.

12
Smart Rabbits: extending RabbitMQ

This chapter covers

- Installing RabbitMQ plugins
- A review of interesting plugins
- Implementing your own custom exchange plugin

At this point you've learned how to use RabbitMQ as an AMQP message broker using what comes out of the box. In chapter 8 you saw that some customization was required in order to have an easier way to manage the broker. You enabled the Management plugin, which includes a slick web interface that adds a bunch of functionality to the server. The process of enabling the plugin is simple: you run a single command at the shell, `rabbitmq-plugins enable rabbitmq_management`, and the plugin is ready to use. Taking that into account, wouldn't it be nice if you could add custom behaviors to the broker?

In this chapter we'll take a deep dive into RabbitMQ plugins, seeing what you can do with them and what features they bring to the table. You'll learn how to enable plugins and, in case you don't need their functionality anymore, you'll also see how to uninstall them. You might be wondering where you can get plugins for

RabbitMQ. Don't worry; we've got you covered. Many cool plugins are out there and you'll see where to get them.

Learning about already existing plugins won't be all. In the second section of the chapter you'll make your own plugins. Yes, you read that right. You'll get your hands dirty programming with Erlang and create your own. Don't worry if you don't know Erlang; we'll cover enough to get you started, but you will feel more comfortable if you already know about it. So let's move onto the next section to pimp up our rabbit.

12.1 RabbitMQ plugins

If you look at a system like RabbitMQ you'll see that the features shipped with it are those that are useful to a large set of users. The same thing happens with server default configurations or with the new characteristics shipped with new broker releases. But what happens when you need something that doesn't come out of the box? For that situation, RabbitMQ can be enhanced by adding plugins. You can find plugins on the internet or create your own. Let's first look at when you might need a plugin, and then we'll see where you can get new plugins for your broker.

12.1.1 What can you do with plugins?

So which use cases go beyond what RabbitMQ provides out of the box? Here's a list of possible scenarios or needs that can be solved by installing a plugin:

- Support for protocols other than AMQP
- Different authentication mechanisms (LDAP, custom database)
- Message replication
- New exchanges and routing algorithms
- Message logging and audition

Let's go through some of these cases.

DIFFERENT PROTOCOLS—STOMP

One area where there has been a lot of experimentation is adding support for other protocols on top of RabbitMQ. As you know, AMQP is the default protocol supported by RabbitMQ, but one size doesn't fit all, so there's also a plugin for the STOMP protocol. STOMP is a simple text-based protocol used for transmitting data across applications. One advantage of STOMP is that it works with other brokers like ActiveMQ. If you have a code base that targets ActiveMQ and STOMP and you want to only use RabbitMQ, then you can start to migrate step by step by using the STOMP plugin. Or if you work with a programming language that lacks an AMQP client but has one for STOMP, then you can start using RabbitMQ by installing this plugin. If you want to learn more about STOMP you can do so on its web page: http://stomp.github.com/.

LDAP AUTHENTICATION

Another use case for RabbitMQ plugins is the need to authenticate to the broker via some method other than plain AMQP. Let's say all the user management in your systems is done via LDAP and you want to continue using it when you connect to

RabbitMQ. That's possible now thanks to the LDAP authentication backend: http://www.rabbitmq.com/plugins.html#rabbitmq-auth-backend-ldap. Install the plugin, add the proper configuration, and you can get going with LDAP authentication.

CUSTOM EXCHANGE TYPES

New protocols and different authentication mechanisms aren't the only things that you can add on top of RabbitMQ. You can go low-level on AMQP and implement your own exchanges with custom routing rules. An interesting example of a custom exchange is the Riak Exchange by Jon Brisbin (https://github.com/jbrisbin/riak-exchange). Riak is a Dynamo-inspired key/value store that offers fault tolerance out of the box. What if you need to log every message that passes through a RabbitMQ exchange for auditing purposes? One way to do that would be to have a fanout exchange and bind an extra queue to it, and then implement the logger using a run-of-the-mill AMQP consumer… or you can let the server handle that for you by using the Riak Exchange which will do just that: log every message to a Riak bucket.[1]

What if you need to replicate messages from one broker to another that lives in a data center miles away? For such use cases there's the RabbitMQ shovel plugin. You specify a queue name on the plugin's configuration and a destination exchange on a remote broker, and it will take care of *shoveling* the messages over the wire to the remote exchange.

That's not all you can do with plugins. You don't have to limit yourself to adding new exchange types or authentication methods. With plugins you can do almost everything that Erlang allows you to do; the limit is your imagination—and judgment. After all, you don't want the broker crashing because you tried to implement some wild ideas on top of it. Now that you know what's doable with RabbitMQ plugins, let's see where to find them.

12.1.2 Where do you find plugins?

The first place to look for RabbitMQ plugins is the page dedicated to them at the RabbitMQ website: www.rabbitmq.com/plugins.html. There you can find a list of *maintained plugins* and a second list of what are called *experimental plugins*. The former are maintained by the RabbitMQ crew and are kept up to date with new broker releases. Also you can file bugs and feature requests via the RabbitMQ mailing list at http://lists.rabbitmq.com/cgi-bin/mailman/listinfo/rabbitmq-discuss. Though you can do the same with the experimental plugins, you can't be sure that there will be an answer to your issues with them.

12.1.3 Installing plugins

You already saw that since RabbitMQ version 2.7.0, installing plugins is easy: just run a command such as `./rabbitmq-plugins enable rabbitmq_management`, restart the server, and that's about it. The plugin is ready to be used! Now the question is what happens when you want to enable a plugin that's not part of the broker distribution.

---

[1] *Buckets* in Riak are a way to organize data in a way similar to the use of tables in SQL databases.

First you'll have to download the plugin's `.ez` files into the `plugins` folder[2] of your RabbitMQ installation and, after you have it there, run the usual `./rabbitmq-plugins enable plugin_name` command.

Let's try these instructions by enabling the STOMP plugin. Move into the `sbin` folder of your RabbitMQ installation and type the following:

```
$ ./rabbitmq-plugins enable rabbitmq_stomp
The following plugins have been enabled:
  rabbitmq_stomp

Plugin configuration has changed. Restart RabbitMQ
for changes to take effect.
```

Now stop the broker in case you had it running:

```
$ ./rabbitmqctl stop
Stopping and halting node rabbit@mrhyde ...
...done.
```

And then start it again to load the new plugin:

```
$ ./rabbitmq-server -detached
Activating RabbitMQ plugins ...
7 plugins activated:
* amqp_client-2.7.0
* mochiweb-1.3-rmq2.7.0-git
* rabbitmq_management-2.7.0
* rabbitmq_management_agent-2.7.0
* rabbitmq_mochiweb-2.7.0
* rabbitmq_stomp-2.7.0
* webmachine-1.7.0-rmq2.7.0-hg
```

As you can see, among the other plugins that were already installed, the server is listing the `rabbitmq_stomp-2.7.0` plugin together with the activated plugins. The STOMP plugin will be up and running with its default configuration. To test that it works as expected, let's connect to RabbitMQ using the STOMP protocol with the default user credentials. Let's do so using `nc`, the *netcat* command-line utility:

```
$ nc localhost 61613
```

The previous command will open a connection to the server. All the input you type now will be sent to the STOMP adapter which will try to parse the frames. Now enter the following to start a session:

```
CONNECT
login:guest
passcode:guest

^@
```

After you input the credentials, you need to add an extra empty line, which will signal an empty body, and then enter ^@ (the Control key together with the *at* symbol or @),

---

[2] If you don't have the plugins folder, just create it inside RabbitMQ's installation directory. This folder can also be safely removed later in case you don't want to use any plugin.

which signals the end of the frame. If everything went well you should get a reply with a new session like this:

```
CONNECTED
session:session-ds/mGfvEV6TkPXPVcUv8YA==
heart-beat:0,0
version:1.0
```

With this small example we end our test of the STOMP plugin. Our goal was to install it and see that with zero configuration you could get it up and running. You can quit the session by entering ^c (Ctrl+C). If you want to learn more about using STOMP with RabbitMQ you can consult the documentation at http://www.rabbitmq.com/stomp.html.

12.1.4 *Removing plugins*

Now let's say you don't need the STOMP plugin anymore and want to remove it. That's easy to achieve by using the same `rabbitmq-plugins` commands that you've been using so far. First you have to disable the plugin by running the following from the `sbin` folder:

```
$ ./rabbitmq-plugins disable rabbitmq_stomp
The following plugins have been disabled:
  rabbitmq_stomp

Plugin configuration has changed. Restart RabbitMQ
for changes to take effect.
```

Then you have to stop the server:

```
$ ./rabbitmqctl stop
Stopping and halting node rabbit@mrhyde ...
...done.
```

And then you can restart the server again:

```
$ ./rabbitmq-server -detached
Activating RabbitMQ plugins ...
6 plugins activated:
* amqp_client-2.7.0
* mochiweb-1.3-rmq2.7.0-git
* rabbitmq_management-2.7.0
* rabbitmq_management_agent-2.7.0
* rabbitmq_mochiweb-2.7.0
* webmachine-1.7.0-rmq2.7.0-hg
```

You can list the enabled plugins to make sure that the STOMP plugin has been disabled:

```
$ ./rabbitmq-plugins list -e
[e] amqp_client                  2.7.0
[e] mochiweb                     1.3-rmq2.7.0-git
[E] rabbitmq_management          2.7.0
[e] rabbitmq_management_agent    2.7.0
[e] rabbitmq_mochiweb            2.7.0
[e] webmachine                   1.7.0-rmq2.7.0-hg
```

You can see that the `list` option displays the enabled plugins along with their versions, and that the STOMP plugin doesn't appear in that list. If you want to learn more about the `rabbitmq-plugins` command you can find its manual page here: http://www.rabbitmq.com/man/rabbitmq-plugins.1.man.html.

Now that you've seen the power of plugins, it's time to create your own plugin. Get your fingers ready because in the next section you'll be coding in Erlang.

12.2   *Making your own plugins*

So far we've discussed what you can do with plugins; now it's time to create your own. The goal will be to add your own custom exchange to RabbitMQ. Why might you need a new exchange type? Imagine that you need to model a chat application with RabbitMQ where you have a global room where all the users connect. Each user gets their own queue that's bound to the global fanout exchange. Every time a new message is sent to the exchange, this message gets fanned out to every queue bound to it. Now what happens when a new client connects to the chat room? Though they will get all the new messages that are sent to the chat room, they won't have any context about what happened before they joined the conversation. Wouldn't it be nice if you could deliver the last 20 messages to the user to give them some context for what's going on in the chat room? With the default elements from AMQP that's not possible. After a message is consumed from a queue, it's not seen anymore in the broker. You can change that if you create an exchange that caches the last 20 messages that it has routed. Then whenever a new user connects to the room (which means a new queue is bound to the exchange) your exchange will deliver the last 20 messages. Figure 12.1 explains the idea: the area of the figure that's separated with a dotted line is what your exchange will add to your application. Though you might not need to implement a chat room using RabbitMQ, there are cases when your new consumers need to know the last value *seen* on this exchange. An easy way to implement that is with this kind of exchange.

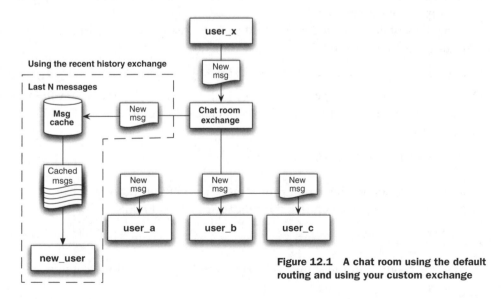

Figure 12.1   A chat room using the default routing and using your custom exchange

In this section you'll implement such an exchange, which will be called *RabbitMQ Recent History Exchange*. As usual, the complete source code for this project can be found with the code that accompanies this book. Look for the folder called `rabbitmq-recent-history-exchange`. In the next section you'll set up your development environment in order to get ready to start creating plugins. Keep in mind that you'll be coding in Erlang.

12.2.1   Getting the RabbitMQ Public Umbrella

To write your own plugins you'll need to set up a basic development environment to build your plugins upon. The RabbitMQ developers have facilitated such a task for you by creating an environment in what's called the *RabbitMQ Public Umbrella* (from now on let's call it *umbrella*). Installing it is a matter of checking out its repository and then adding your own plugin into that project structure. To get the umbrella code you'll have to set up *Mercurial*, which is a distributed revision control system similar to Git. Mercurial is the system used by the RabbitMQ developers to publish and manage their open source code. If you already have it installed, then you're good to go. Mercurial is a multiplatform system, so you should be able to install it for your platform. The installation procedure is simple; please go to the Mercurial website (http://mercurial.selenic.com/) and download the version that suits your computer. Don't worry if you haven't used Mercurial before; you'll be using just a couple of commands to get the umbrella source code.

If you've been following along with the book code examples, then you probably have Python installed already; if not, it's time to do so because some tools under the umbrella require it (including Mercurial itself). See the Python website for installation instructions: http://www.python.org/. The last requirement is to have Erlang installed on your machine; if you can run RabbitMQ, then you must have it installed as well. As with Python, please consult the Erlang website to get installation instructions: http://www.erlang.org/.

Now let's obtain the umbrella's source code. Assuming you installed Mercurial, you can get the code with the following command:

```
$ hg clone http://hg.rabbitmq.com/rabbitmq-public-umbrella/
```

Once the repository has been cloned to your computer, it's time to get the projects contained inside it. Run the following commands, but grab a cup of coffee since it may take a while:

```
$ cd rabbitmq-public-umbrella
$ make co
```

As an optional step to check that your setup is working properly, you can run the following two commands to compile the `rabbitmq-stomp` plugin:

```
$ cd rabbitmq-stomp/
$ make
```

If everything went well you should see your console output ending like this:

```
[elided] generate deps
[elided] fix test deps
sed -i -e 's|build/deps.mk|$(DEPS_FILE)|' build/deps.mk
rm -rf build/dep-ezs
mkdir -p build/dep-ezs
....
many lines trimmed out
....
touch dist/.done.0.0.0
touch dist/.done
```

The next thing to do is to create the folder structure for your plugin. Type `cd ..` to move back to the umbrella folder before continuing to the next section.

12.2.2 Setting up the folder structure

You'll build your plugin following the Open Telecom Platform (OTP) coding standards—you'll follow a certain folder structure, file naming conventions, and source code organization using several programming patterns that fit Erlang. Since this is a book about RabbitMQ, we won't have time to cover Erlang in detail but if you're curious and want to learn more, we recommend the book *Erlang and OTP in Action* from Manning (http://manning.com/logan/) or *Learn You Some Erlang for Great Good* (http://learnyousomeerlang.com/). The code presented will be easy to grasp even if you don't have any Erlang experience, but be warned that some techniques may seem strange if you've never used Erlang or functional programming before.

The folder structure for the plugin is simple. Since you're going to call it *RabbitMQ Recent History Exchange*, create a folder inside the umbrella project named `rabbitmq-recent-history-exchange`. Inside it you'll need one folder to hold your source code called `src`. It's that simple:

```
cd ..
mkdir rabbitmq-recent-history-exchange
cd rabbitmq-recent-history-exchange
mkdir src
```

The next step will be to include the umbrella build system into your project.

12.2.3 Including the plugin build system

To be able to use the umbrella build system, you need to add a couple of files to your project root folder. The first file is called `Makefile` and will reference the umbrella make file. Add the following content to it:

```
include ../umbrella.mk
```

By referencing the `umbrella.mk` file, you benefit from all commands already created for you. There are commands that can package your plugin as an `.ez` file, and others that can run your plugin inside the broker directly from the project folder, making it easier to test your plugin. There are commands to clean up the built files and much more. For a full list of options, consult the file `README.makefiles` inside the umbrella folder.

Now that your `Makefile` is in place, you can add your `package.mk` file that will contain the plugin-specific configuration options for the build system. Create that file inside your project folder and add the following content to it:

```
DEPS:=rabbitmq-server rabbitmq-erlang-client
RETAIN_ORIGINAL_VERSION:=true
```

As you can see, this is as simple as it can get. What you did here is specify the plugin dependencies in the `DEPS` macro and set the `RETAIN_ORIGINAL_VERSION` macro to true to tell the build system to pick up the plugin version number out of the version number that you'll soon assign to the plugin. Since you're going to build a custom exchange, you need some functionality that's already present on the `rabbitmq-server` project and other features from the `rabbitmq-erlang-client`; therefore, you specify in your `package.mk` file that your plugins depend on those two projects. The cool thing here is that the umbrella build system will take care of resolving the dependencies for you. Now that you have everything ready to start coding your plugin, let's continue by writing the application specification file.

12.2.4 *Creating the Erlang application file*

Now that you have the basic requirements in place, let's create the application specification file. You may be wondering what that is—what's an application, after all? Erlang programs are structured as applications where the modules that implement its functionality are held. Things like the list of Erlang modules included with the application or the configuration options are specified in the *application specification* file. When you create your application specification file, you need to indicate a list of the Erlang modules included in your application, something that's a bit tedious. Luckily this step can be simplified by using *application specification templates* that later are automatically filled with such information by the umbrella build system. This means that you don't have to worry about keeping the list of modules up to date; the build system will do that for you. So although in a normal Erlang project you'll create a plain application file, in this case you'll create a template for it and let the umbrella system fill in the information automatically. Let's create this template file inside the `src` folder and call it `rabbitmq_recent_history_exchange.app.src`. The file will have the following content:

```
{application, rabbitmq_recent_history_exchange,
 [{description, "RabbitMQ Recent History Exchange"},
  {vsn, "0.1.0"},
  {modules, []},
  {registered, []},
  {applications, [kernel, stdlib, rabbit, mnesia]}]}.
```

What you have here is an Erlang `tuple`, a compound data type that holds a fixed number of Erlang values (terms).[3] If you simplify that structure you can see that it has the following shape:

```
{application, application_name, [{key1, val1}, ..., {keyN, valN}]}.
```

---

[3] If you want to know more about Erlang data types, consult http://www.erlang.org/doc/reference_manual/data_types.html.

That's a tuple with its first element made of the atom called `application`—atoms are like *symbols* in Ruby or *keywords* in Clojure. The second element is an atom that holds the application name. Finally, the third element is an Erlang list, delimited by the characters [and]. This list is said to be a `property list` because it holds tuples made of keys and values. If you see the contents in detail, you have, for example, the description property `{description, "RabbitMQ Recent History Exchange"}` with the information of what the application is doing. You can have any string there serving as the description. The `vsn` value specifies the version number of your application. Since you've just created it, you'll tag it as *0.1.0*. Then comes the list that will hold the Erlang modules used by your app. As we already said, this list will be automatically filled by the umbrella build system. The property `registered` tells which processes will be registered by your application, which for this example you'll keep as an empty list. Finally, you specify which applications must be running for the plugin to work properly. You require the Erlang `kernel` and the standard library `stdlib`. On the RabbitMQ side, you need the broker running; therefore you add the `rabbit` application there. As a last requirement, because you'll use the Erlang Mnesia database, you also add it there.

Before starting to write the exchange logic, let's make sure the `Makefile` is set up properly. Type `make` inside your plugin folder. You should start seeing a lot of output on your command line. That's normal: it's the build system *making* all your plugin dependencies like the Erlang AMQP client and the broker itself. After the process is finished, you'll notice that you have some new folders in your project root. The most interesting one is called `dist` or *distribution* folder, where your final plugin files will be put. Try the following command at the terminal:

```
$ ls dist
amqp_client-0.0.0.ez   rabbit_common-0.0.0.ez
rabbitmq_recent_history_exchange-0.1.0-rmq.ez
```

There you have your plugin files together with their dependencies. Though your plugin still lacks functionality, you could at least test that the build system is properly set up. After you have your plugin final version, you'll have to copy those files into the `plugins` folder of your RabbitMQ installation. Now let's start writing some Erlang code.

12.3 Creating your custom exchange module

Source code in Erlang is organized inside modules. Modules hold functions that implement the features offered by your applications. There are no classes or packages like in Java or C#, which makes the structure flat and simple. Your plugin will need only one module containing the custom exchange implementation. You'll create a file called `rabbit_exchange_type_recent_history.erl` inside the `src` folder and will add content to it as you progress with this section.

How do you know what goes inside an exchange? How can RabbitMQ know what functions to call in your module in order to route messages through the exchange, bind queues to it, and so on? In *object-oriented programming* you have the concept of *interfaces* where you define a set of methods that your classes must implement as part of the contract. So, for example, to implement the *Visitor* pattern you can check the `Visitor` interface that will tell you that you need to provide a `Visit` method, an `Iterator` will have to implement the methods `hasNext` and `next`, and so on. In Erlang you have the same concept but with a different name: *behaviour*. Note the special British spelling in that word.

An Erlang *behaviour* will specify which functions a module has to implement and export, so code calling your module knows what to expect from it. Another difference from the OOP world is that Erlang has no concept of visibility like in Java; for example, there are no public/protected/private modifiers. What you have is just a list of functions that your module exports. So if your module implements functions `foo`, `bar`, and `baz` but only exports `foo`, then `bar` and `baz` can't be called from outside. Just telling which functions a module has to export is one part of the story; the other is the number of arguments a function accepts. Erlang has the concept of *function arity*—the number of arguments a function takes. Erlang accepts functions with the same name but with different arity; thus a behaviour can specify function `foo/1` and `foo/2`, which are different functions. When specifying function names, put a forward slash between the function name and its arity. Now coming back to the question that fired the discussion on behaviours: how do you know what goes inside an exchange? RabbitMQ exposes an exchange behaviour called `rabbit_exchange_type` that tells which functions you need to implement to have a well-behaved exchange. Since your exchange will be a beefed-up fanout exchange that will cache the last 20 messages, you'll base your implementation in the code for the actual fanout exchange that comes with the broker, which will simplify the task.

In figure 12.2 you can see what you have to do differently from the default fanout implementation. First, you need to cache routed messages. Whenever your exchange routes a message, you'll keep it on some database. That will be done in the function called `route/2`. Then, when a queue is bound to your exchange, you have to deliver the cached messages to it in case you have any. That will be handled in the function `add_binding/3`. Finally, when your exchange is deleted, you have to drop the cache to avoid memory leaks, which will be handled by the function `delete/3`. Note that you have to implement other functions as well. The ones mentioned in the figure are those that differ from the fanout exchange default implementation. As a last implementation detail you'll use *Mnesia*, the Erlang built-in database that's already used by RabbitMQ to store bindings and exchange meta information. You'll implement your exchange step by step and then, at the end, we'll show you the complete source code for the module.

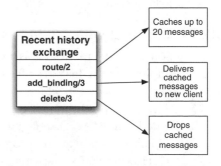

Figure 12.2 Specific functions of recent history exchange

Now let's create the file `rabbit_exchange_type_recent_history.erl` inside the src folder and add the following content to it.

Listing 12.1 `rabbit_exchange_type_recent_history.erl`

```
-module(rabbit_exchange_type_recent_history).              ◁──❶ Module declaration
-include_lib("rabbit_common/include/rabbit.hrl").                  ◁─┐
-include_lib("rabbit_common/include/rabbit_exchange_type_spec.hrl").  │ Import
                                                                       │ required
-behaviour(rabbit_exchange_type).                                   ❷ │ headers
                                                                     
-export([description/0, serialise_events/0, route/2]).      ◁──┐
-export([validate/1, create/2, delete/3, add_binding/3,          │ Module
         remove_bindings/3, assert_args_equivalence/2]).         │ exported
-export([setup_schema/0]).                                     ❹ │ functions
```

Specify ❸ behaviour points to `-behaviour(rabbit_exchange_type).`

First, you provide the name of your module ❶, which has to match the filename minus the `.erl` extension. Then, you include a couple of libraries that your module requires ❷ and define that your module implements the `rabbit_exchange_type` behaviour ❸. Finally, you declare the list of functions that your module exports ❹. Note that you have several `export` declarations in this code. You do that for readability's sake, since you could provide just one `export` with all the functions there. Each export has an Erlang list inside delimited by the square brackets `[]` where you have a comma-separated list of function names of the form *function_name/arity*. For example, you have to implement a function called `description` that doesn't take any arguments, a function called `route` that accepts two arguments, and so on. The first two `export` declarations are what the `rabbit_exchange_type` behaviour requires, whereas the last one that includes `setup_schema` is related to your module only. As you can see, you can export more functions than those required by the behaviour that you're implementing. Now let's continue with the rest of the code.

12.3.1 *Registering your exchange with RabbitMQ*

For RabbitMQ to pick up your exchange and be able to use it, it has to know about its existence. RabbitMQ maintains a registry where all the exchange types with their respective module names are tracked. Let's say you publish a message to a fanout exchange. What RabbitMQ will do is to go to the registry and check which module implements the fanout exchange. When it has the module name, it will proceed to call the routing function on that module. In this case, you need to find a way to add your exchange to that registry to make it available for the broker. RabbitMQ supports the concept of *boot steps*—a series of steps that have to be called while the server starts up. You'll add one boot step to your module and then RabbitMQ will *magically* execute it and add your exchange to the `rabbit_registry`. Add the following code to the module to accomplish that.

Listing 12.2 `rabbit_exchange_type_recent_history.erl`

```
-rabbit_boot_step({rabbit_exchange_type_rh_registry,
[{description, "recent history exchange type: registry"},
   {mfa, {rabbit_registry, register,
            [exchange, <<"x-recent-history">>,
             ?MODULE]}},
   {requires, rabbit_registry},
   {enables, kernel_ready}]}).

-rabbit_boot_step({rabbit_exchange_type_rh_mnesia,
   [{description, "recent history exchange type: mnesia"},
     {mfa, {?MODULE, setup_schema, []}},
     {requires, database},
     {enables, external_infrastructure}]}).

-define(KEEP_NB, 20).
-define(RH_TABLE, rh_exchange_table).
-record(cached, {key, content}).
```

① Register exchange

② Initialize database

③ Define constants and records

A `rabbit_boot_step` **①** has the following components: a `description` telling what the boot step is about (note that this is for documentation; it doesn't matter what you put there as long as it's a string). Next is the `mfa` or `module function arguments` section, where you invoke the function `register` in the `rabbit_registry`, passing as arguments your exchange type and the module related to it. Your exchange type at the AMQP level will be called `x-recent-history`. According to the AMQP spec, all the custom elements that you add to the protocol need to have the x- prefix. Finally come the `requires` and `enables` parts, where you tell RabbitMQ that in order to register your exchange, the `rabbit_registry` has to be running already (which is obvious) and that your exchange is a requirement for the `kernel_ready` event to be fired—boot steps depending on the `kernel_ready` event will have to wait for your exchange to be initialized.[4]

You also take advantage of the `rabbit_boot_step` system to initialize your plugin **②**. Since your plugin will use Mnesia to store the cached messages, you add an extra step here to set up the database schema for your plugin; the `mfa` part of the boot step will invoke the function `setup_schema` that belongs to your exchange module. The `?MODULE` piece that you see there works similar to a C macro, so in this case it will be expanded to your module name. Since the function `setup_schema` doesn't require any arguments, you provide an empty list `[]`.

Finally, you define a couple of macros, `KEEP_NB` and `RH_TABLE` **③**, which stand for the number of messages that you want to keep in the cache and the name of the Mnesia table that you'll create. Speaking of Mnesia tables, you need to define the schema for a table, and you do that with the `-record` declaration at the end. The records that you'll store will be called `cached` and they'll have two elements: the `key` and the `content`. In the `key` property, you'll store the exchange name and in the `content` property you'll keep a list of the last 20 messages that passed through the

---

[4] If you want to learn more about the RabbitMQ boot process you can consult the following document: https://github.com/videlalvaro/rabbit-internals/blob/master/rabbit_boot_process.md.

exchange. That will provide you with an easy-to-access map from exchange name to cached messages. When the time comes to deliver the last 20 messages from the cache, you'll need to look up the message list by your exchange name. Let's take a look now at the `setup_schema/0` function.

Listing 12.3   `rabbit_exchange_type_recent_history.erl`

```
setup_schema() ->                                            <-- ❶ Function definition
  case mnesia:create_table(?RH_TABLE,                        <--
          [{attributes, record_info(fields, cached)},            ❷ Create
            {record_name, cached},                                 table
            {type, set}]) of
      {atomic, ok} -> ok;                                    <-- ❸ Creation succeeded

      {aborted, {already_exists, ?RH_TABLE}} -> ok           <-- ❹ Creation failed
 end.
```

The code in this function is simple to understand. First you have the function header ❶ with the function name, the list of arguments that go between parentheses (in this case you have none), and the arrow `->` that indicates what follows is the function body. There you have a `case` expression with the following shape:

```
case Expr of
 Pattern1 ->
  Body1;
 ...;
 PatternN ->
  BodyN
end
```

Erlang will evaluate `Expr`, and the `Body` part that gets executed will depend on the result of that expression; you mark the end of the case expression with the word `end`. As you can see, this works similarly to switch/case statements in other languages. In this function the `Expr` will be the call to `mnesia:create_table` ❷. Let's look at it in detail:

```
mnesia:create_table(?RH_TABLE,
        [{attributes, record_info(fields, cached)},
          {record_name, cached},
          {type, set}])
```

Here you create a table with the name `rh_exchange_table` because that's the value your `?RH_TABLE` macro will expand to. The attributes or `columns` of your table will be the fields of the `cached` record—key and content fields that you defined earlier. You tell Mnesia that the name of the record used will be `cached` and that the type of your table will be `set`, which means that there won't be any duplicated values. If you store a new value with the same key, then the old value will be overwritten by the new value.

Coming back to your `setup_schema` function, if the result of `Expr` is `{atomic, ok}` ❸ that means your table was created, so you return `ok`. Note that in Erlang, as with many functional languages, there are no `return` keywords. Functions implicitly return the result of the last expression. Now if `mnesia:create_table` returned {aborted, {already_exists, ?RH_TABLE}} ❹, you'll also return ok becuase the table is already present in Mnesia, probably from a previous RabbitMQ startup, so there's nothing else to do there.

12.3.2 *Implementing the exchange behaviour*

Now it's time to start implementing the exchange behaviour. You'll add a bunch of functions whose implementation is simple, since you'll be reusing the default implementation provided by RabbitMQ. Let's add the following functions to your module.

Listing 12.4 `abbit_exchange_type_recent_history.erl`

```
description() ->                                              ❶ Exchange description
  [{name, <<"recent-history">>},
   {description, <<"List of Last-value caches exchange.">>}].
                                                             ❷ Binding event
serialise_events() -> false.                                   serialization

remove_bindings(_Tx, _X, _Bs) -> ok.                           Miscellaneous
validate(_X) -> ok.                                          ❸ functions
create(_Tx, _X) -> ok.
                                                             ❹ Exchange argument
assert_args_equivalence(X, Args) ->                            equivalence
  rabbit_exchange:assert_args_equivalence(X, Args).
```

First you have a function called description ❶ that's only used for informative purposes. It returns a property list having the exchange name and its description. Simple! The next function is serialise_events ❷, which is used by RabbitMQ to determine whether it has to serialize the binding events that your exchange accepts, and because in this case you don't need such functionality, you return false. The implementation of remove_bindings, validate, and create ❸ is straightforward. You return the atom ok because you don't need to do any bookkeeping when such operations happen to your exchange; RabbitMQ will perform the default actions. Finally, you delegate the call to assert_args_equivalence to the implementation provided by RabbitMQ's rabbit_exchange module ❹. You won't get into details regarding these functions but if you want to know more, consult the file called rabbit_exchange_type.erl inside the server source code, which has an explanation for each of the behaviour functions.

Now that you've implemented the basics, it's time to define the functions that will add that extra set of functionalities to your exchange. As you know, you need to modify the way that the functions route/2, delete/3, and add_binding/3 work. Let's start with by adding the code for route/2.

Listing 12.5 Message routing—`rabbit_exchange_type_recent_history.erl`

```
route(#exchange{name = XName},                               ❶ Extract exchange name
      #delivery{message = #basic_message{
                              content = Content               ❷ Extract message content
      }}) ->
cache_msg(XName, Content),                                    ❸ Cache message
rabbit_router:match_routing_key(XName, ['_']).                ❹ Route message
```

As the name of the function implies, route takes two parameters: the exchange record and the message that's being routed. A record in Erlang works similar to a struct in C: it's a data structure that has fields mapping to values. One of the advantages of records is that you can access their values by field name. Erlang has a technique called *pattern matching* that can be used to extract bits of information out of data structures, which simplifies data access and removes the need for temporary variables. In this case you're just interested in the exchange name, so though the function takes a record with all the exchange information, by putting the code #exchange{name = XName} in the function header, you can extract the name value and *bind it* to the variable XName ❶. Then you can use the variable that holds the exchange name in the rest of the function body. Once you get used to this Erlang technique, you'll see how it simplifies code. You use the same idea to extract the message content in the second argument to your function ❷ and bind the value to the Content variable. That variable will get the message delivery content—the AMQP message properties and payload.

The body of the function is simple. First you call the function cache_msg/2, passing the exchange name and the message content ❸. You'll soon see the code of that function. Once the message is cached, you call the default rabbit_router ❹ to provide your exchange with the same behaviour as provided by the fanout exchange. The next step will be to write the code for cache_msg/2 and the auxiliary function called store_msg/2. Add the following code to your module file.

Listing 12.6 rabbit_exchange_type_recent_history.erl

```
cache_msg(XName, Content) ->                                    Anonymous
  rabbit_misc:execute_mnesia_transaction(                       function as
                                                                argument

    fun () ->

      Cached = get_msgs_from_cache(XName),         <---  Get cached messages

      store_msg(XName, Cached, Content)            <---  Store messages
    end).
store_msg(Key, Cached, Content) ->
  mnesia:write(?RH_TABLE,
    #cached{key = Key,                                          Prepend
                                                               message
      content = [Content|lists:sublist(Cached, ?KEEP_NB-1)]},   to list
    write).
```

The first function, cache_msg/2, takes two parameters: the exchange name and the message content. In this function you need to access Mnesia to retrieve the messages that may be in the cache and append to them the latest message. Because your exchange can be called concurrently, you need to run the read and update operations inside a transaction to ensure that you have consistent data. RabbitMQ provides a helper function for that called rabbit_misc:execute_mnesia_transaction/1. That function takes a function as argument and runs it in the context of a Mnesia transaction. As with many functional languages, Erlang provides the ability to define anonymous functions, or funs as they're are called in the Erlang world. Functions are first-class citizens, which means they can be passed as normal values to other functions and can also be returned by functions. If you've used JavaScript, then you've probably used some anonymous functions when working with callbacks. The simplified syntax for an Erlang fun is like this:

```
fun(Arg1, Arg2, ...., ArgN) ->
    Expr1,
    Expr2
    ....,
    ExprN
end
```

The fun in this code doesn't take any arguments since it *closes over* the arguments passed to the cache_msg function. The first thing this fun will do is to retrieve the cached messages by calling the helper function get_msgs_from_cache/1, which takes the exchange name as argument. You bind the result of that function call to the variable Cached and then pass that code to the function store_msg/3 that will take care of storing the data. By having these two separate steps, you can reuse the code that retrieves the data from Mnesia and the code that stores data in Mnesia as well.

The function store_msg/3 is also simple. It calls the function write/3 from the mnesia module. The first argument is the table name; the second argument is the record that you want to store. Note that you use the exchange name as the value for the key field. To store the cached content, you dynamically create an Erlang list using the syntax [Head|Tail]. The head of the list will be the new cached element and the tail will be a sublist of the last ?KEEP_NB - 1 elements that have already been cached. By doing that, you make sure to have at most 20 elements in your cache. You may wonder why you prepend the new element to the list head. Lists in Erlang are implemented as linked lists, so it's cheaper to prepend elements to the list first and then do a *list reverse* when you want to deliver the messages in the same order as they arrived. The last parameter to the Mnesia function is write, which is used to ask Mnesia for a write lock to the ?RH_TABLE table. Now let's see the code for the get_msgs _from_cache/1 function. Add the following code the your module file.

> **Listing 12.7   rabbit_exchange_type_recent_history.erl**

```
get_msgs_from_cache(XName) ->
  rabbit_misc:execute_mnesia_transaction(
    fun () ->
      case mnesia:read(?RH_TABLE, XName) of
        [] ->

          [];                                                    ➊ Return an
          [#cached{key = XName, content=Cached}] ->                  empty list

          Cached                                                 ➋ Return the
      end                                                            cached content
    end).
```

The code in this function is fairly simple, too. Again you use the execute_mnesia_transaction/1 function, passing a fun that has a case expression inside. The case expression will call mnesia:read/2 by providing it the table and the exchange names. If the database returns an empty list denoted by [], you return that empty list ❶. If you get a list with one element being the #cached record, you extract from the record the *exchange name* and the *content*. Now you might be wondering why you associate the value of the key field with the variable XName. This again has to do with pattern matching in Erlang. In this case you use this technique as a sanity check to ensure that you got a value that's associated with the exchange name. How does that work? When your function is called, the variable XName (which is the only argument the function takes) will be bound to the value passed to the function. In Erlang, as with many functional languages, variables *don't vary*. Variables work the same way as variables do in high school math. The value bound to XName can't be changed during the scope and lifetime of your function execution. So the only way the second expression of case will match is if the value contained in the key field matches the contents of the XName variable. By doing that you make sure that you get back from Mnesia the values that you cached for your current exchange. Even if this seems complex at the beginning, it will simplify your code a lot later; you won't need to add needless if/then/else cases to your code because you'll pattern match variables in advance. If the pattern match fails, then your code won't be executed at all. Coming back at the code, you can see the second part of the case expression returns the cached content ❷.

The function get_msgs_from_cache/1 ends the description of the code needed by the exchange to route and cache messages. Now it's time to see what you have to do when somebody deletes one of your custom exchanges. The following code implements the delete/3 function. Let's add it to the module.

Listing 12.8 rabbit_exchange_type_recent_history.erl

```
delete(_Tx, #exchange{ name = XName }, _Bs) ->
  rabbit_misc:execute_mnesia_transaction(
    fun() ->
      mnesia:delete(?RH_TABLE, XName, write)
    end),
  ok.
```

The delete/1 function is simple too. RabbitMQ will call it whenever the exchange has to be deleted. Though it takes three arguments in this case, you'll only use the second one to extract the value of the exchange name and then use it to delete from Mnesia the information belonging to that exchange. Keep in mind that there can be many instances of your custom exchange type, each caching different messages. To prevent memory leaks, whenever any instance of your exchange type is removed from the server you have to take care to delete the messages associated with its name. The next callback to implement is the one used to bind queues to your exchange. Add this code to your source file.

Listing 12.9   `rabbit_exchange_type_recent_history.erl`

```erlang
add_binding(_Tx, #exchange{ name = XName },
            #binding{ destination = QName }) ->
  case rabbit_amqqueue:lookup(QName) of                    ❶ Obtain
    {error, not_found} ->                                     queue Pid

      queue_not_found_error(QName);
    {ok, #amqqueue{ pid = QPid }} ->
      Cached = get_msgs_from_cache(XName),
                                                            ❷ Convert
      Msgs = msgs_from_content(XName, Cached),                messages

      deliver_messages(QPid, Msgs)
  end,
  ok.
```

The function `add_binding/3` will be called by RabbitMQ whenever a binding is added to your exchange and lets you perform extra operations for the binding. For this use case, a new binding means that a new client connected to the exchange, so it's time to deliver the messages in the Mnesia cache. Basically all the code you've seen before was to support this function. To deliver messages to a queue, you need its `Pid` or *process ID*. A `Pid` acts as an address where you can send messages (Erlang messages, not AMQP messages). You can use a queue `Pid` to deliver messages by delegating to the queue module the actual message delivery to the consumer. Keep in mind that in RabbitMQ, consumers subscribe to queues, so at the exchange level you have no such concept as *consumers*. To obtain a queue `Pid`, you call the helper function `rabbit _amqqueue:lookup/1` that takes the queue name as parameter ❶ and returns either its `Pid` or a tuple containing the atoms `{error, not_found}`. If RabbitMQ can't find the queue you're looking for, then you return a protocol error to the user by calling the function `queue_not_found_error/1`. If you get the actual `QPid`, retrieve the messages' content contained in the cache and transform them to actual AMQP messages by calling the function `msgs_from_content/2` ❷, which will return a list of AMQP messages. Finally, you pass those messages over to the function `deliver _messages/2`, which will iterate over the list of messages and will deliver each one to the queue. After you handle message delivery, you return the atom `ok` back to the broker to signal that the binding operation succeeded.

To finish with the implementation, let's take a look a the helper functions used in the previous code.

Listing 12.10   `rabbit_exchange_type_recent_history.erl`

```erlang
queue_not_found_error(QName) ->                          ❶ Protocol error

  rabbit_misc:protocol_error(
    internal_error,
    "could not find queue '~s'",
    [QName]).

msgs_from_content(XName, Cached) ->
```

Creates an AMQP message ③

```
        lists:map(
          fun(Content) ->
            {Props, Payload} = rabbit_basic:from_content(Content),
            rabbit_basic:message(XName, <<"">>, Props, Payload)
          end, Cached).
    deliver_messages(Queue, Msgs) ->
      lists:map(
        fun (Msg) ->
          Delivery = rabbit_basic:delivery(false, false, Msg, undefined),
          rabbit_amqqueue:deliver(Queue, Delivery)
        end, lists:reverse(Msgs)).
```

② **Creates message properties and content**

④ **Wraps message as a "delivery"**

⑤ **Delivers message to queue**

The first function is a simple helper used to send a protocol error to the client ❶. It takes the queue name as argument and uses it to format a string that tells the user that the queue can't be found. Then you have the function msgs_from_content/2 that generates a list of AMQP messages out of the content received. Keep in mind that you pass to this function a list of Content values; therefore you must map over that list applying the fun that you define in there to each of the elements of the list. When you call the map function, you have to remember to reverse the list of messages to get them in the same order as they were received. To get the list in reverse order, you call the Erlang function lists:reverse/1.

An AMQP message is composed of a set of properties and the payload. You extract those from the cached content by calling rabbit_basic/from_content/1 ❷, which returns a tuple with the message payload and its properties. The next thing to do is to add to the message the name of the exchange that routed it and the routing key used to route the message. In this case you have a blank routing key denoted by the empty binary term: <<"">>.[5] You accomplish that by calling the function rabbit_basic: message/4 ❸, where you pass the message properties and payload and you get back a proper AMQP message.

Last but not least you have the helper function deliver_messages/2 that takes a queue Pid and a list of messages, and maps over that list to deliver each of the messages to the queue. The first thing your function does is wrap the message as a delivery ❹ by calling the function rabbit_basic:delivery/4. This function takes four arguments: the first tells whether the message delivery is mandatory, which you set as false; the second says that the message isn't immediate; the third is the actual message; and the last parameter is the message sequence ID, which in this case is undefined. After you have your message delivery created, you finally send it to the queue by calling the function rabbit_amqqueue:deliver/2 that takes the queue Pid and the Delivery as parameters ❺.

---

[5] For the purposes of this chapter let's say that binaries are an efficient way to represent strings in Erlang. For more information on binaries and other Erlang data types, see the nice introduction given by the book *Learn You Some Erlang for Great Good*: http://learnyousomeerlang.com/starting-out-for-real#bit-syntax:.

12.3.3 *Compiling your custom exchange*

That code completes your custom exchange. As you can see, it's easy to extend RabbitMQ and add new exchange types. You just have to follow a couple of rules imposed by the Erlang behaviour that you want to implement. To ease your implementation, you could even base your exchange on the fanout type, making things easier for you. Let's recap what you just did: you overrode the implementations for message routing, queue binding, and exchange deletion to be able to cache and deliver messages. In order to have clean code and keep your functions short, you wrote a couple of helpers to access Mnesia whether you needed to write to the cache or to read messages from it.

Now let's try to compile and run RabbitMQ with your custom exchange plugin. Luckily the umbrella build system includes a command that allows you to run your plugin directly into the broker by automatically installing your plugin. Type the following command in your plugin folder:

```
$ make run-in-broker
```

You'll see a lot of output when you press Enter. First your plugin will be built and, if everything went well, RabbitMQ will be launched. You should see a message like the following confirming that your plugin was enabled:

```
Activating RabbitMQ plugins ...
2 plugins activated:
* amqp_client-0.0.0
* rabbitmq_recent_history_exchange-0.1.0-rmq
```

The usual RabbitMQ logo will appear and after the *rabbit registry* is started, you should see the following output:

```
external infrastructure ready
starting plugin registry                                   ...done
starting auth mechanism cr-demo                             ...done
starting auth mechanism amqplain                            ...done
starting auth mechanism plain                               ...done
starting statistics event manager                          ...done
starting logging server                                    ...done
starting exchange type direct                              ...done
starting exchange type fanout                              ...done
starting exchange type headers                             ...done
starting recent history exchange type: registry            ...done
starting exchange type topic                               ...done
```

Pay attention to the line that says: `starting recent history exchange type: registry` `...done`. That's your plugin seamlessly integrated with the broker. Finally you'll be left at the Erlang command line. For now, don't enter anything there. Later you'll see how to close it and exit Erlang. Before you write a consumer and a publisher, let's see the complete listing for your custom exchange module.

Listing 12.11 `rabbit_exchange_type_recent_history.erl`

```erlang
-module(rabbit_exchange_type_recent_history).
-include_lib("rabbit_common/include/rabbit.hrl").
-include_lib("rabbit_common/include/rabbit_exchange_type_spec.hrl").

-behaviour(rabbit_exchange_type).

-export([description/0, serialise_events/0, route/2]).
-export([validate/1, create/2, delete/3, add_binding/3,
         remove_bindings/3, assert_args_equivalence/2]).
-export([setup_schema/0]).

-rabbit_boot_step({rabbit_exchange_type_rh_registry,
[{description, "recent history exchange type: registry"},
  {mfa, {rabbit_registry, register,
          [exchange, <<"x-recent-history">>,
           ?MODULE]}},
  {requires, rabbit_registry},
  {enables, kernel_ready}]}).

-rabbit_boot_step({rabbit_exchange_type_rh_mnesia,
  [{description, "recent history exchange type: mnesia"},
    {mfa, {?MODULE, setup_schema, []}},
    {requires, database},
    {enables, external_infrastructure}]}).

-define(KEEP_NB, 20).
-define(RH_TABLE, rh_exchange_table).
-record(cached, {key, content}).

description() ->
  [{name, <<"recent-history">>},
    {description, <<"List of Last-value caches exchange.">>}].

serialise_events() -> false.

route(#exchange{name = XName},
      #delivery{message = #basic_message{
                            content = Content
                           }}) ->
  cache_msg(XName, Content),
  rabbit_router:match_routing_key(XName, ['_']).

validate(_X) -> ok.
create(_Tx, _X) -> ok.

delete(_Tx, #exchange{ name = XName }, _Bs) ->
  rabbit_misc:execute_mnesia_transaction(
    fun() ->
      mnesia:delete(?RH_TABLE, XName, write)
    end),
  ok.

add_binding(_Tx, #exchange{ name = XName },
            #binding{ destination = QName }) ->
  case rabbit_amqqueue:lookup(QName) of
    {error, not_found} ->
      queue_not_found_error(QName);
```

```erlang
    {ok, #amqqueue{ pid = QPid }} ->
        Cached = get_msgs_from_cache(XName),
        Msgs = msgs_from_content(XName, Cached),
        deliver_messages(QPid, Msgs)
    end,
    ok.

remove_bindings(_Tx, _X, _Bs) -> ok.

assert_args_equivalence(X, Args) ->
    rabbit_exchange:assert_args_equivalence(X, Args).

setup_schema() ->
    case mnesia:create_table(?RH_TABLE,
             [{attributes, record_info(fields, cached)},
              {record_name, cached},
              {type, set}]) of
        {atomic, ok} -> ok;
        {aborted, {already_exists, ?RH_TABLE}} -> ok
    end.

%%private
cache_msg(XName, Content) ->
    rabbit_misc:execute_mnesia_transaction(
      fun () ->
        Cached = get_msgs_from_cache(XName),
        store_msg(XName, Cached, Content)
      end).

get_msgs_from_cache(XName) ->
    rabbit_misc:execute_mnesia_transaction(
      fun () ->
        case mnesia:read(?RH_TABLE, XName) of
          [] ->
            [];
          [#cached{key = XName, content=Cached}] ->
            Cached
        end
      end).

store_msg(Key, Cached, Content) ->
    mnesia:write(?RH_TABLE,
      #cached{key     = Key,
              content = [Content|lists:sublist(Cached, ?KEEP_NB-1)]},
      write).

msgs_from_content(XName, Cached) ->
    lists:map(
      fun(Content) ->
          {Props, Payload} = rabbit_basic:from_content(Content),
          rabbit_basic:message(XName, <<"">>, Props, Payload)
      end, Cached).

deliver_messages(Queue, Msgs) ->
    lists:map(
      fun (Msg) ->
        Delivery = rabbit_basic:delivery(false, false, Msg, undefined),
        rabbit_amqqueue:deliver(Queue, Delivery)
      end,  lists:reverse(Msgs)).
```

```
queue_not_found_error(QName) ->
  rabbit_misc:protocol_error(
    internal_error,
    "could not find queue '~s'",
    [QName]).
```

Now that your exchange is running, it's time to test it. Let's write a publisher and a consumer to give it a try.

12.3.4 *Taking your plugin for a test drive*

To test your custom exchange you'll create a couple of PHP scripts: one with a consumer and the other with a producer. Your test will consist of starting a consumer and then running the producer in a separate terminal window publishing 100 messages to your recent history exchange. The expected result is that your consumer receives and consumes all the messages. In a normal AMQP scenario, you shouldn't see those messages anymore in the server. In this case since you're using your custom exchange, you should have the last 20 messages still available in the exchange cache. To prove this, you'll start another consumer in a separate window and bind its queue to your exchange. By doing that, you expect to receive the last 20 messages. Let's create a file called recent_history_consumer.php and add the following code there.

Listing 12.12 Recent history exchange consumer

```php
<?php

require_once('../path/to/lib/php-amqplib/amqp.inc');

define('HOST', 'localhost');
define('PORT', 5672);
define('USER', 'guest');
define('PASS', 'guest');
define('VHOST', '/');

$exchange = 'rh-exchange';

$conn = new AMQPConnection(HOST, PORT, USER, PASS, VHOST);
$ch = $conn->channel();

$ch->exchange_declare($exchange,               ◁─────┐  Declare
        'x-recent-history',                           │  recent
        false,                                        │  history
        true,                                       ❶  │  exchange
        false);

list($queue,,) = $ch->queue_declare('');

$ch->queue_bind($queue, $exchange);            ◁─────┐  Bind
                                                      │  queue to
$consumer = function($msg){                         ❷  │  exchange
    echo $msg->body, "\t";
};

$ch->basic_consume(                            ◁─────┐  Subscribe
        $queue,                                     ❸  │  to queue
        '',
```

```
          false,
          true,
          false,
          false,
          $consumer);

echo "consuming from queue: ", $queue, "\n";

function shutdown($conn, $ch){
  $ch->close();
  $conn->close();
}

register_shutdown_function('shutdown', $conn, $ch);

while(count($ch->callbacks)) {
    $ch->wait();
}
?>
```

<4> **Wait for incoming messages**

The code here is similar to previous consumers that you've already seen in the book. An important detail is that when you declare the exchange **❶**, you specify its type as x-recent-history to tell RabbitMQ that you want to use your custom exchange. Keep in mind that if you're running the broker without your plugin installed, then this code will throw an exception and fail because RabbitMQ won't be able to find the module for that exchange type. After you create your exchange, you declare an anonymous queue and bind it to the exchange **❷**. Then you start consuming from the queue **❸**, passing the $consume callback to the basic_consume method. Your callback will echo to STD_OUT the content of the messages received. Finally, you wait on the channel for incoming messages **❹**.

Let's continue coding your producer by creating a file called recent_history_producer.php with the following code inside.

Listing 12.13   Recent history exchange producer

```php
<?php

require_once('../path/to/lib/php-amqplib/amqp.inc');

define('HOST', 'localhost');
define('PORT', 5672);
define('USER', 'guest');
define('PASS', 'guest');
define('VHOST', '/');

$conn = new AMQPConnection(HOST, PORT, USER, PASS, VHOST);

$channel = $conn->channel();

for($i=0; $i<100; $i++) {
  $msg = new AMQPMessage('msg_'.$i,
        array('content_type' => 'text/plain'));
  $channel->basic_publish($msg, 'rh-exchange');
}
```

Publish 100 messages ❶

```
$channel->close();
$conn->close();
?>
```

As with your consumer, this code is similar to other producers that you've already created in the book. What you do here is send 100 messages ❶ to the exchange called rh-exchange that you created in your previous script. To be able to identify each message, you tag them with the value of your loop variable. Now let's open three terminal windows to test this code. Keep in mind that you should have left RabbitMQ running from the previous call to make run-in-broker.

Open a terminal window, cd into the folder where you saved the previous PHP code, and type

```
$ php recent_history_consumer.php
consuming from queue: amq.gen-C56UdaXBTQdIeSEkiUPiZQ==
```

That will start a consumer and output the queue name from where it's consuming. Keep in mind that the queue name might be different in your machine.

Then, on another terminal, you can launch the producer and send 100 messages over RabbitMQ. Type the following:

```
$ php recent_history_producer.php
```

If everything went well and the messages got routed through the exchange to your consumer, then in the first window you should see output like the following:

```
$ php recent_history_consumer.php
consuming from queue: amq.gen-nipi9vrRRoEOr/ZKI1kuaw==
msg_0    msg_1    msg_2    msg_3    msg_4    msg_5    msg_6
msg_7    msg_8    msg_9    msg_10   msg_11   msg_12   msg_13
msg_14   msg_15   msg_16   msg_17   msg_18   msg_19
... omitted output
msg_71   msg_72   msg_73   msg_74   msg_75   msg_76   msg_77
msg_78   msg_79   msg_80   msg_81   msg_82   msg_83   msg_84
msg_85   msg_86   msg_87   msg_88   msg_89   msg_90   msg_91
msg_92   msg_93   msg_94   msg_95   msg_96   msg_97   msg_98
msg_99
```

Now if you switch to the last window and start a second consumer, you should get the last 20 messages. Let's try that:

```
$ php recent_history_consumer.php
consuming from queue: amq.gen-V9qcoRYbOuSnWmgNx7DfXg==
msg_80   msg_81   msg_82   msg_83   msg_84   msg_85   msg_86   msg_87
msg_88   msg_89   msg_90   msg_91   msg_92   msg_93   msg_94   msg_95
msg_96   msg_97   msg_98   msg_99   msg_80   msg_81   msg_82   msg_83
msg_84   msg_85   msg_86   msg_87   msg_88   msg_89   msg_90   msg_91
msg_92   msg_93   msg_94   msg_95   msg_96   msg_97   msg_98   msg_99
```

Wow. The experiment just worked! Let's see what happened. First, you started your consumer, which declared the exchange named rh-exchange; that consumer bound an anonymous queue to it and then subscribed to that queue. Then, you started a

```
● ○ ○                    Terminal — php — 104×11
mrhyde:chapter-12 mrhyde$ php recent_history_consumer.php
consuming from queue: amq.gen-nipi9vrRRoE0r/ZKI1kuaw==
msg_0   msg_1   msg_2   msg_3   msg_4   msg_5   msg_6   msg_7   msg_8   msg_9   msg_10  msg_11  msg_12 m
sg_13   msg_14  msg_15  msg_16  msg_17  msg_18  msg_19  msg_20  msg_21  msg_22  msg_23  msg_24  msg_25 m
sg_26   msg_27  msg_28  msg_29  msg_30  msg_31  msg_32  msg_33  msg_34  msg_35  msg_36  msg_37  msg_38 m
sg_39   msg_40  msg_41  msg_42  msg_43  msg_44  msg_45  msg_46  msg_47  msg_48  msg_49  msg_50  msg_51 m
sg_52   msg_53  msg_54  msg_55  msg_56  msg_57  msg_58  msg_59  msg_60  msg_61  msg_62  msg_63  msg_64 m
sg_65   msg_66  msg_67  msg_68  msg_69  msg_70  msg_71  msg_72  msg_73  msg_74  msg_75  msg_76  msg_77 m
sg_78   msg_79  msg_80  msg_81  msg_82  msg_83  msg_84  msg_85  msg_86  msg_87  msg_88  msg_89  msg_90 m
sg_91   msg_92  msg_93  msg_94  msg_95  msg_96  msg_97  msg_98  msg_99
```

```
○ ○ ○                    Terminal — bash — 104×12
mrhyde:chapter-12 mrhyde$ php recent_history_producer.php
mrhyde:chapter-12 mrhyde$ php recent_history_producer.php
mrhyde:chapter-12 mrhyde$
```

```
● ○ ○                    Terminal — php — 104×11
mrhyde:chapter-12 mrhyde$ php recent_history_consumer.php
consuming from queue: amq.gen-V9qcoRYbOuSnWmgNx7DfXg==
msg_80  msg_81  msg_82  msg_83  msg_84  msg_85  msg_86  msg_87  msg_88  msg_89  msg_90  msg_91  msg_92 m
sg_93   msg_94  msg_95  msg_96  msg_97  msg_98  msg_99  msg_80  msg_81  msg_82  msg_83  msg_84  msg_85 m
sg_86   msg_87  msg_88  msg_89  msg_90  msg_91  msg_92  msg_93  msg_94  msg_95  msg_96  msg_97  msg_98 m
sg_99
```

Figure 12.3   Testing the recent history exchange

separate window, published 100 messages, and as expected those messages were delivered to your initial consumer. Finally, you started another consumer in a separate window and without the need to publish any new messages, the last 20 messages were delivered to the consumer. Let's look at figure 12.3 to see how both tests look when run at the same time.

With this, you finish the exercise of creating your own plugin, namely your own custom exchange. Now it's time to stop the RabbitMQ instance that you've been using for testing the plugin. To do that, type q(). at the Erlang command line. Note that the dot . at the end is necessary. If you don't include it, then the Erlang interpreter will keep waiting for more input. When you're back at the shell command line, you can type ls dist/ to see the product of your hard work: your plugin's .ez files.

```
$ ls dist/
amqp_client-0.0.0.ez
rabbit_common-0.0.0.ez
rabbitmq_recent_history_exchange-0.1.0-rmq.ez
```

If you want to install the plugin in your broker, then copy the file rabbitmq_recent_history_exchange-0.0.0.ez into the plugin folder[6] of your

---

[6] The files rabbit_common-0.0.0.ez and amqp_client-0.0.0.ez are only needed while building your plugin; they don't need to be deployed into the server's plugin folder because the contents of those files are already shipped with RabbitMQ.

RabbitMQ installation and then run the following command followed by a server restart:

```
rabbitmq-plugins enable rabbitmq_recent_history_exchange
```

If you wish to uninstall the plugin, you'll have to first delete any exchange that you've declared with the type x-recent-history and then you can proceed to disable the plugin followed by a server restart. You can, if you want, remove the rabbitmq_recent _history_exchange plugin files from the plugins folder.

12.4 Summary

If you thought that you were limited to the factory defaults when using RabbitMQ, then with this chapter you learned otherwise. Many plugins are out there for RabbitMQ, including officially supported ones like the Management plugin or the STOMP plugin, which can add extra features and new protocols to the server, and community-provided plugins like the Riak Exchange. You also went all the way down the rabbit hole and implemented your own plugin. Of course we wanted to give you something that goes beyond a mere Hello World project, so you created your own custom exchange. Along the way you had a quick overview of Erlang programming, which can help later if you ever want to dig deeper into RabbitMQ's source code to learn more about its own internal behavior. To create your plugin, you learned about the RabbitMQ Public Umbrella build system, which can be used to build the broker from source as well as other plugins. All in all, now you can make the little rabbit behave as you choose.

Being able to bend RabbitMQ completely to your will through your own custom code is the pinnacle of Rabbit knowledge … and the end of our journey. You started with humble intentions: to free yourself from tight coupling and synchronous communications between your applications. Now you can go far beyond that and build industrial-strength messaging architectures that can power the next world-changing app. Whether you're really writing the next successful dog walking app, changing the way doctors help patients, or helping a traveling dad see his daughter from the road, we hope you'll see the possibilities for messaging everywhere you build software. Most of all, we hope that what we've written has helped you, so that you can focus on *using* RabbitMQ instead of digging it out yourself. As our journey together has ended, your journey with Rabbit is just beginning and there's a whole world of messaging ahead. If you need any help along the way, we'd love to hear from you (and help where we can) on the *RabbitMQ in Action* forums. Enjoy Rabbit!

appendix A
Using Rabbit
from Java and .NET

Though we chose Python and PHP for their clarity and suitability as teaching languages, we realize there are a lot of .NET and Java programmers out there. Also, most of the AMQP clients for different languages are similar in their interfaces. But the Java and .NET clients diverge significantly enough from the other language clients that they warrant some advice on how to map the examples in *RabbitMQ in Action* to those languages. With that in mind, we'll translate a few examples from the book into their .NET and Java equivalents. Specifically, we'll show you how the Hello World example would look in C#. Also, we'll reimagine the alerting and RPC examples from chapter 4 in C# and Java, respectively. In each case, our goal is to stick as closely as possible to the structure, comments, and naming conventions of the original Python and PHP examples. Our hope is that this will help you build a mental map so that when you look at any other example in the book, you can easily translate that into how it would work in Java or .NET. As with the other examples in the book, all of the source code for this appendix is available for download in the book's Github repository: https://github.com/rabbitinaction/sourcecode. In the repository, you'll find not only the .java and .cs source files, but also Visual Studio projects for the .NET examples that are ready to be built with msbuild. Without further ado, let's look at converting the Hello World example from chapter 2 into C#.

A.1   *Saying hello again (library options and Hello World)*

Though the .NET universe has a plethora of languages to choose from that can leverage the RabbitMQ.NET client, we'll focus on C#. In particular, all of the .NET examples in this appendix assume you're using version 4.0 of the .NET framework (including C# 4.0). But before you can dive into writing your C# Hello World, you have to first install the RabbitMQ.NET client.

The most recent version of the .NET Rabbit client will always be found at http://www.rabbitmq.com/dotnet.html, and in our case we'll use version 2.7.0. On the .NET client download page you'll find both autoinstaller (.MSI) and .ZIP packaged versions of the client. We recommend using the .MSI for convenience, so download the .MSI installer and run it (see figure A.1). The examples will assume it's been installed into the default location (C:\Program Files\RabbitMQ\DotNetClient).

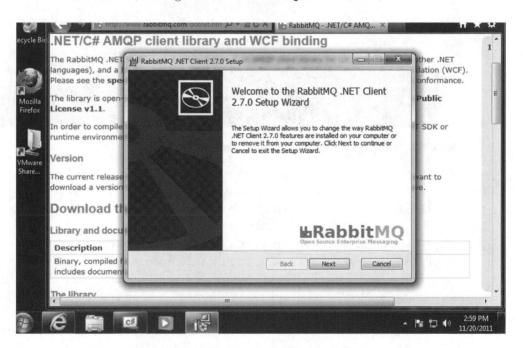

Figure A.1   Installing the Rabbit .NET client

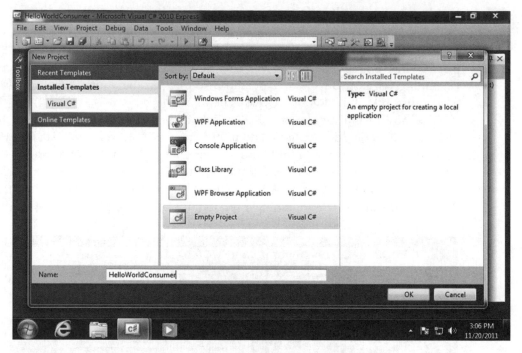

Figure A.2   Creating the HelloWorldConsumer project

Now that you have the client installed, go ahead and create the Visual Studio project (choose Empty Project) for your Hello World consumer, as in figure A.2.

The last thing you need to do before starting to write your code is to add a reference to the RabbitMQ.NET client in your project. Otherwise, Visual Studio (or msbuild) won't be able to find it. First, right-click on References under your new project in the Solution Explorer and select Add Reference (see figure A.3).

Next select the Browse tab (see figure A.4) and navigate to C:\Program Files \RabbitMQ\DotNetClient\bin (or to the alternate location where you installed the client). Then select RabbitMQ.Client.dll and click OK.

With RabbitMQ.Net added to your project, create a new file in your project called hello_world_consumer.cs to contain the Hello World consumer. First you'll put the imports into the consumer:

```
using System;
using System.Text;

using RabbitMQ.Client;
using RabbitMQ.Client.Events;
```

Importing RabbitMQ.Client gives you access to the classes for creating connections and channels (IConnection and IModel), and also for managing consumption subscriptions (QueueingBasicConsumer). You also have to import RabbitMQ.Client .Events so you can access the arguments that are passed back to your consumer when a message delivery event occurs.

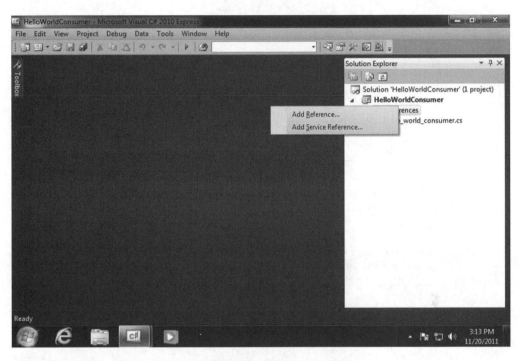

Figure A.3   Adding a reference to the Visual Studio project

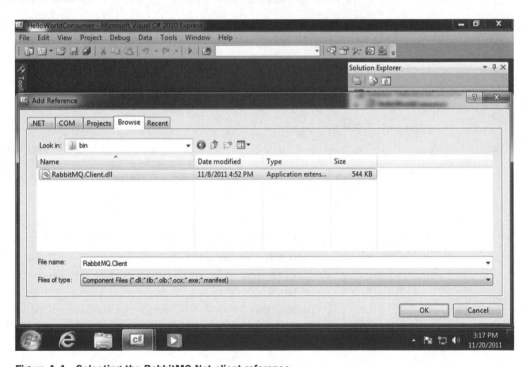

Figure A.4   Selecting the RabbitMQ.Net client reference

Since your RabbitMQ server will likely not be on the same box as your consumer, you'll collect the Rabbit host to connect to as a command-line argument to the consumer:

```
namespace HelloWorld {
    class Consumer {

        public static void Main(string[] args) {

            if(args.Length < 1) {
                Console.WriteLine("Must supply hostname.");
                Environment.Exit(-1);
            }
```

Now that you have started the class (`HelloWorld.Consumer`) that will form your consumer and collected the RabbitMQ hostname to connect to, let's connect to the server and start creating your messaging fabric.

Listing A.1   Creating the messaging fabric for your consumer

```
var conn_factory  = new ConnectionFactory();

conn_factory.HostName = args[0];
conn_factory.UserName = "guest";
conn_factory.Password = "guest";                       ❶ Establish
                                                         connection
                                                         to broker
IConnection
    conn = conn_factory.CreateConnection();
IModel chan = conn.CreateModel();                      ❷ Obtain channel

chan.ExchangeDeclare("hello-exchange",                 ❸ Declare exchang
                ExchangeType.Direct,
                true,
                false,
                null);

chan.QueueDeclare("hello-queue",                       ❹ Declare queue
            false,
            false,
            false,
            null);                                     ❺ Bind queue
                                                         and exchange
chan.QueueBind("hello-queue",                            on key hola
            "hello-exchange",
            "hola");
```

The first thing your consumer does is create a `ConnectionFactory` object that will generate and manage the actual connection to the broker. After you've used the factory to create the connection ❶, you then use the connection object (`conn`) that's returned to create the channel ❷. You may notice that the channel object (`chan`) is of type `IModel`, which represents the AMQP channel you'll use. This is unlike any other Rabbit client library (including the Java client), which all use the word *channel* to describe their representation of an AMQP channel.[1] So don't be confused when you see the word *model* used in various classes in the RabbitMQ.NET client; it always refers to a channel.

With your channel created, you're ready to start declaring the exchange and queue that will form the fabric for your Hello World consumer and producer. As with the original Hello World consumer in chapter 2, you want your exchange (hello-exchange) to be declared ❸ as a direct exchange that's durable but not autodelete. The second argument in the ExchangeDeclare call specifies that the exchange type should be direct (ExchangeType.Direct). In the RabbitMQ.NET client, exchange types are specified using constants from the ExchangeType class. If you wanted hello-exchange to be a fanout exchange instead of a direct exchange, for example, you'd use ExchangeType.Fanout instead.[2]

You then create ❹ your nondurable, non-autodelete queue (hello-queue) with QueueDeclare, and bind it ❺ to hello-exchange on the routing key hola.

Finally, you're ready to subscribe to hello-queue and start processing messages.

Listing A.2   Subscribe and process messages

```
QueueingBasicConsumer                                     ◁──── Subscribe
    consumer = new QueueingBasicConsumer(chan);          ❶ consumer
String consumer_tag = chan.BasicConsume("hello-queue",
                                        false,
                                        consumer);

while(true) {                                            ◁──❷ Start consuming
    BasicDeliverEventArgs                               ◁──── Process
        evt_args = (BasicDeliverEventArgs)                    incoming
                      consumer.Queue.Dequeue();         ❸ messages
    IBasicProperties msg_props = evt_args.BasicProperties;

    String
        msg_body = Encoding.ASCII.GetString(evt_args.Body);

    chan.BasicAck(evt_args.DeliveryTag,                 ◁──── Message
                      false);                            ❹ acknowledgement

        if(msg_body == "quit") {
            chan.BasicCancel(consumer_tag);            ◁──── Stop consuming more
            break;                                      ❺ messages and quit
        } else
```

---

[1] The use of *model* to describe a channel in the .NET client is a historic holdover from the early days of AMQP when the thought was that other transports besides TCP (HTTP, SCTP, and so on) might be used for AMQP. Since the channel concept is specific to the TCP transport, the .NET client was architected to use the more generic term *model* for the same concept. Now that TCP is only transport for AMQP, all of the newer clients use the channel term.

[2] ExchangeType is a convenience class. You can alternatively pass a string containing the exchange type to ExchangeDeclare. For example, instead of specifying ExchangeType.Direct you could've passed the string "direct" to ExchangeDeclare.

```
                Console.WriteLine("Message Body: " + msg_body);

        }

        Environment.Exit(0);
        }
    }
}
```

There are a lot of moving parts in this last piece of your consumer, so let's break it down. First you set up ❶ your consumer object (consumer) using the QueueingBasic-Consumer convenience class. QueueingBasicConsumer divorces the actual arrival of subscribed messages from the act of processing them with your code. When the channel object receives a new message that consumer is subscribed for, it fires consumer's HandleBasicDeliver method. This receives the message and stuffs it into a thread-safe SharedQueue instance inside of the consumer object. This means new subscribed messages can stream into consumer unblocked by the actions of your code actually processing those messages from the SharedQueue. With consumer created, you start the consumption by invoking BasicConsume on the channel with consumer as an argument. This tells the channel to subscribe to hello-queue and, when messages arrive from the subscription, to stuff them into consumer's SharedQueue.

Though consumer does the heavy lifting of receiving subscribed messages, you still need to process those messages yourself and acknowledge their receipt back to the broker. In Python with the Pika client, you'd create a function to do the processing and pass it as a callback to basic_consume. But as you've seen ❶, QueueingBasic-Consumer doesn't use a callback/event-based model. Instead, when messages arrive they're placed into a SharedQueue inside consumer and it's up to you to poll that SharedQueue and strip off messages for processing. Your polling mechanism in this case is an ❷ infinite while loop (while(true) {}) that endlessly polls the next message from consumer, processes it, and starts over again. To remove a message from the queue ❸, you call Dequeue() on the Queue property of consumer. This returns a

---

BasicConsume

You can call BasicConsume multiple times with different queues to subscribe to the same consumer object. This will cause all messages from the different subscriptions to be placed in the same SharedQueue in the consumer object. You can then use the BasicDeliverEventArgs object passed with each message to determine which queue it arrived from during processing (since they'll all be mixed together in the SharedQueue). You'd want to take this approach because consumer.Queue .Dequeue() will halt execution waiting for a message if the SharedQueue is empty. The effect would be that if you had multiple sequential Dequeue() calls on different consumer objects, the Dequeue() on the first consumer object would prevent the subsequent consumer object Dequeue() calls from being reached until the first consumer object/subscription received a message. By using a single consumer object for multiple subscriptions, you only need one Dequeue() call to service all the subscriptions without blocking each other.

BasicDeliverEventArgs object (evt_args) containing the AMPQ message properties (including headers), message body, and the delivery tag you'll need to acknowledge the message. After you have evt_args, you break it apart into an IBasicProperties object (msg_props) containing the headers and message properties (like .Content-Type and .DeliveryMode), as well as the message body (msg_body), which in this case is an ASCII-encoded string.

At this point, you've successfully decoded the message's body and extracted its properties, so you can let Rabbit know that the message was successfully consumed ❹ by calling chan.BasicAck with the message's delivery tag (evt_args.DeliveryTag). You may notice that you also passed a second argument false to BasicAck. This tells BasicAck you'll only be acknowledging one message at one time. Finally, the only thing left to do with your decoded message is print its contents to the user or terminate ❺ the app if the message contained quit.

With your Hello World consumer converted to .NET, you need to convert your producer so that you have something to consume! As has been the case throughout these examples, the producer is much simpler than the consumer. You'll use the same imports as before, but add your Producer class instead (you can create the hello_world_producer.cs file in a new Visual Studio project or add it to the one you created for the consumer).

Listing A.3   Publishing messages in .NET

```
namespace HelloWorld {
    class Producer {

        public static void Main(string[] args) {            ❶ Collect
                                                                server and
            if(args.Length < 2) {                               message
                Console.WriteLine("Must supply hostname and " +
                                  "message text.");
                Environment.Exit(-1);
            }

            var conn_factory  = new ConnectionFactory();

            conn_factory.HostName = args[0];
            conn_factory.UserName = "guest";
            conn_factory.Password = "guest";                 ❷ Establish
                                                                connection
            IConnection conn = conn_factory.CreateConnection();  to broker
            IModel chan = conn.CreateModel();

            chan.ExchangeDeclare("hello-exchange",        ❸ Declare exchange
                                 ExchangeType.Direct,
                                 true,
                                 false,                       ❹ Create
                                 null);                          plaintext
                                                                 message
            string msg_body = args[1];
            IBasicProperties msg_props = chan.CreateBasicProperties();
            msg_props.ContentType = "text/plain";

            chan.BasicPublish("hello-exchange",        ❺ Publish message
                              "hola",
```

```
                             msg_props,
                             Encoding.ASCII.GetBytes(msg_body));

             Environment.Exit(0);
          }
       }
    }
```

In addition to the broker to connect to, you also need to collect the message to publish from the command line ❶. Then you're ready to connect ❷ and declare hello-exchange ❸ to make sure you have a place to publish to. Creating your message ❹ to publish is similar to the steps you used to process the message, just in reverse. First, you grab the message contents from the command line and store them in the string msg_body. Next, you create an IBasicProperties object (msg_props) to store your message's publishing properties and set the message's content type to text/plain so that the consumer knows the message body is plain ASCII text. Finally, you publish ❺ the message (msg_body) into hello-exchange with the routing key hola along with the message properties you set in msg_props. You may notice that as a part of publishing the message, you first converted it into a byte array using Encoding.ASCII.Get-Bytes. AMQP (and RabbitMQ by proxy) is agnostic about the contents of the message body. The only requirement is that it be a sequence of 8-bit bytes. Because of this, the BasicPublish command in the Rabbit .NET client will only accept byte arrays for the message body.

With your C# consumer and producer written, let's build and test them! For this example, the RabbitMQ broker will be located in a different virtual machine (192.168.241.1) than the Windows system hosting your consumer and producer. First fire up two PowerShell instances[3] (see figure A.5), and navigate one to your Hello World consumer project and the other to your Hello World producer. First build and start your consumer:

```
PS > msbuild
Microsoft (R) Build Engine Version 4.0.30319.1
[Microsoft .NET Framework, Version 4.0.30319.1]
Copyright (C) Microsoft Corporation 2007. All rights reserved.
...
Done Building Project "\HelloWorldConsumer.csproj" ...

Done Building Project "\HelloWorldConsumer.sln" (default targets).

Build succeeded.
    0 Warning(s)
    0 Error(s)

Time Elapsed 00:00:00.17
PS > .\bin\Debug\HelloWorldConsumer.exe 192.168.241.1
```

---

[3] You may need to add the full path to your .NET framework to your system's PATH environment variable. For example, the path to the .NET framework on the test system used for the example is C:\Windows \Microsoft .NET\Framework\v4.0.30319.

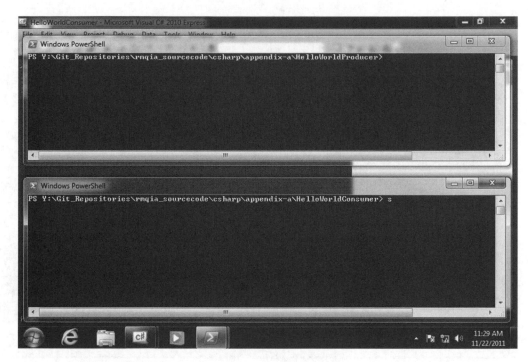

Figure A.5   Create terminals for your consumer and producer tests.

Now in your other terminal build your producer and send a test message:

```
PS \HelloWorldProducer> msbuild
Microsoft (R) Build Engine Version 4.0.30319.1
[Microsoft .NET Framework, Version 4.0.30319.1]
Copyright (C) Microsoft Corporation 2007. All rights reserved.
...
Done Building Project "\HelloWorldProducer.csproj" ...

Done Building Project "\HelloWorldProducer.sln
" (default targets).


Build succeeded.
    0 Warning(s)
    0 Error(s)

PS > .\bin\Debug\HelloWorldProducer.exe 192.168.241.1 \
    "Hello there world!"
PS >
```

Back in your consumer terminal, did it arrive?

```
PS > .\bin\Debug\HelloWorldConsumer.exe 192.168.241.1
Message Body: Hello there world!
```

Ba-da bing! Your C# consumer and producer worked! Since your C# Hello World apps are direct ports of the original Python apps, they'll also work with each other! To try

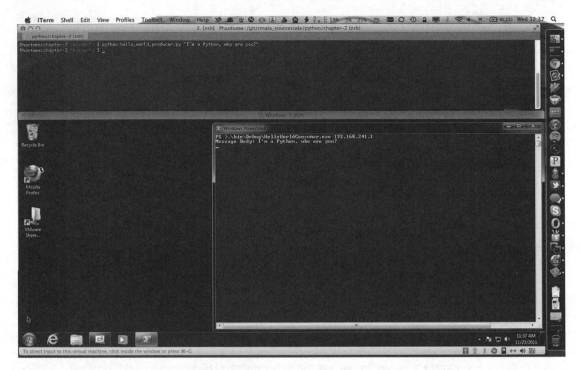

Figure A.6   Cross platform messaging in action!

out some cross-language communication goodness (as seen in figure A.6), try using the `hello_world_producer.py` from chapter 2 to publish a message to the C# consumer that's running!

Now that you have the basics of using RabbitMQ with .NET mastered, let's take a quick run through converting your alerting server from the chapter 4 version to C#.

A.2   *Alerting revisited: porting the alert app to event-oriented .NET*

With Hello World under your belt, you might think we've covered enough RabbitMQ.NET basics for you to be able to mentally translate the examples in the rest of the book. That's 90% true. What we haven't covered is how to consume messages using an event-based approach. In the Python client Pika, all consumers are built using callbacks (event-oriented) that are registered for each subscription and then fired when messages for those subscriptions arrive. As you saw with the C# Hello World consumer, using `QueueingBasicConsumer` to manage subscriptions and message consumption requires a poll-based approach. But if you're a .NET developer and prefer event-oriented programming like us, you're in luck—Rabbit.NET supports event-oriented consumption using `EventingBasicConsumer`.[4] To demonstrate how to

---

[4]   Unfortunately, the RabbitMQ Java client doesn't have an event-oriented consumption interface available.

do event-oriented consumption in .NET, we'll show the relevant parts of the alerting server example from chapter 4 converted to C#. To see a full copy of the alerting server consumer (and producer) in C#, check out the code in our companion example code repository for the book: https://github.com/rabbitinaction/sourcecode.

Before we get started, you'll need to select a .NET JSON library since the original alerting examples communicate using JSON. In this case you'll use the JSON.NET 4.0 library from James Newton-King: http://json.codeplex.com/. After you've installed the latest version from Codeplex, be sure to add a reference to the JSON.NET library in your project (the default installer places it in C:\Program Files\JSON.NET\Bin\Net35).

The primary change when moving to event-oriented consumption in .NET is to use the `EventingBasicConsumer` class for your consumer object rather than using `QueueingBasicConsumer`:

```
EventingBasicConsumer
    c_consumer = new EventingBasicConsumer {Model = chan};
```

Note that `EventingBasicConsumer` doesn't define a constructor, so you set `c_consumer`'s `Model` property to refer to the channel object (`chan`) directly at instantiation time. What makes `EventingBasicConsumer` event-oriented is that it uses C# events and delegates internally, and fires a list of defined callbacks when a message is received for the consumer's subscription. To add a function (`critical_notify` in this case) to that list of callbacks, you add it to the consumer object's `Received` property and then issue `BasicConsume`:

```
c_consumer.Received += critical_notify;
chan.BasicConsume("critical",
                  false,
                   c_consumer);
```

The only requirements for an `EventingBasicConsumer` callback function are that its return type be `void` and that it accept `IBasicConsumer` and `BasicDeliverEventArgs` objects as its two arguments. Let's see what this looks like in the C# version of `critical_notify`.

Listing A.4 Critical notify subscription callback handler

```
private static void critical_notify(IBasicConsumer consumer,
                                    BasicDeliverEventArgs eargs) {

    string[] EMAIL_RECIPS = new string[]                      ❶ Extract
                        {"ops.team@ourcompany.com"};            message
                                                                body and
    IBasicProperties msg_props = eargs.BasicProperties;       ◀ properties
    String msg_body = Encoding.ASCII.GetString(eargs.Body);

    msg_body = JsonConvert.DeserializeObject        ◀─┐        ❷ JSON-decode
                       <string>(msg_body);                       message body

    send_mail(EMAIL_RECIPS,                         ◀─┐        Email
            "CRITICAL ALERT",                                   decoded
            msg_body);                                          message
                                                              ❸ body
```

```
        Console.WriteLine("Sent alert via e-mail! Alert Text: " +
                    msg_body + " Recipients: " +
                    string.Join(",", EMAIL_RECIPS));

    consumer.Model.BasicAck(eargs.DeliveryTag,
                        false);
}
```
◁─┐   **Acknowledge**
 ❹ **message**

Your `critical_notify` callback is fired by `EventingBasicConsumer` for any messages received in the `critical` queue (as with the chapter 4 original). The `EventingBasic-Consumer` object passes in a reference to itself via the `consumer` argument, and then a copy of the received message via the `eargs` argument. As before, you'll extract ❶ the message properties and message body. But because the message body is actually JSON-encoded, you'll use the JSON.NET library ❷ to further decode the message body into a .NET data type. Then you'll send the alert email ❸ and notify the user onscreen. Where things get interesting is ❹ where you acknowledge the message. Since `Basi-cAck` is a method of the channel object, you need to get access to that object in order to acknowledge the message. You do that by way of the `Model` property on the `con-sumer` object that was passed in. As you may remember, the .NET client calls AMQP channels *models*, and the `Model` property of `consumer` contains a reference to the channel that received the message being consumed. So acknowledging your message is as simple as invoking `consumer  .Model.BasickAck()` and supplying the `DeliveryTag` for the message contained in `eargs`. That's all there is to writing a callback function for `EventingBasicConsumer`.

Using event-oriented message consumption in .NET is really that simple. Definitely check out the full code for this C# consumer in the examples repository for *RabbitMQ in Action*. Enough .NET; let's show some love to Java and see how to use Rabbit with the world's most popular bytecode interpreter.

A.3   RPC with your coffee: implementing AMQP RPC with Java

In the last section of this appendix you'll reimplement the RPC client and server from section 4.3 using the RabbitMQ client for Java. The client will send a message containing the client version and the current timestamp encoded as a JSON object. The message will look like this:

```
{"client_name": "RPC Client 1.0",
"time" : 1320846509}
```

When the request has been sent to the server, the client will then wait for the server reply. The server will take the JSON object out of the AMQP message, extract the message timestamp, and then it will reply with the word *Pong!* followed by the original timestamp sent by the client.[5]

---

[5]   In this section you'll implement an RPC client and server to illustrate how to translate the examples from chapter 4. Having said that, it's worth mentioning that the official RabbitMQ Java client implements basic RPC functionality as described here: http://www.rabbitmq.com/api-guide.html#rpc.

A.3.1 Obtaining the Java libraries

The first thing you need to do is to download the latest version of the RabbitMQ Java client. You can go directly to the client download page located here and then select the package that matches your platform: http://www.rabbitmq.com/java-client.html.

For this example you'll download the one named *Binary, compiled for Java 1.5 or newer (zip)*. Create a folder called `java-rpc` and then download the library using `wget`. Alternatively, you can point and click with your browser to get the file downloaded to the new folder:

```
$ mkdir java-rpc
$ cd java-rpc
$ wget http://www.rabbitmq.com/releases/rabbitmq-java-client/\
v2.7.0/rabbitmq-java-client-bin-2.7.0.zip
```

Now that you've downloaded the library, you'll unzip its contents and then copy the `*.jar` files into a folder called `lib` that you'll use to keep the libraries used by the application:

```
$ unzip rabbitmq-java-client-bin-2.7.0.zip
$ mkdir lib
$ cp rabbitmq-java-client-bin-2.7.0/*.jar lib/
```

Since you also need to send JSON messages, download Douglas Crockford's `org.json` Java library:

```
$ wget http://search.maven.org/remotecontent\
?filepath=org/json/json/20090211/json-20090211.jar \
-O lib/json-20090211.jar
```

If you type `ls lib`, you should see the following files inside:

```
$ ls lib/
commons-cli-1.1.jar          commons-io-1.2.jar
json-20090211.jar            junit.jar
rabbitmq-client-tests.jar    rabbitmq-client.jar
```

A.3.2 Setting up the class path

As you know, every time you run a Java program, you have to specify the class path so the JVM knows where to find the packages and the classes required by your program. The class path can start to get lengthy easily, so you'll create a shell variable that will hold the class path information so you don't have to type it over and over again. On Unix-like systems you can create a variable to hold our class path like this:

```
$ export CP=.:./lib/commons-io-1.2.jar:./lib/commons-cli-1.1.jar:\
./lib/rabbitmq-client.jar:./lib/json-20090211.jar
```

On Windows you'll have to replace colons with semicolons in order to separate `.jar` files. The command used is `set` instead of `export`:

```
set CP=.;./lib/commons-io-1.2.jar;./lib/commons-cli-1.1.jar;\
./lib/rabbitmq-client.jar;./lib/json-20090211.jar
```

Whenever you want to run one of your Java consumers/producers, you'll use that class path variable. Now that you have the basic setup out of the way, it's time to code your RPC server and client. In the rest of this section you'll jump right into the Java code. If you want to know more about the library, you can read the online API guide at http://www.rabbitmq.com/api-guide.html, and the Javadocs are located here: http://www.rabbitmq.com/releases/rabbitmq-java-client/v2.7.0/rabbitmq-java-client-javadoc-2.7.0/.

A.3.3   *Creating an RPC Server*

As with every Java program, first you need to import the classes that you'll use in your program, so create a file called Client.java inside the `java-rpc` folder. We'll describe the code of this class step by step, and then at the end we'll provide the whole source file. Let's start by describing the `import` directives:

```
import com.rabbitmq.client.ConnectionFactory;
import com.rabbitmq.client.Connection;
import com.rabbitmq.client.Channel;
import com.rabbitmq.client.QueueingConsumer;
import com.rabbitmq.client.QueueingConsumer.Delivery;
import com.rabbitmq.client.AMQP.BasicProperties;
import org.json.JSONObject;
```

As you can see in that snippet, you import the `ConnectionFactory`, `Connection`, and `Channel` classes from the RabbitMQ client which are needed to establish a connection to the broker and then to obtain a channel. The classes `QueueingConsumer` and `QueueingConsumer.Delivery` are used to get a RabbitMQ consumer and to manage message deliveries respectively. With the `AMQP.BasicProperties` class, you'll create AMQP properties for your messages. The final class that you include is the `JSONObject` class from the `org.json` package that's used to load JSON objects in memory.

Now let's look at the `init()` method of your class where you'll create the AMQP connection, obtain a channel, and then use that channel to start your AMQP fabric by declaring the exchange, queues, and finally binding them together. Here's the code.

Listing A.5   Server init method

```
public Server init()
throws Exception {                                                    ❶ Create a
  ConnectionFactory factory = new ConnectionFactory();                    connection
  factory.setUsername("rpc_user");
  factory.setPassword("rpcme");
  connection = factory.newConnection();

  channel = connection.createChannel();                               ❷ Create a
                                                                        channel

  channel.exchangeDeclare("rpc", "direct");                           Set up
  channel.queueDeclare("ping", false, false, false, null);          ❸ AMQP fabric
  channel.queueBind("ping", "rpc", "ping");

  consumer = new QueueingConsumer(channel);                           Start
  channel.basicConsume("ping", false, "ping", consumer);            ❹ consumer
```

```
System.out.println(
  "Waiting for RPC calls..."
);

return this;
}
```

The first thing you have to do is create an instance of the ConnectionFactory class ❶ that you'll use to set up your connection. As you can see, the factory accepts calls to methods like setUsername and setPassword where you provide the required connection information. The ConnectionFactory class also has methods like setVirtualHost and so on. In this case you'll connect using the rpc_user name and rpcme password. Once the factory is set up, you can call the method newConnection in order to ȯbtain the connection object, which you then use to get a channel object ❷. As you can see, you don't declare the connection or the channel variables since you'll add them as members of your class.

Then you use the channel to set up your AMQP fabric ❸. First you declare an exchange by calling exchangeDeclare on the channel object. The parameters passed to that method are the exchange name and type. Then you declare a queue called ping. The remainder of the parameters stand for durable, exclusive, autodelete, and extra arguments respectively. As you can see, you created a nondurable, non-autodelete, nonexclusive queue. After the queue is created, you bind it to the ping exchange by using the ping routing key.

The final step of your init method is to start the consumer. First you obtain a new instance of a QueueingConsumer by passing it the channel object ❹. Then you subscribe to the ping queue by calling the basicConsume method. You also use the string ping as your consumer tag and pass the consumer object as the message callback so every time a new message is delivered it'll be sent to your consumer. The mysterious second parameter to the basicConsume method specifies that you're consuming in non-auto-ack mode—you'll issue a message acknowledgment for each message delivery that you receive.

Listing A.6   Serving RPC requests

```
public void serveRequests() {
  while (true) {
    try {

      Delivery delivery = consumer.nextDelivery();          ❶ Get next message
      BasicProperties props = delivery.getProperties();

      channel.basicAck(delivery.getEnvelope().getDeliveryTag(),
                  false);                                    ❷ Acknowledge message
      System.out.println(
        "Received API call...replying..."
      );

      channel.basicPublish(                                 ❸ Reply back to client
        "",
        props.getReplyTo(),
```

```
      null,
      getResponse(delivery).getBytes("UTF-8")
    );

  } catch (Exception e){
    System.out.println(e.toString());
  }
 }
}
```

In this method you enter an endless loop where you process one message at a time. You get the last message sent by the server by calling nextDelivery on the consumer object ❶. The delivery object has both the message payload and the message properties that you'll later use in your method. Then you acknowledge the message back to the server by calling basicAck ❷ where you pass the message delivery tag, which you obtain by first getting the message envelope out of the delivery object and then by chaining the call to getDeliveryTag. You can also use the Envelope object to obtain the exchange used to route the message by calling getExchange or the message routing key by calling getRoutingKey, and so on.

Finally, you send your reply back to the client by calling basicPublish to send a message ❸ to the anonymous exchange using as routing key the reply_to property from the original client request. The null parameter indicates that the message isn't mandatory. The response message itself is created by calling the method getResponse, which you'll implement right away. To sum up what happens in this method: First you get the next delivery out of the consumer. You use that delivery to extract the message properties. You acknowledge the message using the message envelope to get the delivery tag, and after that you publish a reply back to the client. Let's now see the code for the getResponse method.

Listing A.7   Creating the RPC response

```
private String getResponse(Delivery delivery) {
  String response = null;
  try {                                                              ❶ Get next
    String message = new String(delivery.getBody(), "UTF-8");    ◁      body as
                                                                        String
    JSONObject jsonobject = new JSONObject(message);             ◁── Get next body
                                                                  ❷ as String
    response = "Pong!" + jsonobject.getString("time");           ◁
  }
  catch (Exception e){                                                Extract time
    System.out.println(e.toString());                            ❸ value
    response = "";
  }
  return response;
}
```

The method takes a Delivery object as parameter so it can extract the message body ❶ and stores it in the message variable as a string. The next thing you need to do is to parse that string as a JSON object so you can get the timestamp sent by your client ❷ and then send it back together with the string `Pong!` ❸. To extract a property from a `JSONObject` instance, you call the `getString` method, which takes the object property key as parameter to return its value.

Finally, let's see the `main` method of your `Server` class where you instantiate the server so it can wait for client requests. Here's the code.

Listing A.8   Server main method

```
public static void main(String[] args) {
  Server server = null;
  try {
    server = new Server();                          ⟵—— Server initialization
    server.init().serveRequests();
  } catch(Exception e) {
    e.printStackTrace();
  } finally {
    if(server != null) {
      server.closeConnection();                     ⟵—— Resources cleanup
    }
  }
}
```

The code there is simple. Apart from the try/catch/finally logic, you just create an instance of your `Server` class, initialize it by calling `init`, and finally chain the method call to `serveRequests` to start processing messages. The full code of the class is presented next, including the method `closeConnection` that you use in the `finally` block.

Listing A.9   RPC Server full code

```
import com.rabbitmq.client.ConnectionFactory;
import com.rabbitmq.client.Connection;
import com.rabbitmq.client.Channel;
import com.rabbitmq.client.QueueingConsumer;
import com.rabbitmq.client.QueueingConsumer.Delivery;
import com.rabbitmq.client.AMQP.BasicProperties;
import org.json.JSONObject;

public class Server
{
  private Connection connection;
  private Channel channel;
  private QueueingConsumer consumer;

  public Server Server(){
    return this;
  }

  public Server init()
  throws Exception {
    ConnectionFactory factory = new ConnectionFactory();
    factory.setUsername("rpc_user");
    factory.setPassword("rpcme");
    connection = factory.newConnection();
```

```java
    channel = connection.createChannel();
    channel.exchangeDeclare("rpc", "direct");
    channel.queueDeclare("ping", false, false, false, null);
    channel.queueBind("ping", "rpc", "ping");

    consumer = new QueueingConsumer(channel);
    channel.basicConsume("ping", false, "ping", consumer);

    System.out.println(
      "Waiting for RPC calls..."
    );

    return this;
  }

  public void closeConnection() {
    if (connection != null) {
      try {
        connection.close();
      }
      catch (Exception ignore) {}
    }
  }

  public void serveRequests() {
    while (true) {
      try {

        Delivery delivery = consumer.nextDelivery();
        BasicProperties props = delivery.getProperties();

        channel.basicAck(delivery.getEnvelope().getDeliveryTag(),
                         false);
        System.out.println(
          "Received API call...replying..."
        );

        channel.basicPublish(
          "",
          props.getReplyTo(),
          null,
          getResponse(delivery).getBytes("UTF-8")
        );

      } catch (Exception e){
      System.out.println(e.toString());
      }
    }
  }

  private String getResponse(Delivery delivery) {
    String response = null;
    try {
      String message = new String(delivery.getBody(), "UTF-8");
      JSONObject jsonobject = new JSONObject(message);
      response = "Pong!" + jsonobject.getString("time");
    }
    catch (Exception e){
      System.out.println(e.toString());
```

```
      response = "";
    }
    return response;
  }

  public static void main(String[] args) {
    Server server = null;
    try {
      server = new Server();
      server.init().serveRequests();
    } catch(Exception e) {
      e.printStackTrace();
    } finally {
      if(server != null) {
        server.closeConnection();
      }
    }
  }
}
```

Now that you have the server fully implemented, let's compile it by running the following command:

```
$ javac -cp ./lib/rabbitmq-client.jar:./lib/json-20090211.jar \
  Server.java
```

That command should have created your `Server.class` file:

```
$ ls Server.class
Server.class
```

A.3.4 Creating your RPC client

Let's move on now so you can start coding your client. You'll create a file called Client.java and add your code there. As usual, the complete source code will be given at the end of this section. The first thing to add is the list of imports:

```
import com.rabbitmq.client.ConnectionFactory;
import com.rabbitmq.client.Connection;
import com.rabbitmq.client.Channel;
import com.rabbitmq.client.QueueingConsumer;
import com.rabbitmq.client.QueueingConsumer.Delivery;
import com.rabbitmq.client.AMQP.BasicProperties;
import org.json.JSONStringer;
import org.json.JSONException;
```

The only difference here from the previous server code are the JSON libraries that you need to import. Because in the client you have to create a JSON object, you'll import the `JSONStringer` object that lets you create JSON strings in an OOP way. The `JSON-Exception` is required because when you convert the JSON object to a string, it might throw an exception. What follows is the class `init` method:

Listing A.10   Client `init` method

```
public Client init()
throws Exception {
  ConnectionFactory factory = new ConnectionFactory();
  factory.setUsername("rpc_user");
  factory.setPassword("rpcme");
  connection = factory.newConnection();
  channel = connection.createChannel();
  return this;
}
```

The code here is similar to that used by the server. You create an instance of the `ConnectionFactory` object and then set up the user and password. You get a `Connection` instance and from there you obtain a channel object. You keep the channel and the connection objects as members of your class. After you have the connection, you need to set up your consumer.

Listing A.11   Client consumer setup

```
public Client setupConsumer()
throws Exception {

  replyQueueName = channel.queueDeclare().getQueue();
  consumer = new QueueingConsumer(channel);
  channel.basicConsume(replyQueueName, false, consumer);
  return this;
}
```

The important bit from that method is that you declare an anonymous queue and let RabbitMQ generate a queue name for you. You keep that name in the member variable `replyQueueName`. Later you'll use that variable as the value of your `reply_to` message property.

Listing A.12   Sending the RPC request

```
public String call(String message) throws Exception {
  String response = null;

  channel.basicPublish(                          ◁──❶ Send RPC request
    "rpc",
    "ping",
    getRequestProperties(),                      ◁──❷ Add request properties
    message.getBytes()
  );

  System.out.println("Sent 'ping' RPC call. Waiting for reply...");

  while (true) {                                 ◁──❸ Wait for RPC reply
    Delivery delivery = consumer.nextDelivery();
    response = new String(delivery.getBody(), "UTF-8");
    break;
  }

  return response;
}
```

The call method accepts a string as parameter, which will represent the message payload that you want to send to the server. You'll publish that message ❶ to the rpc exchange using the string ping as routing key. You'll create your message properties object by calling the method getRequestProperties ❷. Then you wait for a reply inside the while (true) loop ❸. To receive a message from RabbitMQ you use the same technique that you employed on the server code. After you have the delivery, you get the message body as a string and return that response to whomever called the method. Let's see now how you can create the message properties that will include your replyQueueName as part of the reply_to message's basic properties.

Listing A.13 Creating the message's basic properties

```
private BasicProperties
  getRequestProperties() {
    return new BasicProperties
             .Builder()
             .replyTo(replyQueueName)
             .build();
}
```

This method is simple. You create a BasicProperties object that uses a *builder* technique where you can chain calls to set each of the basic properties that you might need. In this case you'll only set the replyTo property, but you can also use this technique to set properties like correlationId or deliveryMode. Now let's see the main method.

Listing A.14 Client main method

```
public static void main(String[] args) {
  Client client = null;
  String response = null;

  try {
    client = new Client();
    client.init().setupConsumer();
    response = client.call(Client.createRequest());        ◁─❶ Call RPC server
    System.out.println("RPC Reply --- " + response);
  }
  catch (Exception e) {
    e.printStackTrace();
  }
  finally {
    if (client!= null) {
      try {
        client.close();
      }
      catch (Exception ignore) {}
    }
  }
}
```

The code here is similar to that which initializes the server. The interesting bit is how you call the server ❶. After you have the consumer instance, you execute the call method and then wait for a reply from the server. Note that for a user of your RPC client, there's no apparent difference between doing a local method call from an RPC call, so be careful in this regard because an RPC call is many orders of magnitude slower than a local method call. The missing piece of this puzzle is the Client.createRequest code that you use to generate the JSON string you send to the server. Let's see that code now.

Listing A.15   Generating the JSON request

```
public static String createRequest()
throws JSONException {
  float epoch = System.currentTimeMillis()/1000;
  JSONStringer msg = new JSONStringer();
  return msg
         .object()
         .key("client_name")
         .value("RPC Client 1.0")
         .key("time")
         .value(Float.toString(epoch))
         .endObject().toString();
}
```

First you get the current UNIX timestamp, which you need to send with your RPC message. Then you create an instance of the JSONStringer object, which provides an OOP interface to build the JSON object. As you can see there, you create the JSON object and set the client_name and time properties with the values RPC Client 1.0 and Float.toString(epoch) respectively.

Let's sum up how the client works. First you have to instantiate your RPC client inside the main method of your class. After you have a Client instance, you can use the call method to get a reply from the server. The JSON object that you send as a message is constructed inside the createRequest method. During the client initialization, you also declared a queue in the server for the client and kept the queue name in the object state. That name is passed along with your JSON object to the server so the server will know where to reply to. Once you get the reply back from the server, you print it to the console and exit the program. Before terminating the app, you take care to clean up resources by closing the connection. Here's the complete code for the RPC client including the Client.close method.

Listing A.16   RPC client full code

```
import com.rabbitmq.client.ConnectionFactory;
import com.rabbitmq.client.Connection;
import com.rabbitmq.client.Channel;
import com.rabbitmq.client.QueueingConsumer;
import com.rabbitmq.client.QueueingConsumer.Delivery;
import com.rabbitmq.client.AMQP.BasicProperties;
import org.json.JSONStringer;
```

```java
import org.json.JSONException;

public class Client {

  private Connection connection;
  private Channel channel;
  private String replyQueueName;
  private QueueingConsumer consumer;

  public Client init()
  throws Exception {
    ConnectionFactory factory = new ConnectionFactory();
    factory.setUsername("rpc_user");
    factory.setPassword("rpcme");
    connection = factory.newConnection();
    channel = connection.createChannel();
    return this;
  }
  public Client setupConsumer()
  throws Exception {
    replyQueueName = channel.queueDeclare().getQueue();
    consumer = new QueueingConsumer(channel);
    channel.basicConsume(replyQueueName, false, consumer);
    return this;
  }

  public String call(String message) throws Exception {
    String response = null;

    channel.basicPublish(
      "rpc",
      "ping",
      getRequestProperties(),
      message.getBytes()
    );

    System.out.println("Sent 'ping' RPC call. Waiting for reply...");

    while (true) {
      Delivery delivery = consumer.nextDelivery();
      response = new String(delivery.getBody(), "UTF-8");
      break;
    }

    return response;
  }

  public void close() throws Exception {
    connection.close();
  }

  private BasicProperties
    getRequestProperties() {
      return new BasicProperties
                .Builder()
                .replyTo(replyQueueName)
                .build();
  }

  public static String createRequest()
```

```
  throws JSONException {
    float epoch = System.currentTimeMillis()/1000;
    JSONStringer msg = new JSONStringer();
    return msg
            .object()
            .key("client_name")
            .value("RPC Client 1.0")
            .key("time")
            .value(Float.toString(epoch))
            .endObject().toString();
  }

  public static void main(String[] args) {
    Client client = null;
    String response = null;

    try {
      client = new Client();
      client.init().setupConsumer();
      response = client.call(Client.createRequest());
      System.out.println("RPC Reply --- " + response);
    }
    catch  (Exception e) {
      e.printStackTrace();
    }
    finally {
      if (client!= null) {
        try {
          client.close();
        }
        catch (Exception ignore) {}
      }
    }
  }
}
```

Let's compile that code by executing the following command:

```
$ javac -cp ./lib/rabbitmq-client.jar:./lib/json-20090211.jar \
  Client.java
```

If the compilation was successful, then you should have a new `Client.class` file:

```
$ ls Client.class
Client.class
```

Now start your RabbitMQ server so you can test drive your RPC clients and server. Keep in mind that you need the same setup as from chapter 4—you need to have the rpc_user configured in your broker.

A.3.5   *Testing your RPC client and server*

Open two terminal windows and then type the following on the first to start your server:

```
$ java -cp $CP Server
Waiting for RPC calls...
```

Your server should then be ready to accept client requests. Let's move on to the second terminal window, set up the CP variable as explained before, and then type

```
$ java -cp $CP Client
Sent 'ping' RPC call. Waiting for reply...
RPC Reply --- Pong!1.32087475E
```

You'll see the reply being printed on the screen right away. On the other hand, in the terminal window where the server is running, you should see the following output:

```
Received API call...replying...
```

With this example we finish our coverage of the RabbitMQ client for Java. As an exercise, try to run the Python RPC server with the Java client or vice versa to test the interoperability of both AMQP clients.

A.4   *Summary*

When we started this appendix, you might have had RabbitMQ's basics under your belt, but using those basics from Java and .NET might've proven elusive. Now you've converted the Hello World (chapter 2) and alerting server (chapter 4) examples into .NET, and have a functional RPC client and server in Java that will fully interoperate with their Python originals (chapter 4). We hope this whirlwind jaunt through using Rabbit with Java and .NET has provided the necessary mental map for utilizing all of the concepts and examples in the book with your interpreted bytecode language of choice.

appendix B
Online resources

In this appendix we gathered some interesting online resources that should make your life easier whenever you go looking for some information related to RabbitMQ, whether that's a client library for your favorite programming language or the latest messaging design pattern to use for your current problem. Well, let's be fair: we can't cover all of your needs but we'll make the effort by listing resources that have been helpful to us.

B.1 Websites you should know

Let's start by reviewing some websites:

- *RabbitMQ official documentation*—This is the place to go first if you're looking for information about RabbitMQ. Since we started writing this book, the resources available on the official websites have augmented considerably. See here for more details: http://www.rabbitmq.com/documentation.html.

- *AMQP references*—If you want to get a deeper understanding of AMQP, you can visit the protocol's official website (http://amqp.org/) where you can find the specifications of its various versions (http://amqp.org/resources/download). Apart from those links, the RabbitMQ developers created an AMQP Quick Reference at http://www.rabbitmq.com/amqp-0-9-1-quickref.html. Whenever you want to know what the fourth argument to that AMQP method means, go and check that web page.

- *Enterprise Integration Patterns*—If you're interested in knowing more about messaging and integration patterns, then the book *Enterprise Integration Patterns* written by Gregor Hohpe and Bobby Woolf is the one to read. The small caveat we must mention for an AMQP user is that all the examples are targeted for technologies like JMS or MSMQ. You'll need to translate the concepts slightly. Also many patterns are already part of RabbitMQ itself. The good thing is that you don't need to buy the book to get started. The pattern narratives and diagrams are released under the *Creative Commons*

Attribution License so you can read them online at http://www.eaipatterns.com/ eaipatterns.html. Patterns like *Publish Subscribe* or *Competing Consumers* and many others were covered in the examples we presented in chapter 4.

- *Ruby AMQP gem documentation site*—The Ruby AMQP gem website is filled with documentation and examples of how to use RabbitMQ and AMQP. Examples even have funny rabbit drawings: http://rubyamqp.info/.

- *RabbitMQ development RSS feed*—The RabbitMQ Mercurial repository offers an RSS feed with the latest code changes to the server. It's interesting if you want to keep up with what's going on at the bleeding edge: http://hg.rabbitmq.com/ rabbitmq-server/rss-log.

B.2 Blogs

- *RabbitMQ official blog*—The RabbitMQ team maintains a blog at http:// www.rabbitmq.com/blog/ where you can find them discussing new developments in the broker, providing tips about performance, and much more. Be sure to keep an eye on that blog.

- *Jason's plans*—Jason's own blog was what started it all when we were looking for some examples of how to use RabbitMQ and AMQP back in 2009. His article called "Rabbits and warrens" has been an inspiration for many through the years. From time to time, someone rediscovers it and it pops up again on Twitter. Check it out here: http://blogs.digitar.com/jjww/2009/01/rabbits-and-warrens/.

- *Alvaro's blog*—Alvaro maintains a blog where he discusses messaging and many other software topics. There you can find small articles explaining things like implementing RPC with RabbitMQ and Haskell: http://videlalvaro.github.com/ 2010/10/rpc-over-rabbitmq.html.

B.3 AMQP libraries and related OSS projects

- *Developer tools and learning material*—The RabbitMQ official website has a list of open source projects that are related to RabbitMQ in one way or another: http://www.rabbitmq.com/devtools.html. There you can find links from AMQP libraries to Github repositories offering alternate exchange implementations— even video tutorials created by the community!

B.3.1 Client libraries

Here we list some interesting libraries for AMQP and RabbitMQ in particular:

- *Java*—Besides the official Java client, you have other options to integrate Java and RabbitMQ. The Spring framework offers the Spring AMQP library: http:// www.springsource.org/spring-amqp.

  The Mule ESB also offers integration with AMQP and RabbitMQ. You can find more details at https://github.com/mulesoft/mule-transport-amqp/ blob/master/GUIDE.md.

Finally, LShift, the company that originally created RabbitMQ, has an experimental RabbitMQ component for Apache Camel: https://github.com/lshift/camel-rabbitmq.

- *.Net/C#*—For C# you have the official client that was covered in the previous appendix, and Spring AMQP also provides a library to use with their Spring Integration framework. The link is the same as for Java: http://www.spring-source.org/spring-amqp.

  Apart from that library, Mike Hadlow created a library called EasyNetQ that he presents at https://github.com/mikehadlow/EasyNetQ/wiki/Introduction. The goals for his library were to have *"Zero or at least minimal configuration"* and a *"Simple API."*

- *Python*—In the book we used the library called *Pika*. Marek Majkowski, one of the RabbitMQ developers, started working on a new one called *Puka* and he explains the design reasons behind his new library at http://www.rabbitmq.com/blog/2011/07/08/puka-rethinking-amqp-clients/.

- *C*—For C there's a library called `rabbitmq-c` written and maintained by David Wragg, which also works for RabbitMQ. The library has been wrapped by C++ and Objective-C users as well. The library is hosted at the RabbitMQ Mercurial repository: http://hg.rabbitmq.com/rabbitmq-c/.

- *PHP*—For PHP we used the `php-amqplib` client library, which is a pure PHP implementation. There's also a PECL extension for AMQP that you can find at http://pecl.php.net/package/amqp. At the time of this writing, that library is under heavy development. Keep in mind that it depends on the `rabbitmq-c` library.

  Another pure PHP library is worth mentioning due to its active development and documentation efforts by its author. It's called *amqphp* and can be found at https://github.com/braveSirRobin/amqphp.

- *Ruby*—For Ruby you can try the *Ruby AMQP Gem* that we mentioned earlier (http://rubyamqp.info/). If you're using JRuby there's an alternate library called *hot_bunnies* that you can find at https://github.com/ruby-amqp/hot_bunnies. The good news is that it's maintained by one of the AMQP Gem authors too.

- *Erlang*—If you need to use RabbitMQ from Erlang, the language in which RabbitMQ is written, a client library is offered by the RabbitMQ team. This library is used by most of the RabbitMQ plugins, so chances are you're using it indirectly in your RabbitMQ installation. Details on its usage can be found on the RabbitMQ official website: http://www.rabbitmq.com/erlang-client-user-guide.html.

- *JavaScript, Node.js, and web messaging*—Though JavaScript is a frontend language, lately server-side frameworks have appeared that present the language as an interesting choice for backend programming. Node.js is a server that allows you to write server-side code in JavaScript, and as you can imagine we didn't have to wait long before someone wrote an AMQP client for it. The main library is called *node-amqp* and it's maintained by Theo Schlossnagle, the author of the book *Scalable Internet Architectures*. More on the library here: https://github.com/postwait/node-amqp.

There's also a library called Rabbit.js, which implements several messaging patterns for the web. It was created by Michael Bridgen, one of the RabbitMQ developers. More details here https://github.com/squaremo/rabbit.js.

- *Clojure*—For Clojure you have a library called *langohr*, which was created by Michael Klishin, one of the maintainers of the Ruby AMQP Gem and the hot_bunnies library. The library design is built on top on his experience writing the Ruby clients. The library wraps the Java official library into idiomatic Clojure. Here's the Github repository: https://github.com/michaelklishin/langohr.

- *Scala*—For Scala there's an AMQP library that can be used directly with the AKKA Scalability framework. Documentation for the library can be found in its repo at http://doc.akka.io/docs/akka-modules/1.3.1/modules/amqp.html.

- *Haskell*—If you want to use RabbitMQ with Haskell, take a look at this package on hackage: http://hackage.haskell.org/package/amqp. There's a getting started guide here: http://videlalvaro.github.com/2010/09/haskell-and-rabbitmq.html.

- *NoSQL*—RabbitMQ has also been integrated with some NoSQL databases; most notable is the work by Jon Brisbin, who's been working on bridging RabbitMQ with Riak. There's an alternate RabbitMQ exchange that logs messages into Riak at https://github.com/jbrisbin/riak-exchange. Also, if you want to receive change notifications of what's going on in your Riak database, Jon wrote a Riak post-commit-hook. More information here: https://github.com/jbrisbin/riak-rabbitmq-commit-hooks.

B.4 Discussions and mailing lists

- *Mailing list*—If you want to get in touch with the RabbitMQ community, including its developers, there are a couple of places you can head to. First there's the official mailing list at http://lists.rabbitmq.com/cgi-bin/mailman/listinfo/rabbitmq-discuss. The list is very active and you can find answers to your questions, sometimes even the same afternoon. If you're having trouble with RabbitMQ, that's the best place to go if you want to ask for help.

- *IRC channel*—If you prefer more live communication there's the #rabbitmq IRC channel on the http://freenode.net/ network. Feel free to chime in; there are always members from the community who are willing to help.

- *Twitter*—Finally, if you want to know what people are saying about RabbitMQ in real time you can subscribe to the #rabbitmq hash tag on Twitter: http://twitter.com/#!/search?q=%23rabbitmq.

B.5   *Summary*

With more than 30 links to new resources in this appendix, there's plenty to read if you want to dig even deeper into the rabbit hole. We provided a selection of links from interesting websites and blogs and a small commentary on each of the libraries that we mentioned here. You can see that with RabbitMQ and AMQP, you don't need to be locked into a particular language solution. Finally, if you want to get in touch with the community, you can do so via traditional email, direct IRC chat, or keep track of what's happening with RabbitMQ users in real time via Twitter.

appendix C
Installing RabbitMQ
on Windows

As with most programs that originate on UNIX, installing RabbitMQ on Windows is different than the installation instructions we covered in chapter 1. Fortunately, the kind folks at Rabbit HQ have provided MSI-based installers that make the process rather painless. But before you install Rabbit, you must first install a recent version of Erlang from http://www.erlang.org/download.html. Generally, the latest version of Erlang available from erlang.org will work with the latest version of RabbitMQ. So go ahead and grab the download labeled Windows Binary File (see figure C.1).

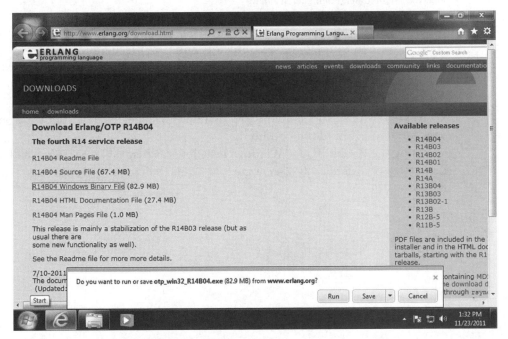

Figure C.1 Downloading the Erlang for Windows installer

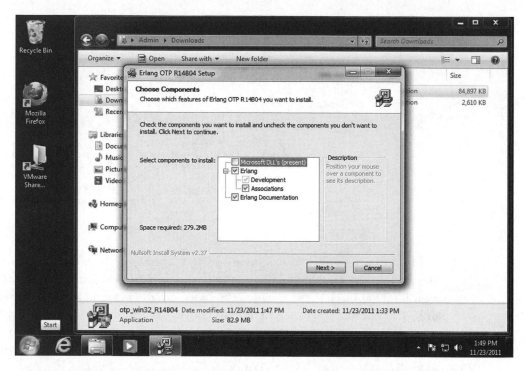

Figure C.2   Installing Erlang for Windows

After you've downloaded the Erlang installer (`otp_win32_R14B04.exe` in this case), you'll browse to your Downloads directory and run it (see figure C.2).

All of the defaults in the Erlang for Windows installer are acceptable when using Rabbit, so click Next (or Finish) on all the stages of the installer wizard to deploy a default installation of Erlang.

Next, download the RabbitMQ for Windows installer (see figure C.3) from http://www.rabbitmq.com/download.html.

Using the RabbitMQ for Windows installer is as easy as the Erlang installer: run the downloaded installer file (see figure C.4) and click through the stages using the defaults.

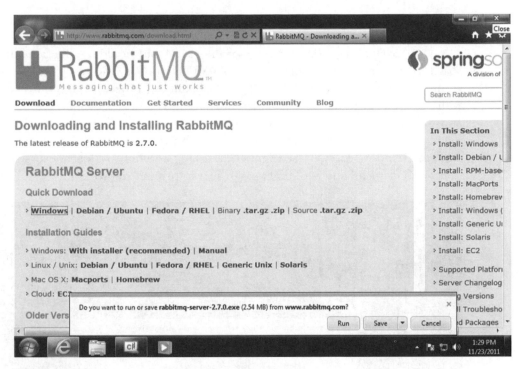

Figure C.3   Downloading the RabbitMQ for Windows installer

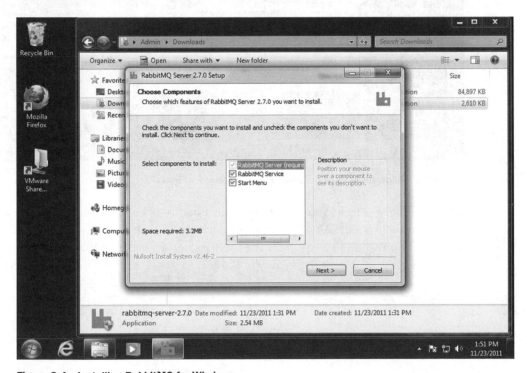

Figure C.4   Installing RabbitMQ for Windows

When the installer finishes, you'll have a fully functional copy of RabbitMQ running as a Windows service! If you open up a command prompt and run `cd C:\Program Files\RabbitMQ Server\rabbitmq_server-2.7.0` you should see the same directory structure as on any other platform RabbitMQ supports. One thing that's different from the UNIX versions of RabbitMQ is that utilities in the `.\sbin` subdirectory end with `.bat`. For example, instead of running `.\sbin\rabbitmqctl`, on Windows you'd run `.\sbin\rabbitmqctl.bat`. Also, the first time you run any of the utilities (like `rabbitmqctl.bat`) that communicate with Rabbit via Erlang, you'll receive a warning from the Windows Firewall (see figure C.5) asking whether to allow network access for `erl.exe`. Go ahead and allow `erl.exe` to access "private" networks.

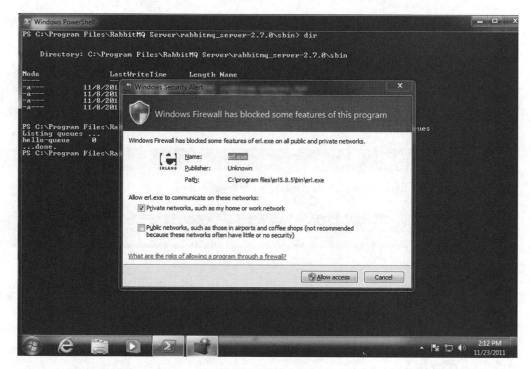

Figure C.5   Allow network access for erl.exe in Windows Firewall.

That's all there is to it! You now have a fully functional copy of RabbitMQ running on your Windows system! All of the examples in this book will work as well with the Windows version of Rabbit (especially the .NET examples in appendix A) as they do with the UNIX version. That's the beauty of Rabbit!

index